Learning

C

Neill Graham

McGRAW-HILL, INC.

New York St. Louis San Francisco Auckland Bogotá
Caracas Lisbon London Madrid Mexico Milan
Montreal New Delhi Paris San Juan Singapore
Sydney Tokyo Toronto

This book was set in Postscript Bembo and Univers 67 type by Octavo.
Development and production management were provided by Cole and
Associates.
The editors were Eric Munson and Elliot Simon;
production coordination was done by Simon and Assocs.
The cover was designed by Advanced Presentations.
The interior was designed by Seventeenth Street Studios and Octavo.
Illustrations were done by Advanced Presentations and Octavo.
Printing and binding was done by R.R. Donnelley & Sons Company.

LEARNING C

2 3 4 5 6 7 8 9 0 DOHDOH 9 5 4 3 2

ISBN   0-07-023981-9

Library of Congress Cataloging-in-Publication Data

Graham, Neill, (date).
    Learning C / Neill Graham.
        p.   cm.
    Includes bibliographical references and index.
    ISBN 0-07-023981-9
    1. C (Computer program language)   I. Title.
QA76.73.C15G74   1992
005.13'3—dc20   91-45897

Contents

3
Types and Conversions

4
Arrays and Pointers

5
Pointers and Strings

CONTENTS

Preface

This book is an introduction to C for readers who are already acquainted with at least one programming language (which will probably be Pascal). The only reason for such a prerequisite is that this book focuses more on the details of C than on the elements of programming. No background is assumed in any other area of computing, such as computer science or system programming. Important computing concepts, such as variables and pointers, are reviewed briefly before being used, a practice for which we ask the indulgence of readers with more experience.

About C

C is now the most popular language for professional software development on minicomputers and microcomputers. Many programmers who formerly used assembly language or Pascal have switched to C, and some existing software products have actually been translated into C from Pascal or assembly language.

Although C provides most of the features one expects of a higher-level language, it also offers the low-level access to hardware and software that is characteristic of assembly language (and that is required for all system programming and much application programming). Some languages that offer this low-level access are so hardware specific that they can be used on only one kind of computer (assembly language is, of course, the prime example). C seems to have hit the right level of generality in that it offers the low-level access that programmers need yet can be (and has been) implemented on a wide variety of main frames, minicomputers, and microcomputers.

A recently developed ANSI (American National Standards Institute) standard for C will make it even easier to port (move) C programs from one computer to another. The computer industry is moving toward the ANSI version of C as fast as possible, considering the amount of existing software that is written in older versions. To avoid confusion, this book covers only ANSI C and the style of programming that is recommeded for it. Readers who have mastered ANSI C should have little difficulty understanding the programming styles used in older versions of the language.

Because C does not put the programmer in a straitjacket, programmers have more opportunities for making errors, a fact for which the language is often criticized. Yet powerful tools always require more care in their use than less capable ones. A high-performance automobile or airplane is far more demanding of the driver or pilot than a lower-performance machine. The solution is to make sure that driver, pilot, and programmer are properly trained in the use of their respective tools, including any necessary safety precautions. Like a conscientious driving or flying instructor, this book points out a number of areas in which the careless student is likely to get into trouble.

Newcomers to the language are sometimes intimidated by C programs, which look so different from programs in Pascal-style languages. Yet these differences are often superficial, reflecting merely different notations for the same underlying concepts. This book frequently points out the similarity of C constructions to those found in other languages (without, however, demanding knowledge of any particular other language).

About This Book

To get the student writing nontrivial C programs as quickly as possible, Chapters 1 and 2 focus on those features of C that have close counterparts in other languages. Only a few of C's idiosyncrasies, including the increment, decrement, and compound assignment operators, are introduced in these chapters. Only two data types, `int` and `double`, are introduced. To heighten the sense of familiarity, some of the examples and exercises were deliberately chosen from among such old standbys as Fibonacci's rabbit problem and finding the number of grains of wheat paid to the inventor of chess.

After Chapters 1 and 2 have brought the reader up to speed in C programming, Chapter 3 takes some time to explore some details of the language. Following a brief introduction to hardware memory organization (which influences so much of C), the remaining arithmetic data types are introduced. Conversions between arithmetic types are also introduced, as are the additional conversion specifiers that enable `scanf()` and `printf()` to handle the types introduced in this chapter. In addition to the topics mentioned in the chapter titles, most of the remaining chapters have sections devoted to filling in background details about some aspects of the language.

Once we get beyond the elements of C, our attention invariably shifts to pointers and arrays, which are central to all advanced applications of the language. Chapter 4 introduces these two closely related concepts, but focuses mainly on array processing. Chapter 5 introduces pointer arithmetic and string processing, with some of the string library functions providing examples of both. Although the main topic of Chapter 6 is structures, pointers and arrays are never far from our thoughts.

So far, we have only used the standard input, output, and error streams, although file redirection has been suggested for systems that have that capability. Chapter 7 explores the C model of files and streams and shows the student how to open files in various modes, obtain file names from command-line parameters, read and write binary data, and use positioning functions for direct access. Functions with varying numbers of arguments and conditional preprocessor directives are the two "extra" topics discussed in this chapter.

Four appendices provide additional information. Appendix 1 lists C keywords and Appendix 2 gives the precedence, associativity, and arity (number of operands) of C operators. Appendix 3 describes a typical integrated development environment, in the hopes that newcomers will prefer this modern tool to the old-fashioned command-line compilers so beloved by many current C programmers. Appendix 4 introduces the *memory models* used with MS-DOS, one of two most popular operating systems for C programming (the other is UNIX, the operating system under which C was developed).

For Further Reading describes some sources of additional information, including the all-important ANSI standard.

Acknowledgments

I wish to thank the following for their helpful comments on the manuscript: Timothy J. McGuire, Texas A&M University; Greg M. Perry, Tulsa Junior College; Paul W. Ross, Millersville University, Millersville, Penna.; Vincent F. Russo, Purdue University; and Phillip C-Y. Sheu, Rutgers University.

1

Getting Started

WE BEGIN WITH the basic elements found in most programming languages: identifiers, types, values, variables, functions, expressions, and provisions for input and output. The C versions of these are largely similar to their counterparts in other languages. The greatest differences are in the input-output facilities, which vary considerably from language to language.

FUNCTIONS

A C program is a collection of *functions*, which play the same roles that functions, procedures, and subroutines do in other languages. When we run a program, the system first calls the function main(), which every C program must define. Function main(), in turn, can call other functions, which can call still other functions, and so on as needed to accomplish the purpose of the program. Thus function main() plays the same role in C as the "main program" does in some other languages.

As can be seen in the previous paragraph, this book uses a distinctive typeface for elements of a C program, such as main(). Also, the name of a function is followed by a pair of parentheses. The latter convention lets us see at a glance that names such as main(), printf(), and scanf() represent functions rather than other elements of a C program.

In some other languages, such as Pascal, Basic, and Fortran, the term *function* is reserved for subprograms that return a value. Other terms, such as *procedure* and *subroutine*, are used for subprograms that do not return a value. In C, however, all such subprograms are known as functions. The definition of each individual function determines whether or not it returns a value.

To save us from having to "reinvent the wheel" every time we write a program, all C implementations come with a large *library* of predefined functions. Additional libraries can be created by the programmer or purchased from third-party developers.

THE HELLO-WORLD PROGRAM

It is traditional to begin the study of C with a program that prints the message "Hello, world!" Listing 1-1 shows our version of the hello-world program. Working through this listing line-by-line will acquaint us with the structure of a C program.

Comments

The first two lines of Listing 1-1 are *comments*, which explain the program to human readers but are ignored by the compiler. In C, comments are enclosed by the symbols /* and */:

```
/* This is a comment */
```

A comment can extend over several lines:

```
/* Now is the time
   for all good programmers
   to use more and better comments */
```

Nested comments—comments within comments—are *not* allowed. The following will produce one or more error messages:

```
/* This is an /* invalid */ comment */
```

Our hello-world program (Listing 1-1) begins with two comments:

```
/* File hello.c */
/* Say hello to user */
```

The first comment gives the name of the *source file*—the disk file in which the program is stored (Listing 1-1 is just a printout of this disk file). Although the reader seldom actually needs to know these file names, mentioning them in comments emphasizes the correspondence between listings and disk files. Including such comments in your own programs will help you keep track of which listings go with which files.

The second comment describes briefly what the program does. As is often done, the comment is phrased as the command we might give the computer if it could understand English.

Listing 1-1

```
/* File hello.c */
/* Say hello to user */

#include <stdio.h>

int main(void)
{
    printf("Hello, world!\n");
    return 0;
}
```

Header Files, Preprocessing, and `#include` *Directives*

Every function must be declared before it is called; the *declaration* contains information that the compiler may need to call the function properly. This requirement applies to library functions as well as those defined by the programmer.

To help us declare library functions, the C implementation provides *header files* containing the necessary declarations for various parts of the library. For example, the header file `math.h` contains declarations for mathematical functions, the header file `stdio.h` contains declarations for standard input and output functions, and so on. We sometimes use the names of the header files to refer to different parts of the library. We speak of the functions declared in `math.h` as the *math library*, the functions declared in `stdio.h` as the *stdio library*, and so on.

The C compiler provides a simple way of effectively inserting header files into source files. The first phase of compilation is *preprocessing*, which manipulates the text read from the source file before sending it on to the remaining phases of compilation. Some of these manipulations can be controlled with *preprocessing directives*, all of which begin with the symbol #.

An `#include` directive designates a file whose contents are to be inserted into the program text. When the preprocessor encounters an `#include` directive, it replaces the directive by the contents of the designated file. This replacement takes place only in the text that is being passed on to the rest of the compiler. The original source file and the file that was included both remain unchanged.

The third line of the hello-world program includes the header file `stdio.h`:

```
#include <stdio.h>
```

The file `stdio.h` contains the declaration for `printf()`, the library function that the program calls to print the hello-world message. Note that the file name is enclosed by a less-than sign and a greater-than sign, which serve as angle brackets.

When C programmers say that one file *includes* another, they always mean that the one file contains an `#include` directive that names the other file. They do *not* mean that the one file contains a copy of the contents of the other file.

Defining `main()`

The remainder of the hello-world program defines the function `main()`. A function definition has the following form:

> *heading*
> {
>   *declarations (if any)*
>   *statements*
> }

The *heading* provides the information needed to call the function: the name of the function, the types of arguments (if any) that it requires, and the type of value (if any) that it returns.

The heading is followed by the *body* of the function, which specifies the action the function will take when it is called. The body of the function is a *block,* which is a series of declarations and statements delimited by the braces { and }. The braces play the same role in C as do the words **begin** and **end** in many other languages.

The hello-world program declares `main()` as follows:

```
int main(void)
{
    printf("Hello, world!\n");
    return 0;
}
```

The heading

```
int main(void)
```

gives the name of the function as `main`. The `void` in parentheses means that the function takes no arguments. The `int` indicates that the function returns an integer value (`int` is the most frequently used of C's numerous integer data types).

The body of the function is a block containing two statements:

```
{
  printf("Hello, world!\n");
  return 0;
}
```

Each statement ends with a semicolon. The first statement, which calls the library function `printf()`, will be discussed in more detail shortly. The second statement causes `main()` to return a value of 0 to the system. The value returned by `main()` is a *return code* that indicates whether the program ran successfully. Customarily, a return code of 0 indicates a successful run.

Because of the special role of `main()`, its definition can be abbreviated somewhat:

```
main()
{
  printf("Hello, world!\n");
}
```

The full heading `int main(void)` can be shortened to `main()`; the return type defaults to `int`, and no information is provided about possible arguments. If the return code is not used by the system, which is often the case, the `return` statement also can be omitted. The abbreviated form, which was standard in pre–ANSI versions of C, is so widely used that the reader needs to be able to recognize it. However, we will continue to use the unabbreviated form recommended for ANSI C, and we suggest that the reader do likewise.

Strings, Escape Sequences, and calling `printf()`

Pieces of text, such as `Hello, world!`, are stored as *strings*. We can represent a string in a C program by a *string literal*, which consists of the characters of the string enclosed in quotation marks. For example, the message `Hello, world!` can be represented by the string literal

```
"Hello, world!"
```

Some characters that we may wish to include in string literals do not have conventional graphics such as a, b, and c. Such a character can be represented by an *escape sequence*, which consists of a backslash, \ , followed by a letter or number representing the character. A case in point is the *newline character*, which causes the output device to start a new line. The newline character is represented by the escape sequence \n. If the string represented by

```
"Hello, world!\n"
```

is sent to an output device, the device will print `Hello, world!` on the current line, then go to the beginning of the following line.

We call a function by writing the name of the function followed by a pair of parentheses. The paired parentheses are known as the *function-call operator*. Inside the parentheses are listed any argument values that are to be passed to the function.

The library function `printf()` is a powerful function for formatting and printing output. It can be called with different numbers of arguments depending on how it is being used. The simplest use of this function is to call it with a single argument, which is a string to be printed. For example, the function call

```
printf("Hello, world!\n")
```

calls `printf()` and passes it the string represented by the string literal `"Hello, world!\n"`. When called, `printf()` writes the message `Hello, world!` and starts a new line.

The functions in `stdio.h` access input and output devices via *streams*. Each stream is connected to a source or destination for data, such as a keyboard, a display, a printer, or a disk file. Data read from or written to a stream comes from or goes to the device or file to which the stream is connected. The function `printf()` writes to the standard output stream, `stdout`, which is normally connected to the user's display. By changing this connection (we'll see how later), we could send the output from our program to a printer, a disk file, or even a communcations link rather than to the user's display.

The preceding function call is a C *expression,* which could conceivably be part of a larger expression. If we wish to use an expression as a statement, rather than as part of a larger expression, we convert it to an *expression statement* by following it with a semicolon. For example, the hello-world program uses the expression statement

```
printf("Hello, world!\n");
```

to print the desired message. An expression statement *always* ends with a semicolon, regardless of where it may occur in the program (such as embedded within another statement).

Note that `printf()` does not automatically cause the printer to start a new line after a string has been printed. For example, the statements

```
printf("abc");
printf("def");
printf("ghi");
```

print

```
abcdefghi
```

If we wish the strings printed on separate lines, we must include new-line characters in the string literals:

```
printf("abc\n");
printf("def\n");
printf("ghi\n");
```

These statements produce the output

```
abc
def
ghi
```

and cause the output device to start a new line after the third line is printed.

Newline characters can be embedded within a string. For example, the preceding output can also be produced by the single statement

```
printf("abc\ndef\nghi\n");
```

EDITING, COMPILING, AND LINKING

The text of a C program is stored in one or more source files. For simple programs, such as most of the examples in this book, a single source file will suffice. For large programming projects, however, multiple source files are the rule. Different source files contain logically distinct parts of the program and may have been written by different programmers. Source files are created and revised with the aid of a *text editor*.

We use a C *compiler* to translate each source file into a machine-coded *object file*. Each source file is compiled separately. If we need to make changes in a source file, then only that source file needs to be recompiled. This is one reason for using multiple source files: it is generally much faster to recompile one source file than to recompile all the program text for a large project.

The *linker* combines the object files with one another and with the code for any library functions called by the program. The output from the linker is an *executable file*, which contains all the machine code for the program and is ready to be run on the computer. Even for a program with only one source file, linking is still needed to combine the code in the object file with the code for whatever library functions the program calls.

Unfortunately, the detailed commands for editing, compiling, and linking vary too much between implementations for us to consider them here. However, it is worth mentioning two different kinds of implementation: command-line implementations and integrated development environments.

A *command-line implementation* is so called because each software tool, such as a text editor, compiler, or linker, must be invoked by typing an operating system command line. The programmer must invoke a text editor and use it to create or modify each source file. Next, the compiler must be invoked for each source file to translate it into an object file. The linker is then run to produce the executable file. Finally, the C program can be run on the computer to see if it executes properly. If it does not, or if error messages were encountered in any of the preceding steps, the programmer must return to the text editor to locate the errors and make necessary corrections.

Many operating systems provide *scripting* facilities (UNIX scripts, MS-DOS batch files) that allow new operating system commands to be defined in terms of existing commands. Command-line implementations often use these facilities to provide simplified commands for common situations. For example, there may be a single command for compiling, linking, and executing a program that has only one source file. Also, many command-line implementations provide a *make* utility, which will automatically compile and link all the source files in a programming project. The make utility recompiles only those source files in which changes have been made.

An *integrated development environment (IDE)* is a single software tool that can be used for editing, compiling, linking, executing, and debugging C programs. (The term *integrated programming environment (IPE)* is also used.) Normally, the IDE serves as a text editor, allowing us to create and modify source files. When we are ready to compile, link, or execute, however, we can do so with commands to the IDE rather than with operating system command lines. Generally, an IDE will do whatever work is necessary to carry out our commands. For example, if we tell it to execute a program, it will first do any compiling and linking necessary to produce an executable file. Like the make utility, the IDE will recompile only those source files in which changes have been made, and will relink only if one or more source files had to be recompiled. An online help facility provides easy access to information about IDE commands, compiler and linker error messages, and the C library.

IDEs also provide help for debugging. When the compiler discovers errors, the erroneous statements are highlighted on the screen. During execution, the programmer can monitor the values of selected variables and can trace the flow of control—the order in which program statements are executed.

Some old hands at C programming love their command-line compilers and would rather fight than switch. Newcomers, however, are urged to explore the power and convenience of integrated development environments. A typical microcomputer IDE is described in Appendix 3.

IDENTIFIERS

As in most other programming languages, C programmers must devise names for such program elements as variables and functions. These names, or *identifiers*, must be formed according to certain rules:

- An identifier can contain only letters, digits, and the underscore character, `_`. Thus `amount` and `hit_count` are valid identifiers but `$_amount` and `employee_#` are not.

- An identifier must begin with a letter of the alphabet or an underscore character. Thus `_dos_call` is a valid identifier but `1st_round` is not.

- Identifiers that begin with an underscore are reserved for the implementation and should not be defined by the programmer. Thus you should not define an identifier `_dos_call`, but you can use it if it is already defined by the implementation.

- An identifier must not be the same as one of the *keywords* listed in Appendix 1. Thus `int` and `void` are not valid identifiers, because they are keywords.

- C distinguishes between uppercase and lowercase letters, so that `amount`, `Amount`, and `AMOUNT` are three different identifiers.

- Only the first 31 characters of an identifier are significant—that is, are used in distinguishing one identifier from another. Thus

  `very_very_very_long_identifier_1`

and

```
very_very_very_long_identifier_2
```

are considered the same because they agree in their first 31 characters.

■ An identifier defined by the programmer should not be the same as one already defined in the library. For example, `printf` should not be used as a programmer-defined identifier because it is already the name of a library function.

The last rule can be hard to follow because of the large number of identifiers defined in the library. Reference manuals listing all library identifiers are available for each implementation. Also, you can use the help facility of an integrated development environment to check whether a particular identifier is defined in the library: if the help facility cannot retrieve information about an existing definition, you can assume that the identifier is available for your use.

If the compiler or linker seems to be having trouble with a particular identifier, check whether it conflicts with an identifier defined in the library. Alternatively, you can simply change all occurrences of the identifier (with your text editor's search-and-replace command) and see if the problem goes away.

DEFINING, DECLARING, AND CALLING FUNCTIONS

Listing 1-2 shows a slightly more elaborate greeting program that defines three functions: `main()`, `say_hello()`, and `say_goodbye()`. The program prints a four-line message:

```
Hello, everybody!
Best wishes to all!
I've got to go now.
So long, and have a nice day!
```

When the program is run, `main()` calls `say_hello()` to print the first two lines of the message and calls `say_goodbye()` to print the last two lines.

The function `say_hello()` is defined as follows:

```
void say_hello(void)
{
 printf("Hello, everybody!\n");
 printf("Best wishes to all!\n");
}
```

Listing 1-2

```
/* File greet.c */
/* Illustrates function definitions and declarations */

#include <stdio.h>

void say_hello(void);
void say_goodbye(void);

int main(void)
{
    say_hello();
    say_goodbye();
    return 0;
}

/* Extend greetings and best wishes */

void say_hello(void)
{
    printf("Hello, everybody!\n");
    printf("Best wishes to all!\n");
}

/* Take leave */

void say_goodbye(void)
{
    printf("I've got to go now.\n");
    printf("So long, and have a nice day!\n");
}
```

The name of the function, say_hello, is an identifier formed according to the rules given in the preceding section. The void in parentheses says that the function takes no arguments; the void preceding the function name says that the function does not return a value. When the function is called, the two statements in the block are executed, each printing one line of the desired message. The function say_goodbye() is defined similarly.

Recall that functions must be declared before they are called. This requirement is met by collecting the required declarations at the beginning of the source file. Declarations for library functions are obtained by including the appropriate header files. It is up to us, however, to write declarations for functions defined later in the source file.

A function declaration (also known as a *function prototype*) consists of the function-definition heading followed by a semicolon (rather than by the body of the function). Thus the functions `say_hello()` and `say_goodbye()` are declared as follows:

```
void say_hello(void);
void say_goodbye(void);
```

An easy way to create such declarations is to use the copying facilities of your text editor to copy each function-definition heading to the point where the declaration is required. Don't forget, however, to place a semicolon at the end of each declaration.

In Listing 1-2, the declarations for `say_hello()` and `say_goodbye()` are grouped near the beginning of the source file, along with the directive that includes the header file containing the declaration for `printf()`. Note that `main()` does not have to be declared, because it is not called from within the source file.

Function `main()` calls `say_hello()` and `say_goodbye()` with the following expression statements:

```
say_hello();
say_goodbye();
```

The parentheses are required even though the functions take no arguments. Each pair of parentheses is a function-call operator; without them, the functions will not be called.

VALUES, VARIABLES, AND EXPRESSIONS

Having explored the overall structure of C programs, we now turn to some of the details of the language. In this section we focus on the mechanisms for storing, retrieving, and manipulating numerical values.

Types and Values

Like many other languages, C classifies data values as belonging to different *data types* (or just *types*). The type of a value determines how it is stored in memory and what operations can be carried out on it.

In C, numbers belong to *arithmetic types,* which are further divided into *integer types* for whole numbers and *floating types* for floating-point numbers—numbers that can contain a decimal point. C has a relatively large number of arithmetic types (12), to ensure that it can accommodate the various-size integers and floating-point numbers that might be available on a particular computer.

For now, we will confine ourselves to one integer type, `int`, and one floating type, `double` (which stands for "double precision"). The range of values for type `int` vary among implementations. Typical ranges are −32,768 to 32,767 for small (16-bit) computers and about −2 billion to 2 billion for large (32-bit) computers. Type `double` typically offers a precision of about 15 significant digits, which is enough so that we don't have to worry about precision for most straightforward calculations.

Arithmetic constants (which represent arithmetic values in programs) can be written either in everyday arithmetical notation or in the *exponential notation* widely used in programming languages. Integer constants are distinguished by not containing a decimal point and not using exponential notation. The presence of either a decimal point or exponential notation signals a floating-point constant.

Unless the programmer specifies otherwise (with a suffix, as discussed in Chapter 3), integer constants represent values of type `int`, and floating-point constants represent values of type `double`. This is true for integer constants only if they lie within the range of values allowed for type `int`. For example, `0`, `1`, `800`, and `12345` represent values of type `int`, whereas `3.5`, `.045`, and `1925.34` represent values of type `double`. When exponential notation is used, the letter `E` can be either uppercase or lowercase, as in `23.1e25` and `7.3E-20`. Note that `25e10` is a floating-point constant even though no decimal point is present.★

All arithmetic constants represent positive values. Constructions such as `-100` and `-3.14` are allowed, but each is an expression in which the negation operator, `-`, is applied to a positive arithmetical constant (`100` or `3.14`).

Variables and Assignment

As in other languages, a *variable* is a memory location named by an identifier. The value stored in the memory location is the current *value of the variable*. This value can be changed by an *assignment* operation, which stores a new value in the memory location.

★For readers who haven't yet encountered exponential notation, the number following the `E` or `e` specifies how many places the decimal point is to be moved. If this number—the *exponent*—is positive, the decimal point is moved to the right. Thus `7.2345e3` is equivalent to `7234.5`, and `2e4` is equivalent to `20000`. If the exponent is negative, the decimal point is moved to the left. Thus `6.38e-4` is equivalent to `.000638`, and `2e-4` is equivalent to `.0004`. Exponential notation is also known as *scientific notation* or *floating-point notation*.

In C, a variable must always be declared before it is used. The declaration must specify the data type of the value of the variable. The implementation needs to know the data type for two reasons: (1) to determine the size of the corresponding memory location, and (2) to interpret properly the bit patterns that are stored in that location.

The declarations

```
int count;
double amount;
```

declare count as an int variable (one whose value has type int) and amount as a double variable (one whose value has type double). Note that the name of the type precedes the name of the variable, and each declaration ends with a semicolon. The variable names are identifiers formed according to the rules already given.

We can declare several variables of the same type by listing their names in a single declaration. The variable names are separated by commas. For example,

```
int i, j, k;
```

declares i, j, and k as int variables, and

```
double w, x, y, z;
```

declares w, x, y, and z as double variables.

When we declare a variable, we can give it an initial value by following the variable name with an equal sign and the desired value. For example, the declarations

```
int count = 100;
double amount = 29.95;
```

cause count to have an initial value of 100 and amount an initial value of 29.95. Likewise,

```
int i = 30, j = 40, k = 50;
```

causes i, j, and k to have the respective initial values 30, 40, and 50.

The equal sign is also the *assignment operator* in C. (Readers accustomed to another assignment operator, such as : =, must take particular care to use = when writing in C.) Although C has an assignment *operator*, it does not have a special assignment *statement*. Instead, the assignment operator is used in expressions in much the same way as other operators, such as + and -. For example, the expression

```
count = 150
```

assigns the value 150 to the variable count.

We have already seen that we can change an expression into a expression statement by following the expression with a semicolon. Thus

```
count = 150;
```

is a statement that assigns 150 to count. We can consider this an example of a C "assignment statement." However, it is not a special kind of statement, but just another expression statement formed by placing a semicolon after an expression.

Declarations in a block must be placed at the beginning of the block, before the statements. For example, the block

```
{
  int count = 100;
  double amount = 29.95;

  count = 150;
  amount = 49.95;
}
```

declares count with an initial value of 100 and amount with an initial value of 29.95. The declarations are followed by two statements. The first statement changes the value of count to 150 and the second changes the value of amount to 49.95.

Variables declared within a block are called *local variables*. A local variable can be referred to only from within the block in which it is declared; its name is not defined outside the block. We can use the same name for different local variables as long as they are declared in different blocks. Variables declared in different blocks have nothing to do with one another, regardless of whether they have the same or different names.

Arithmetic Operators

Table 1-1 shows the arithmetic operators in C. With the possible exception of the remainder operator, %, these operators are the same as used in most other programming languages.

When +, -, and * are applied to two integers, the operation is carried out using integer arithmetic, and the result is an integer. If either or both operands are floating-point numbers, however, the operation is carried out using floating-point arithmetic, and the result is a floating-point number.

The effect of the division operator, /, differs for integer and floating-point operands. If both operands are integers, / computes only

	Integer Types	Floating Types
Table 1-1	**Integer Types**	**Floating Types**
Arithmetic Operators	+ *addition*	+ *addition*
	− *subtraction*	− *subtraction*
	* *multiplication*	* *multiplication*
	/ *integer division: quotient*	/ *floating-point division*
	% *integer division: remainder*	

the integer quotient; the remainder is discarded. Thus the value of 9/2 is 4. If either or both operands are floating-point numbers, however, a floating-point division is done, yielding a floating-point result. Thus 9/2.0, 9.0/2, and 9.0/2.0 all evaluate to 4.5.

The % operator computes the remainder of two integers (the remainder operator is not defined for floating-point operands). For example, 9%2 evaluates to 1, the remainder obtained when 9 is divided by 2.

Expression Evaluation

Like most other programming languages, C allows expressions containing more than one operator, such as

    3+4*5

To understand how this expression will be evaluated, we need to know how the operands will be grouped with the operators. In particular, we need to know if 4 is an operand of + or *. The desired grouping can be indicated with parentheses. If the expression is written as

    (3+4)*5

4 is an operand of +, and the expression evaluates to 7*5, or 35. On the other hand, if the expression is written as

    3+(4*5)

4 is an operand of *, and the expression evaluates to 3+20, or 23.

In the absence of parentheses, we need rules to determine how an expression will be evaluated. Many computer language textbooks state these rules in terms of the order in which operations will be carried out. An example is the familiar rule that multiplications and divisions are carried out before additions and subtractions. But such rules can be misleading in C, because the C compiler has considerable leeway as to the order in which operations are actually carried out. Therefore, we will state our rules in terms of the order in which operators are grouped with operands. Given such a grouping, the C compiler is free to determine the most efficient order in which to carry out the indicated calculations.

Aside from this slightly different point of view, the rules for evaluating C expressions are very similar to those for other languages. Every C operator has a *precedence* and an *associativity*, which are given in Table A2-1 in Appendix 2. Operators are grouped with operands in order of decreasing precedence: first the highest-precedence operators are grouped with their operands, then the operators with next highest precedence, and so on. The associativities determine the groupings for operators having the same precedence.

For example, as we expect, the multiplication and division operators have higher precedence than the addition and subtraction operators. In

```
3*4+5*6
```

the two * operators are grouped with their operands before the + operator. Thus the operands 4 and 5 are grouped with the * operators rather than with the +. We can indicate the resulting grouping with parentheses:

```
(3*4)+(5*6)
```

The addition, subtraction, multiplication, and division operators all have *left-to-right associativity*, so operators with the same precedence will be grouped from left to right. For example, in

```
9-3-2-1
```

the left-most operator is grouped first:

```
(9-3)-2-1
```

then the next operator to the right, and so on, to give the grouping

```
((9-3)-2)-1
```

The expression evaluates to 3. If the operators had been grouped from right to left, the value of the expression would have been 7.

Operators can be classified according to the number of operands each takes. In C, we find *unary operators* (which take one operand), *binary operators* (which take two), and a single *trinary operator* (which takes three operands). The addition, subtraction, multiplication, and division operators are all binary. There are two unary arithmetic operators, which are listed in Appendix 2 as *unary +* and *unary −*. These are the + and − operators that c   ar in expressions such as

+3*5 and 2/-4. The unary + operator has no effect; the unary − operator changes the sign of its operand. As mentioned earlier, even such simple expressions as +10 and −25 involve the unary + and − operators, because signs are not included as parts of C constants.

As Appendix 2 shows, the unary arithmetic operators have higher precedence than the binary arithmetic operators. For example, in an expression such as

```
-3*5+2*-4
```

the unary − operators are grouped first:

```
(-3)*5+2*(-4)
```

The multiplication operators, which have the next highest precedence, are grouped second:

```
((-3)*5)+(2*(-4))
```

In C, all *prefix* unary operators—that is, unary operators that precede their operands—associate from right to left. For example, in

```
-+-25
```

the right-most operator is grouped with its operand first, then the next operator to the left is grouped, and so on:

```
-(+(-25))
```

More About Variables and Assignments

For most operators, any operands that are variables are replaced by their values and the operator is applied to those values. For example, in evaluating

```
i+j*k
```

i, j, and k are replaced by their current values, and those values are used to compute the value of the expression.

The assignment operator, =, is different. The right operand of = is like that of any other operator: the right operand can be a constant, a variable, or an expression, and its value is computed before the operator is applied. The left operand of =, however, must be a variable—it must name a memory location in which a new value can be stored. The current value of the left operand is not used; instead, it is discarded and replaced by the value being assigned.

For example, when

```
i = j
```

is evaluated, j is replaced by its current value, and that value is stored in the memory location named by i. On the other hand,

```
3 = 5
```

and

```
(3+2) = 10
```

are invalid, because neither 3 nor (3+2) names a memory location.

An assignment expression, such as i=5, yields a value, just as do expressions such as 3+5 and 4*3. The value of an assignment is the value that was assigned to the variable. Thus i=5 evaluates to 5 in the same way that 3+5 evaluates to 8 and 4*3 evaluates to 12. Because an assignment yields a value, it can be used as part of a larger expression. For example,

```
3+(i=5)*4
```

has the value 23, because the assignment has the value 5. When this expression is evaluated, the value 23 is computed as the value of the expression, and the value 5 is assigned to i.

Side Effects

Traditionally, the primary purpose of an expression is computing a value. Any other effect of evaluating the expression, such as assigning a value to a variable, is called a *side effect*. For example, the expression 7*2 has no side effects—it merely computes the value 14. On the other hand, (i=7)*(j=2) has two side effects. In addition to computing the value 14, it also assigns 7 to i and 2 to j.

We already know how to convert an expression into an expression statement by following the expression with a semicolon. When the expression statement is executed, the expression is evaluated and the value of the expression is discarded. Any side effects, however, still take place. For example, when the statement

```
x = 3.5;
```

is executed, the value of the expression (which is 3.5) is discarded. However, the side effect of assigning 3.5 to x still takes place.

If an expression has no side effects, the corresponding expression statement will have no effect whatever. For example,

```
3*5;
```

is a valid expression statement. Its execution will have no effect, however, because the value of the expression will be discarded and there are no side effects to be carried out. Many compilers will issue a warning message for an expression statement that has no effect.

The assignment operator has a lower precedence than most other C operators. This means that, normally, the entire expression to the right of the assignment operator represents the value to be assigned. For example, in

```
i = 3+4*5;
```

the operators, in order of decreasing precedence, are *, +, and =. Therefore, the grouping is

```
i = (3+(4*5));
```

and the value of (3+(4*5)) will be assigned to i.

The associativity of the assignment operator is right to left. This allows us to write *multiple assignments*—assignments that assign the same value to several variables. For example, in the statement

```
i = j = 5;
```

the expression is grouped as

```
i = (j = 5);
```

The subexpression (j = 5) assigns 5 to j, and the value of the subexpression (also 5) is assigned to i. Thus 5 is assigned to both i and j.

Likewise, the expression

```
i = j = k = m+n;
```

is grouped as

```
i = (j = (k = (m+n)));
```

The subexpression (m+n) is evaluated, and its value is assigned, in turn, to k, j, and i.

Dangers of Side Effects

We must use considerable caution in writing expressions containing assignment operators. The problem is that the value and side effects of such an expression can depend on the order in which assignments and other operations are carried out—an order that we cannot in general predict. We already know that the C compiler has considerable leeway as to the order in which it evaluates different parts of an expression. The situation is even worse for side effects. Except for a few special operators, we can say nothing about when or in what order side effects take place during the evaluation of an expression.

To see the kind of problem that can arise, consider the statement

```
i = (i = 5) + 7;
```

The assignment operator in parentheses assigns `i` the value 5; the other assignment operator assigns `i` the value 12 [remember that the value of (`i = 5`) is 5]. Because we cannot know the order in which the two assignments are carried out, we cannot predict whether the value of `i` will be 5 or 12 after the statement has been executed.

Because of such problems, we should generally confine ourselves to assignments that compute a value and then assign it to one or more variables, as in

```
i = j + 2*k;
```

and

```
i = j = k = 3*m - 4*n;
```

Such assignments are always safe. More complex assignment expressions must be studied carefully (by both the programmer and by someone trying to understand the program) to guarantee that they yield the desired value and side effects.

INPUT AND OUTPUT

The stdio library provides a number of input and output functions, the most generally useful of which are `scanf()` for input and `printf()` for output.

Output with `printf()`

We have seen how to use `printf()` to print the string that is supplied as its first (and, so far, only) argument. However, we can do far more with this string than merely print it character by character. The first argument of `printf()` is a *format string*, which can contain *conversion specifications* describing how other values are to be converted into printed form. The values to be converted are supplied as additional arguments to `printf()`. When the format string is printed, each conversion specification is replaced by the corresponding converted value.

A conversion specification always begins with a `%` sign. The simplest conversion specifications for the data types we have studied so far are `%d` for type `int`, `%f` for type `double`, and `%s` for strings.

For example, the statement

```
printf("%d plus %d equals %d\n", 20, 30, 50);
```

prints

```
20 plus 30 equals 50
```

When the format string is printed, the first %d is replaced by 20, the second by 30, and the third by 50.

The arguments of printf(), like all function arguments, can be represented by variables or expressions. For example, the statements

```
x = 2.5;
y = 3.5;
printf("The product is %f\n", x * y);
```

print

```
The product is 8.750000
```

Unless we specify otherwise, an f conversion prints a floating-point number with six decimal places.

Field Widths, Justification, and Precision

When we insert a printed value in running text, we do not want it to take up any more space than necessary. When arranging values in columns or positioning them on preprinted forms, however, it is convenient if each printed value occupies a fixed-size *field*. To this end, we can precede the character that specifies a conversion by a *field width*, which specifies how many character positions the printed value must occupy. The printed value is padded with a sufficient number of spaces to make up the specified field width.

By default, a printed value is *right-justified* in its field. That is, it is *preceded* by any spaces needed for padding, so that the value is moved as far to the right in its field as possible. For example,

```
printf("%6d", 25);
```

precedes the printed 25 with four spaces, so that the printed value is right-justified in a six-character field.

A minus sign preceding the field width causes the printed value to be *left-justified*—positioned as far to the left as possible in the field. For example,

```
printf("%-10s", "Price");
```

prints `Price` followed by five spaces so that the printed value is justified in a 10-character field.

The field width can be followed by a decimal point and a *precision*. For an `f` conversion, the precision specifies the number of decimal places to be printed. For example,

```
printf("%7.3f", 8.75);
```

prints `8.750` right-justified in a seven-character field. We can specify the precision even if the field width is omitted. Thus

```
printf("%.3f", 8.75);
```

prints `8.750` in a five-character field (that is, the five-character value is printed without any padding).

To arrange printed values in columns, use the same field width for a column heading and for all the items in the column. Left-justify strings and right-justify numbers. For example, the statements

```
printf("%-10s    %-7s\n\n", "Item", "Price");
printf("%-10s    %7.2f\n", "Computer", 1999.95);
printf("%-10s    %7.2f\n", "Typewriter", 249.98);
printf("%-10s    %7.2f\n", "Paper", 5.99);
```

produce the following printout:

```
Item          Price

Computer     1999.95
Typewriter    249.98
Paper           5.99
```

A precision can also be specified for some other kinds of conversions. For `%d` conversion, the precision specifies the *minimum* number of digits to be printed. Leading zeros will be printed if necessary to make up the specified number of digits. For `%s` conversion, the precision specifies the *maximum* number of characters to be printed. The string to be printed will be truncated on the right if it contains more than the specified number of characters. For example,

```
printf("%.5d", 25);
```

prints

```
00025
```

and

```
printf("%.4s", "computer");
```

prints

    comp

Note the decimal point in each format string.

Input with `scanf()`

The input function `scanf()` is similar to `printf()` in that input is controlled by a format string whose conversion specifications give the type to which each input value should be converted. Just as `printf()` writes to the standard output stream `stdout`, which is normally connected to the user's display, so `scanf()` reads from the standard input stream `stdin`, which is normally connected to the user's keyboard.

For most types, the letters that specify conversions are the same for `scanf()` and `printf()`. Unfortunately, one of the types we are using is an exception. The conversion specifier for type `double` is `f` for output and `lf` (`l` is an ell) for input. Thus a value written with the conversion specification `%f` would be read with `%lf`.

Another major difference between `scanf()` and `printf()` results from the way arguments are passed in C. C passes arguments *by value*: when a function is called, the argument expressions are evaluated, and the value of each is passed to the function. In particular, if an argument is a variable, the function receives a copy of the variable's value. The function has no access to the variable itself and so cannot assign it a new value.

Every memory location has an *address*,[*] which is used to designate that location for the purpose of storing data in it or retrieving data from it. If a function is to assign a new value to a variable, then we must provide it with the *address of the variable*—that is, the address of the corresponding memory location. Many languages have special argument-passing mechanisms that pass the addresses of variables without the user's necessarily being aware of it (Pascal's variable parameters are an example). C avoids such hidden mechanisms: if a function needs the address of a variable, we must supply the address explicitly as an argument.

Addresses are calculated with the *address-of* operator, `&`: if `x` is a variable, then `&x` is the address of `x`. This address is a value and can be passed to functions just like any other argument value. For example, the statement

    scanf("%lf", &x);

---

[*]Addresses are discussed in more detail in Chapter 3.

reads a floating-point number, converts it to type `double`, and stores it in the variable `x` whose address is supplied as an argument. Likewise, the statement

```
scanf("%d%d%d", &i, &j, &k);
```

reads three integers, converts them to type `int`, and stores them in variables `i`, `j`, and `k`. Values to be read are separated by *whitespace*, which can consist of spaces, tabs, and newlines. Before reading a number, `scanf()` skips any preceding whitespace; therefore, numerical input values can be typed on one or more lines and separated by any number of spaces.

The all-too-common error of omitting the address-of operator always causes the program to malfunction. For example, if we write

```
scanf("%d", i); /* Wrong! */
```

then `scanf()` will be passed the *value* of `i` rather than its *address*. Because `scanf()` receives an invalid address, it will try to store the input value in some unexpected and unintended memory location. The program will certainly not work as intended, and it may very well crash. (Systems with memory protection will crash any program that tries to access a memory location not specifically reserved for the program's use.)

Computing Areas and Perimeters

After our study of input, output, and expressions, we are now finally in a position to write a program that inputs data, carries out calculations, and outputs results. The program in Listing 1-3 calculates the area and perimeter of a rectangle. The declarations

```
double length, width;   /* Data */
double area, perimeter; /* Results */
```

declare the four variables that will be used in the program. All the variables have type `double`. Note that the declarations are placed at the beginning of the block, preceding all statements.

The statements

```
printf("Enter length: ");
scanf("%lf", &length);
printf("Enter width: ");
scanf("%lf", &width);
```

Listing 1-3

```
/* File rectangl.c */
/* Compute area and perimeter of rectangle */

#include <stdio.h>

int main(void)
{
    double length, width;      /* Data */
    double area, perimeter;    /* Results */

    printf("Enter length: ");
    scanf("%lf", &length);
    printf("Enter width: ");
    scanf("%lf", &width);

    area = length * width;
    perimeter = 2 * (length + width);

    printf("Area = %.3f\n", area);
    printf("Perimeter = %.3f\n", perimeter);

    return 0;
}
```

prompt the user for the length and width of a rectangle. The values typed by the user are read into the variables length and width. Note that the prompt strings do not end with newlines; this allows the user's response to be typed on the same lines as the prompt.

The area and perimeter are calculated by the statements

```
area = length * width;
perimeter = 2 * (length + width);
```

Each statement calculates a value and assigns it to a variable. In the second statement, the left operand of * is an integer and the right operand is a floating-point number. Therefore, as explained earlier, the multiplication will be carried out with floating-point arithmetic and produce a floating-point result.

The following statements print the results:

```
printf("Area = %.3f\n", area);
printf("Perimeter = %.3f\n", perimeter);
```

Each output value is printed with no padding and with three decimal places. The following is a typical interaction between the program and the user:

```
Enter length: 7.25
Enter width: 4.9
Area = 35.525
Perimeter = 24.300
```

NAMED CONSTANTS AND PREPROCESSOR MACROS

It is good programming practice to define names for numerical constants and use the names rather than the numbers throughout the program. The names indicate the purposes of what would otherwise be mysterious numbers sprinkled throughout the code. And if a constant needs to be changed, it is much easier to change one name definition than to locate and change every occurrence of a numerical constant.

In C, constants are named with the aid of *preprocessor macros* (usually just called *macros*). A macro is an identifier defined to represent a segment of program text. After the definition has been processed, the preprocessor locates each occurrence of the identifier and *expands* it by replacing it with the corresponding text. (Macro identifiers inside string literals are not expanded.) Because preprocessing is always the first stage of compilation, the rest of the compiler sees the program text only after all macros have been expanded.

A macro is defined with the preprocessor directive #define, which is followed by the macro name and the desired definition. For example,

```
#define  PI  3.14159265
```

defines PI to represent the text 3.14159265. It is customary in C to use all capital letters for identifiers that represent constants. Note that there is no punctuation in the definition: one or more spaces separate #define, the macro name, and the text that the name is to represent.

If later in the same source file we write

```
area = PI * radius * radius;
```

the preprocessor will expand this to

```
area = 3.14159265 * radius * radius;
```

It is this expanded statement that is processed by the remainder of the compiler.

Most header files contain macro definitions as well as function declarations. For example, the header file `stdlib.h` defines macros `EXIT_SUCCESS` and `EXIT_FAILURE` to represent the return codes for successful and unsuccessful execution, respectively. Thus, if `stdlib.h` has been included in the source file, we can replace

```
return 0;
```

by

```
return EXIT_SUCCESS;
```

and we can use

```
return EXIT_FAILURE;
```

to return the code for unsuccessful execution.

Listing 1-4 shows a traditional programming example, a program for making change. Such a program needs constants giving the number of cents in each denomination of coin. We use macros to define names for these constants:

```
#define HALF      50
#define QUARTER   25
#define DIME      10
#define NICKEL     5
```

In the program, `change` is the number of cents that remain to be handed back, and `coins` is the number of coins to be returned for a particular denomination. We handle each denomination by dividing `change` by the number of cents in one coin. The quotient of this division is the number of coins to be handed back, which is assigned to `coins`. The remainder of the division is the new value of `change`—the number of cents that remain to be handed back using coins of smaller denominations. The following code handles half dollars:

```
coins = change / HALF;
change = change % HALF;
printf("%-9s %2d\n", "Halves:", coins);
```

The same format string is used for each denomination, thereby arranging the names and numbers of the coins in parallel columns. The following is a typical interaction with the program:

Listing 1-4

```c
/* File change.c */
/* Program to make change */

#include <stdlib.h>
#include <stdio.h>

/* Define values of coins */

#define HALF        50
#define QUARTER     25
#define DIME        10
#define NICKEL       5

int main(void)
{
    int change;   /* Amount of change yet to be returned */
    int coins;    /* Number of coins to be returned for
                        a particular denomination */

    printf("Enter amount of change in cents: ");
    scanf("%d", &change);

    coins = change / HALF;
    change = change % HALF;
    printf("%-9s  %2d\n", "Halves:", coins);

    coins = change / QUARTER;
    change = change % QUARTER;
    printf("%-9s  %2d\n", "Quarters:", coins);

    coins = change / DIME;
    change = change % DIME;
    printf("%-9s  %2d\n", "Dimes:", coins);

    coins = change / NICKEL;
    change = change % NICKEL;
    printf("%-9s  %2d\n", "Nickels:", coins);

    printf("%-9s  %2d\n", "Pennies:", change);

    return EXIT_SUCCESS;
}
```

```
Enter amount of change in cents: 97
Halves: 1
Quarters: 1
Dimes: 2
Nickels: 0
Pennies: 2
```

Note that the program includes `stdlib.h` and uses `EXIT_SUCCESS` as the return code for successful execution.

FUNCTIONS WITH ARGUMENTS

Early in this chapter we saw how to declare functions that take no arguments. We now know enough about such matters as types, variables, initialization, and assignment to see how arguments are handled.

Our example for this section will be the program in Listing 1-5, which computes the so-called size of a rectangular box. *Size* is defined here as in postal regulations: the length (longest dimension) of the box plus its girth (distance around it in the width–height direction). In the program, `main()` handles input and output but calls the function `size()` to compute the size.

We need to consider two kinds of arguments. *Actual arguments* are the values that are passed to a function when it is called. The various values we have passed to the `printf()` function are examples of actual arguments. *Formal arguments* are variables in the function definition that receive the values of the actual arguments when the function is called.

The formal arguments are declared inside the parentheses in the function heading. The argument declarations are separated by commas:

```
double size(double length,
            double width,
            double height)
```

The `double` preceding the function name states that `size()` returns a value of type `double`. Inside the parentheses, `length`, `width`, and `height` are declared as arguments of type `double`.

The formal arguments are treated as local variables that are initialized to the values of the corresponding actual arguments when the function is called. For example, suppose `size()` is called with the statement

```
s = size(8.0, 5.0, 3.0);
```

Then the formal arguments behave like variables declared and initialized as follows:

Listing 1-5

```
/* File size.c */
/* Demonstrate declaring and defining function
   having arguments and return value */

#include <stdlib.h>
#include <stdio.h>

double size(double length,
            double width,
            double height);

int main(void)
{
    double len, wdth, hght, sz;

    printf("Enter length, width, and height: ");
    scanf("%lf%lf%lf", &len, &wdth, &hght);
    sz = size(len, wdth, hght);
    printf("Size is %.2f\n", sz);
    return EXIT_SUCCESS;
}

/* Compute size of rectangular box */

double size(double length,
            double width,
            double height)
{
    double size1, girth;

    girth = 2 * (width + height);
    size1 = length + girth;
    return size1;
}
```

```
double length = 8.0;
double width = 5.0;
double height = 3.0;
```

These declarations are treated as if they were inserted at the beginning of the block that defines the function, thus making the formal arguments local to that block. The only difference between formal arguments and other local variables is that formal arguments are automatically initialized to the values of the corresponding actual arguments.

The body of `size()` uses the values of the formal arguments to compute and return the size:

```
{
  double size1, girth;

  girth = 2 * (width + height);
  size1 = length + girth;
  return size1;
}
```

The `return` statement terminates execution of the function and returns the specified value (here the value of `size1`) as the value of the function. Every function that returns a value must have at least one `return` statement (if it has more than one, the first `return` statement encountered during execution is the one that is effective).

It is worth looking at some alternate ways of writing the body of `size()`. For example, we can use any expression to specify the value that is returned by the `return` statement. In

```
{
  return length + 2*(width + height);
}
```

all the calculations are done in the `return` statement, and no local variables need be declared.

The initial values of local variables can be specified by expressions, which can contain formal parameters and any variables that have already been declared and initialized. The following block for `size()` does all the calculations in the declarations that initialize the local variables:

```
{
    double girth = 2 * (width + height);
    double size1 = length + girth;

    return size1;
}
```

This block contains only one statement, the `return` statement.

We know that a function must be declared before it can be called, and that we can construct the declaration by writing the function heading followed by a semicolon. Following this prescription for `size()` yields

```
double size(double length,
            double width,
            double height);
```

This declaration appears near the beginning of Listing 1-5.

The declaration of a function with arguments can be simplified by omitting the names of the formal arguments. Only the types of the formal arguments are needed in the declaration, not their names. Thus the declaration for `size()` can be simplified to

```
double size(double, double, double);
```

It is a matter of style as to whether the argument names are included in the declaration. If the argument names are well chosen, they can help someone reading the program to understand how the function is used.

In function `main()` of Listing 1-5, `size()` is called by the statement

```
sz = size(len, wdth, hght);
```

We recall that the parentheses in a function call constitute the function-call operator, `()`. This operator is classified as *unary*, because it is applied to only one operand—the function name. (The actual arguments are part of the function-call operator—they are not additional operands.) The function-call operator is classified as a *postfix* operator, because it *follows* its operand instead of preceding it as do prefix unary operators such as unary + and unary -.

As Table A2-1 in Appendix 2 shows, `()` belongs to the group of operators that have the highest possible precedence. This ensures that the function-call operator will always be grouped with the function name. For example, the previous displayed expression is grouped as

```
sz = (size(len, wdth, hght));
```

The function-call operator is applied to the function name, and the value returned by the function is assigned to `sz`. Likewise, the expression

```
3.5 + 10.3*size(5.2, 3.4, 1.2)
```

is grouped as

```
3.5 + (10.3*(size(5.2, 3.4, 1.2)))
```

The value returned by the function is multiplied by 10.3, and the product is added to 3.5.

The actual arguments can be expressions, as in

```
sz = size(3.5 * 7.2, 9.7 - 3.5, -2.2);
```

The expressions are evaluated before the function-call operator is applied, and their values are passed to the function as usual (the argument values are used to initialize the formal arguments).

We do not know the order in which the actual arguments will be evaluated, which can cause problems if any of the argument expressions have side effects. For example, in

```
x = 2.0;
sz = size(x = 3.5, 2.0, x);
```

we cannot predict whether 3.5 or 2.0 will be passed as the value of the third argument. Thus we do well to avoid operators with side effects in expressions representing actual arguments. If we insist on using such an operator, we must make sure that its side effect cannot affect the value of another argument.

If the actual arguments are variables—as in Listing 1-5—the values of the variables are used to initialize the formal arguments. As already mentioned, this flow of data is strictly one-way: the function cannot change the values of the actual arguments. In particular, if the function definition assigns a new value to a formal argument, only the value of the formal argument is changed. The corresponding actual argument is not affected.

EXERCISES

1-1. Write a program to print your name and address as it would appear on an envelope addressed to you.

1-2. Write a string literal that, when printed, will produce the following pattern:

```
* * * * *
+++++

+++++
* * * * *
```

The upper and lower parts of the pattern are separated by a single blank line. After the pattern has been printed, the output device should start a new line.

1-3. Write a program to compute discounts and sales tax. Given the purchase amount and the discount and sales tax rates, the program should print (as on a sales slip) the amount of the purchase, the amount of the discount, the discounted amount, the amount of sales tax, and the total amount to be paid.

1-4. Write a program to input a time in seconds and print it in hours, minutes, and seconds. For example, an input of 10,000 seconds would be printed as 02:46:40, which represents 2 hours, 46 minutes, and 40 seconds. *Hints:* (1) The calculations are similar to those for the change-making program. Define macros for the number of seconds in an hour and the number of seconds in a minute. (2) Each int value should be printed with a minimum of two digits: 0 is printed as 00, 2 is printed as 02, and so on. Recall that the minimum number of digits for a %d conversion can be specified with a precision parameter. (3) The colons should appear in the format string, separating the conversion specifications for the numerical values.

1-5. Write a program to input a radius and a height, then compute the volume of a sphere with the given radius and the volume of a cylinder with the given radius and height. Each volume should be computed by a separate function. The function main() should be confined to input and output and to calling the functions that compute the volumes. Define a macro to represent the constant *pi*.

2

Control Statements and Related Operators

*B*Y GOVERNING the execution of other statements, control statements provide for *iteration* (executing statements repeatedly) and *selection* (choosing which statements will be executed). In support of iteration and selection we need *relational operators* for testing the state of the computation and *logical operators* for formulating more complicated tests. We will also look at the *increment, decrement,* and *compound assignment* operators, which are widely used in connection with iteration statements.

LOGICAL VALUES AND RELATIONAL OPERATORS

A control statement tests the state of the computation by evaluating a control expression; each control expression tests whether or not a certain condition is satisfied. The value of the expression represents the result of the test and determines the action of the control statement.

For most control statements, the result of a test can be represented as *true* (the test succeeded, the condition is satisfied) or *false* (the test failed, the condition is not satisfied). Some languages provide a separate type for *true* and *false* (Pascal's type `Boolean` is an example). C, however, makes use of any type for which zero and nonzero values can be distinguished; zero represents *false* and any nonzero value represents *true*. Although the words *false* and *true* are not part of the C language, we will sometimes use them in our discussions to represent, respectively, zero and nonzero values.

Types for which zero and nonzero values can be distinguished are called *scalar types*. They include the arithmetic types we began discussing in Chapter 1 and the pointer types we will take up in later chapters. A control expression whose value is to represent *true* or *false* must yield a value of a scalar type. The scalar type most commonly used for this purpose is `int`.

Table 2-1

Relational Operators

OPERATOR	CONDITION
==	*is equal to*
!=	*is not equal to*
<	*is less than*
<=	*is less than or equal to*
>	*is greater than*
>=	*is greater than or equal to*

One of the most common tests is to compare two values for equality, inequality, or numerical order. Such tests are performed by the *relational operators*, which yield 0 for *false* and 1 for *true*. Table 2-1 shows the relational operators and the condition that each tests. The operators <, <=, >, and >= are the same as their counterparts in many other languages. The == and != operators are different, however. In most other languages, = (which is the assignment operator in C) is used to compare values for equality. As a result, newcomers to C tend to slip and write = where == is called for. Often the compiler cannot be sure that this is an error, because C does allow = operators to be embedded within expressions. The best the compiler can do is issue a warning if it finds = where == would be more likely.

In C, the exclamation point represents the word *not*. Therefore, the not-equal-to operator is represented by != rather than by <> as in some other languages.

The relational operators have lower precedence than the arithmetic operators. This means that arithmetic expressions serving as operands of a relational operator do not have to be enclosed in parentheses. For example,

```
m + 2 <= 3 * n
```

is grouped as

```
(m + 2) <= (3 * n)
```

and the relational operator compares the values of the two arithmetic expressions. Although the parentheses are not required, using them anyway may make the expression easier to read.

ITERATION

Iteration in C is accomplished with the while, do, and for statements. The C while statement is very similar to its counterparts in other languages; the C for statement, however, is somewhat eccentric. A statement completely equivalent to the C do statement can be found in ANSI Basic. The Pascal `repeat` statement is similar to the C do statement, but the two are not precisely equivalent.*

The `while` Statement

The `while` statement has the following form:

```
while (expression)
    statement
```

Expression is the control expression and *statement* is the controlled statement, the statement whose execution is governed by the `while` statement. The control expression is evaluated before each execution of the controlled statement. If the value of the control expression is *true* (nonzero), the controlled statement is executed, after which the control statement is evaluated again, and so on. If the value of the control expression is *false* (zero), the controlled statement is not executed and the execution of the `while` statement is terminated.

For example, the statements

```
n = 1;
while (n <= 10)
    n = n + 1;
```

step the value of the `int` variable n from 1 to 10. Note that the `while` statement is preceded by a statement to assign n its initial value. Because a `while` statement begins by evaluating the control expression, any variables in the control expression must be given their initial values *before* the `while` statement is executed.

The controlled statement can be a block, thus allowing the execution of more than one statement to be controlled. For example, the statements

```
n = 1;
while (n <= 10)
{
    printf("%3d", n);
    n = n + 1;
}
```

produce the following printout:

```
1   2   3   4   5   6   7   8   9  10
```

---

*The `repeat` statement repeats *until* the given condition *becomes* true, whereas the do statement repeats *while* the given condition *remains* true.

This example shows one way of writing a `while` statement whose controlled statement is a block. Another style, which we will follow in this book, places the opening brace of the block *on the same line* as the `while` and the control expression:

```
n = 1;
while (n <= 10) {
    printf("%3d", n);
    n = n + 1;
}
```

The punctuation of control statements is governed by the following rules: (1) an expression statement always ends with a semicolon (as do certain other statements, such as the `return` statement); (2) a block is *never* followed by a semicolon; and (3) the preceding applies even if the statement or block is part of a control statement. Thus in the preceding examples, the `while` statement that controls a single expression statement ends with a semicolon, whereas those that control blocks do not.

The do Statement

The do statement has the following form (note the semicolon following the parenthesized control expression):

```
do
    statement
while (expression);
```

The `do` statement is similar to the `while` statement except that the control expression is evaluated *after* each execution of the controlled statement rather than before.

The only real difference between `while` and `do` lies in when the control expression is evaluated for the first time. With `while`, the control expression is evaluated before the controlled statement is executed for the first time. With `do`, the control expression is evaluated after the first execution of the controlled statement. For the remaining iterations, both `while` and `do` evaluate the control expression between successive executions of the controlled statement.

We use the `do` statement when the controlled statement must be executed before the control expression can be evaluated. For example, suppose we wish to read and print numbers, terminating this process when a number of 1000 or greater has been read and printed. We cannot test for termination until the current number has been read and printed, so we use the following `do` statement:

```
do {
   scanf("%d", &n);
   printf("%d\n", n);
} while (n < 1000);
```

Note that, in the style used here, the opening and closing braces of the block appear on the same lines as other parts of the do statement.

The for Statement

Like its counterparts in other languages, the C for statement is intended for stepping a control variable through a series of values and executing a controlled statement once for each value. In most languages one need only specify the initial and final values of the control variable and the amount by which its value is to change after each iteration. In C, however, we must supply the actual expressions that assign the control variable its initial value, test for its final value, and change its value after each iteration. This increases the complexity of the C for statement but also increases its flexibility: we have complete freedom to specify the calculations that test for the final value and change the value after each iteration.

The for statement has the following form:

```
for (exp-i; exp-t; exp-s)
   statement
```

Expression *exp-i* assigns the control variable its initial value, *exp-t* tests whether the iterations should continue, and *exp-s* steps the control variable from one value to the next. For example, in

```
for (n = 1; n <= 10; n = n + 1)
   printf("%3d", n);
```

exp-i (n = 1) assigns n the initial value 1, *exp-t* (n <= 10) ensures that the value of n will not exceed 10, and *exp-s* (n = n + 1) increments the value of n after each execution of the controlled statement. The for statement, which prints the integers from 1 to 10, is exactly equivalent to the while statement discussed earlier:

```
n = 1;
while (n <= 10) {
   printf("%3d", n);
   n = n + 1;
}
```

The same expressions are evaluated and the same statements executed in the two versions of the code. In the for statement, however, the expressions that manipulate and test the control variable are gathered together in one place, making the code easier to understand.

In general, a `for` statement is equivalent to the following statements:

```
exp-i;
while (exp-t) {
    statement
    exp-s;
}
```

Exp-t becomes the control expression for the `while` statement. *Exp-i* and *exp-s* are made into expression statements; the initialization statement is executed before the `while` statement, and the stepping statement is executed after each execution of the controlled statement.

Each of the three expressions in a `for` statement can be omitted if it is not needed; if *exp-t* is omitted, the iterations will continue indefinitely. The most common omission is *exp-i*, which is not needed if the control variable has already been initialized by earlier statements. The two semicolons in the `for` statement are retained even when expressions are omitted.

Here is a final example of a `for` statement. The following statements input and compute the sum of 100 integers:

```
sum = 0;
for (n = 1; n <= 100; n = n + 1) {
    scanf("%d", &number);
    sum = sum + number;
}
```

INCREMENT, DECREMENT, AND COMPOUND ASSIGNMENT OPERATORS

These operators carry out a computation and assign the result to a variable. They are particularly convenient for iteration, where each execution of the controlled statement usually computes new values for one or more variables. Our preceding iteration examples, which do not use these operators, seem unnecessarily cumbersome to an experienced C programmer. They are reminiscent of the stilted speech of a foreigner who has mastered the vocabulary and grammar of a language but has yet to learn the local idioms.

Compound Assignment Operators

A *compound assignment operator* consists of a C operator followed by an = sign, as in +=, -=, *=, and so on. Compound assignment operators are available for many C operators, including all arithmetic operators. A compound assignment operator carries out the indicated operation, then assigns the result to its left operand, which must be a variable. Specifically, for the arithmetic operators, we have

m += n	*is equivalent to*	m = m + n
m -= n	*is equivalent to*	m = m - n
m *= n	*is equivalent to*	m = m * n
m /= n	*is equivalent to*	m = m / n
m %= n	*is equivalent to*	m = m % n

Like the plain assignment operator, =, each compound assignment operator both yields a value and has a side effect. The value is the one computed by applying the arithmetic (or other) operator to the two operands; the side effect consists of assigning this value to the variable on the left. For example, if the value of m is 4 and the value of n is 3, both m += n and m + n yield the value 7. However, m += n changes the value of m to 7, whereas m + n does not change the value of either of its operands

Expression statements such as

```
m += 5;
m *= 10;
```

are common. We can think of each statement as changing the value of the m in a certain way. For example, the first statement increases the value of m by 5, and the second multiplies the value of m by 10.

The compound assignment operators have the same precedence and associativity as =. As with =, an arithmetic expression to the right of the assignment operator is evaluated, and its value is assigned to the variable on the left. For example,

```
m *= n+5;
```

is grouped as

```
m *= (n+5);
```

The statement multiplies the value of m by the value of n+5.

In our earlier code for summing the integers from 1 to 100, the statement

```
sum = sum + number;
```

could have been written more compactly and idiomatically as

```
sum += number;
```

This is the version that would normally be used by experienced C programmers.

The Increment and Decrement Operators

We know that

```
n = n + 1
```

can be written more compactly as

```
n += 1
```

However, we can do even better. C provides an *increment operator* ++, which adds 1 to the value of a variable, and a *decrement operator* --, which subtracts 1 from the value of a variable. The following three expressions are equivalent:

```
n = n + 1
n += 1
++n
```

Likewise, the following expressions are equivalent:

```
n = n - 1
n -= 1
--n
```

The increment and decrement operators can be used as prefix operators (as in ++n and --n) or as postfix operators (as in n++ and n--). The equivalences just given illustrate the prefix operators, which increment or decrement the value of a variable and return the new value of the variable as the value of the expression. For example, if the value of n is 25, ++n changes the value of n to 26 and yields 26 as the value of the expression. Likewise, if the value of m is 10, --m changes the value of m to 9 and yields 9 as the value of the expression.

The postfix operators increment or decrement the value of a variable, just as do the prefix operators. With the postfix operators, however, the value of the expression is the *old* value of the variable—the value before the increment or decrement operator was applied. For example, if the value of n is 30, both ++n and n++ change the value of n to 31. However, the value of the expression ++n is 31 (the new value of n), whereas the value of n++ is 30 (the old value of n). The prefix and postfix versions of -- behave in like manner.

When the value returned by an increment or decrement operator is not used (when the operator is applied only for its side effect), we are free to use either the prefix or the postfix version. For example, the two statements

```
++n;
n++;
```

are equivalent, as are the two statements

```
--n;
n--;
```

In such statements C programmers seem to prefer the postfix operator. However, this is just a stylistic preference. When the value is discarded, the prefix and postfix operators have the same effect.

On the other hand, if we use the value returned by the increment or decrement operator, we must choose the prefix or postfix operator depending on the value we need. For example, the statements

```
m = ++n;
m = n++;
```

are *not* equivalent. Both increment the value of n. But the first assigns to m the new, incremented value of n, whereas the second assigns the old, unincremented value.

As Appendix 2 shows, the precedence and associativity of the increment and decrement operators differ for the prefix and postfix versions. The prefix increment and decrement operators have the same precedence and right-to-left associativity as other prefix unary operators, such as unary + and unary -. The postfix increment and decrement operators have the same precedence and left-to-right associativity as other postfix unary operators, such as the function-call operator.★

Note that both the prefix and postfix increment and decrement operators have higher precedence than binary operators such as the arithmetic and assignment operators. For example, the preceding assignment statements are grouped as

```
m = (++n);
m = (n++);
```

As we have already assumed, the result returned by the increment or decrement operator is assigned to the variable.

★Giving the postfix increment and decrement operators a different precedence and associativity than the corresponding prefix operators is an innovation of ANSI C. In older compilers and textbooks, the postfix increment and decrement operators have the same precedence and associativity as the prefix operators.

The following version of the code for summing the integers from 1 to 100 uses both ++ and +=:

```
sum = 0;
for (n = 1; n <= 100; n++) {
    scanf("%d", &number);
    sum += number;
}
```

This is the way most C programmers would write the code. We could have used prefix ++ instead of postfix ++ in the for statement (why?).

EXAMPLES USING ITERATION

Our first two examples of iteration are both based on *Fibonacci's rabbit problem:* Suppose that a pair of rabbits becomes fertile at the age of one month, and each fertile pair has exactly one pair of offspring each month. If we start with one fertile pair, and if none of the rabbits die, how many pairs will we have after a year's time? The problem is easily generalized to allow for any initial mix of fertile and nonfertile pairs, and to allow the rabbits to reproduce for any number of months. Also, we can consider the inverse problem: If we need a given number of pairs, how long must the rabbits reproduce to produce the required number?

Because each fertile pair has one pair of offspring each month, the number of pairs at the beginning of next month is the number of pairs at the beginning of this month *plus* the number of those pairs that were fertile. Because a newly born pair becomes fertile in one month's time, the number of *fertile* pairs at the beginning of this month equals the *total* number of pairs at the beginning of last month.

Let variables last, this, and next hold the number of pairs at the beginning of each of the corresponding months. According to the preceding discussion, the value of last is the number of fertile pairs, that is, the number of pairs that will have offspring during the current month. We thus calculate the number of pairs at the beginning of next month by

```
next = this + last;
```

When we advance to a new month, what was this month becomes last month and what was next month becomes this month. The values of the variables must be updated accordingly:

```
last = this;
this = next;
```

We begin the calculation by setting `this` to the initial number of pairs and `last` to the initial number of fertile pairs. The preceding three statements are then executed once for each month that the rabbits are allowed to reproduce.

Program for Rabbit Problem

The program in Listing 2-1 computes the number of pairs after the rabbits have reproduced for a given number of months. The user can

Listing 2-1

```c
/* File months.c */
/* Solve Fibonacci rabbit problem */

#include <stdlib.h>
#include <stdio.h>

int main(void)
{
    int last, this, next;   /* Pairs */
    int months, m;          /* Months */

    printf("Initial number of pairs? ");
    scanf("%d", &this);
    printf("Initial number of fertile pairs? ");
    scanf("%d", &last);
    printf("Number of months? ");
    scanf("%d", &months);

    for (m = 1; m <= months; m++) {
        next = this + last;
        last = this;
        this = next;
    }

    printf("After %d months you will have %d pairs\n",
            months, this);
    return EXIT_SUCCESS;
}
```

specify the initial numbers of pairs and fertile pairs. The following exchange with the program solves Fibonacci's original rabbit problem:

```
Initial number of pairs? 1
Initial number of fertile pairs? 1
Number of months? 12
After 12 months you will have 377 pairs
```

The program uses a `for` statement to carry out the calculation for the required number of months:

```
for (m = 1; m <= months; m++) {
    next = this + last;
    last = this;
    this = next;
}
```

Note the use of the postfix `++` operator to increment the value of `m` after each iteration.

Program for Inverse Rabbit Problem

The program in Listing 2-2 computes the number of months that the rabbits must reproduce to equal or exceed a given number of pairs:

```
Initial number of pairs? 1
Initial number of fertile pairs? 1
How many pairs do you need? 1000
After 15 months you will have 1597 pairs
```

This program uses a `while` statement to repeat the monthly calculation as long as the required number of pairs has not been reached or exceeded:

```
while (this < needed) {
    next = this + last;
    last = this;
    this = next;
    months++;
}
```

Note the use of the postfix `++` operator to count the number of months that the rabbits must reproduce.

Listing 2-2

```c
/* File pairs.c */
/* Solve inverse Fibonacci rabbit problem */

#include <stdlib.h>
#include <stdio.h>

int main(void)
{
    int last, this, next, needed;  /* Pairs */
    int months = 0;

    printf("Initial number of pairs? ");
    scanf("%d", &this);
    printf("Initial number of fertile pairs? ");
    scanf("%d", &last);
    printf("How many pairs do you need? ");
    scanf("%d", &needed);

    while (this < needed) {
        next = this + last;
        last = this;
        this = next;
        months++;
    }

    printf("After %d months you will have %d pairs\n",
            months, this);
    return EXIT_SUCCESS;
}
```

Program for Computing Amount in Bank Account

The program in Listing 2-3 computes the balance in a bank account after a given number of months has elapsed:

```
Starting balance: 1000
Monthly deposit: 100
Annual percentage rate: 7
Number of months: 48
Balance after 48 months: $6875.18
```

Listing 2-3

```
/* File balance.c */
/* Compute amount in bank account */

#include <stdlib.h>
#include <stdio.h>

#define APR_TO_MDR   1200.0   /* For converting annual
                                 percentage rate to
                                 monthly decimal rate  */

int main(void)
{
    double balance;              /* Current balance */
    double deposit;              /* Monthly deposit */
    double annual_pcnt_rate;     /* Annual percentge rate */
    double rate;                 /* Monthly decimal rate */
    double interest;             /* Interest for this month */
    int months;                  /* Number of months */
    int m;                       /* Current month */

/* Get input data from user */

    printf("Starting balance: ");
    scanf("%lf", &balance);
    printf("Monthly deposit: ");
    scanf("%lf", &deposit);
    printf("Annual percentage rate: ");
    scanf("%lf", &annual_pcnt_rate);
    printf("Number of months: ");
    scanf("%d", &months);

/* Compute new balance */

    rate = annual_pcnt_rate / APR_TO_MDR;

    for (m = 1; m <= months; m++) {
        balance += deposit;
        interest = balance * rate;
        balance += interest;
    }

/* Print balance */

    printf("Balance after %d months: $%.2f\n",
            months, balance);
    return EXIT_SUCCESS;
}
```

The program assumes that interest is compounded monthly, but it is not hard to adapt to other periods such as daily, quarterly, or annually. The heart of the program is a `for` statement that makes a deposit and computes interest each month:

```
for (m = 1; m <= months; m++) {
    balance += deposit;
    interest = balance * rate;
    balance += interest;
}
```

Note the use of postfix ++ to increment the value of m and the two uses of += to update the value of `balance`. The last two controlled statements could be combined:

```
balance += balance * rate;
```

The multiplication would be carried out before the addition and assignment are performed.

SELECTION STATEMENTS AND THE CONDITIONAL OPERATOR

Selection statements select from among one or more alternatives the action that the computer is to carry out; the selection is based on the value of a control expression. C has three selection statements: the `if` statement, the `if-else` statement, and the `switch` statement. The `if` and `if-else` statements are very similar to their counterparts in other languages. The `switch` statement plays the same role as (but is not precisely equivalent to) the `case` statement in other languages. There is also an operator for selection, the *conditional operator*, which is the only trinary operator in C.

The `if` and `if-else` Statements

The `if` statement has the form

```
if (expression)
    statement
```

The control expression is evaluated first. If the value of the control expression is *true*, the controlled statement is executed; if the value is *false*, the controlled statement is ignored.

Consider the following example:

```
if (count > MAX_COUNT)
    printf("Overflow\n");
```

If the value of count exceeds that of MAX_COUNT, the message Overflow is printed. If the value of count does not exceed that of MAX_COUNT, no message is printed. As with other control statements, the controlled statement can be a block:

```
if (count > MAX_COUNT) {
    printf("Overflow\n");
    count = 0;
}
```

Adding an else part to the if statement gives us the if-else statement:

```
if (expression)
    statement-1
else
    statement-2
```

If the value of the control expression is *true*, *statement-1* is executed; if the value of the expression is *false*, *statement-2* is executed. For example, the following statement increments the value of a counter if its maximum count has not been reached; if the maximum count has been reached, the statement resets the counter to 0 and prints an error message:

```
if (count < MAX_COUNT)
    count++;
else {
    printf("Overflow\n");
    count = 0;
}
```

Nested if and if-else Statements

The controlled statement in an if or if-else statement can itself be an if or if-else statement. We say that statements are *nested* when a controlled statement is the same kind of statement as the control statement in which it is embedded. Nested if-else statements allow us to construct multiway selections, such as the following:

```
if (expression-1)
    statement-1
else if (expression-2)
    statement-2
else if (expression-3)
    statement-3
else if (expression-4)
    statement-4
else
    statement-5
```

There can be as many `else if` parts as we wish. Only one of the statements is selected for execution. The expressions are evaluated in the order shown; the first expression to yield a nonzero value (*true*) causes the corresponding statement (and only that statement) to be executed. If all the expressions yield zero (*false*), the statement in the final `else` part is executed. If there is no final `else` part, then no statement is executed when all the expressions yield *false*.

For example, the following checks the number of decimal digits in a positive integer `n`:

```
if (n < 10)
    printf("One digit\n");
else if (n < 100)
    printf("Two digits\n");
else if (n < 1000)
    printf("Three digits\n");
else
    printf("Four or more digits\n");
```

The order in which the tests are performed is important. The test for two digits will work only if we have already eliminated the possibility of one digit. The test for three digits will work only after we have eliminated the possiblities of one or two digits, and so on.

The Dangling *else* Problem

Many other nesting schemes are possible, but some can be difficult for programmers to write correctly and for readers to understand. One pitfall for the unwary is the infamous *dangling-else problem*, which is also present in Pascal.

Let *e1* and *e2* stand for control expressions and let *s1* and *s2* stand for statements. Consider the following nested statements, which we write all on one line so as not to give away their structure:

```
if e1 then if e2 then s1 else s2
```

(This is the way the compiler would see the nested statements, because any line breaks or indentation would be ignored.)

The question at hand is, does the the `else` part belong to the first `if` statement or the second? Nothing we have discussed so far resolves this ambiguity. Instead, we must use the following special rule: *each `else` part goes with the nearest `if` statement that does not already have an `else` part.* Thus "`else s2`" is part of the second `if` statement, and the nested statements should be indented as follows:

```
if e1 then
    if e2 then
        s1
    else
        s2
```

We will only be fooling ourselves if we inadvertently write

```
if e1 then
    if e2 then
        s1
else                    /* Incorrect indentation */
    s2
```

The compiler will, of course, follow the given rule rather than our incorrect indentation. If we incorrectly assume that the statement works as we have written it, the resulting bug will be hard to find, because the program text will not reflect the actual behavior of the program.

Because of such pitfalls, there is much to be said for confining ourselves to the multiway-selection nesting scheme described previously, rather than making up our own nesting schemes on the spur of the moment.

The `switch` and `break` Statements

Another approach to multiway selection is the `switch` statement, which corresponds to the `case` or `select` statements in other languages. The `switch` statement has the following general form:

```
switch (expression)
    statement
```

The controlled statement is normally a block, one or more of whose statements are preceded by *case labels*. Each case label represents a possible value for the control expression; for example, the case label

```
case 25:
```

corresponds to the value 25. If the value of the control expression is equal to the value given in one of the case labels, the computer begins execution of the block immediately after the case label rather than at the beginning of the block. No two of the case labels can specify the same value.

In the following examples, each ellipsis (...) represents any number of statements. In

```
switch (2) {
case 1:
    . . .
case 2:
    . . .
case 3:
    . . .
}
```

execution of the block begins immediately after the label `case 2:`, rather than at the beginning of the block. In

```
switch (3) {
case 1:
    . . .
case 2:
    . . .
case 3:
    . . .
}
```

execution of the block begins immediately following the label `case 3:`.

If none of the case labels corresponds to the value of the control expression, then none of the statements in the block are executed. Thus in

```
switch (5) {
case 1:
    . . .
case 2:
    . . .
case 3:
    . . .
}
```

the entire block is skipped.

The case label `default:` corresponds to any value of the control expression that is not represented by another case label. Thus in

```
switch (5) {
case 1:
   ...
case 2:
   ...
default:
   ...
}
```

execution will begin following `default:` because none of the other case labels corresponds to the value of the control expression.

The control expression determines only where execution of the block begins. If we do not specify otherwise, all the statements between the selected case label and the end of the block will be executed. Usually this is not what we want. Instead we want a separate set of statements executed for each case. After executing the statements for the selected case, we want to leave the block and continue with the rest of the program.

We accomplish this with a `break` statement, which directs the computer to exit from a `switch` statement or an iteration statement and to continue with the rest of the program. The statements for each case should end with a `break` statement:

```
switch (2) {
case 1:
   ...
   break;
case 2:
   ...
   break;
case 3:
   ...
   break;
}
```

In this example, only the statements for case 2 are executed. In our previous version of this example, without the `break` statements, the statements for both case 2 and case 3 are executed. The `break` statement at the end of the block *can* be omitted. However, because of the disaster that will result if a `break` statement is accidentally omitted, we suggest that you form the invariable habit of terminating *every* case with a `break` statement.*

For example, suppose the value of n is a nonnegative integer representing the number of items (of some kind) that the user has requested from a program. The program can comment on the user's request with the following `switch` statement:

```
switch (n) {
case 0:
    printf("What, you don't need any?\n");
    break;
case 1:
    printf("Are you sure that one is enough?\n");
    break;
case 2:
    printf("Two should do nicely.\n");
    break;
case 3:
    printf("Do you really need three?\n");
    break;
default:
    printf("My, we're greedy today, aren't we.\n");
    break; /* Optional but recommended */
}
```

What is the printout for each value of n? What would the printout be if the `break` statements were omitted?

The Conditional Operator

The conditional operator has three operands, which are separated by the symbols ? and : as follows:

exp-c ? *exp-t* : *exp-f*

Exp-c is the control expression; its value determines which of the two following expressions will be evaluated. If *exp-c* yields *true*, *exp-t* is evaluated and its value is returned by the conditional operator. If *exp-c* yields *false*, *exp-f* is evaluated and its value is returned.

*In December 1989, long-distance telephone service in the United States was disrupted by a software problem in the AT&T electronic switching system, which is programmed in C. The problem was reportedly traced to a misuse of a `break` statement in a `switch` state-

For example, the following expression yields the maximum of the values of m and n:

```
m >= n ? m : n
```

If the value of m is greater than or equal to the value of n, the value of m is returned. Otherwise, the expression yields the value of n. Likewise, the expression

```
m >= 0 ? m : -m
```

returns the absolute value of m. If the value of m is positive, that value is returned. If the value of m is negative, the value of -m is returned.

The conditional operator has lower precedence than the operators commonly used for computing and testing results, such as the arithmetic and relational operators. Therefore, those operators can be used freely in *exp-c*, *exp-t*, and *exp-f* without those expressions having to be parenthesized. For example,

```
m > 0 ? m + 5 : 2*m
```

is grouped as

```
(m > 0) ? (m + 5) : (2*m)
```

Thus m > 0 is the control expression, and its value will determine whether the value of m + 5 or of 2*m is returned.

On the other hand, the conditional operator has higher precedence than the assignment operators. For example,

```
n = m >= 0 ? m : -m;
```

is grouped as

```
n = ((m >= 0) ? m : (-m));
```

The conditional expression computes the absolute value of m, which is then assigned to n.

As is often the case, however, optional parentheses—those that precedence considerations would allow us to omit—often improve the readability of an expression. For example,

```
n = m >= 0 ? m : -m;
```

is undoubtedly easier to read if written as

```
n = (m >= 0 ? m : -m);
```

or even as

```
n = ((m >= 0) ? m : -m);
```

The control expression, *exp-c*, is evaluated, and all its side effects are carried out, before *exp-t* or *exp-f* is evaluated. The conditional operator is the first operator we have encountered whose operands are evaluated in a specified order. We will encounter several more such operators in this chapter. All of these operators are exceptional, however. For most C operators, we can say nothing about the order in which the operands will be evaluated.

EXAMPLES USING SELECTION STATEMENTS

Listings 2-4, 2-5, and 2-6 illustrate selection statements as well as several other features of C.

Computing Gross Wages

The program in Listing 2-4 computes the weekly gross wages for workers who are paid by the hour. By long tradition, hours in excess of 40 are overtime, and workers are paid time-and-a-half for overtime—each overtime hour is counted as an hour and a half. In the program, REG_LIMIT is the 40-hour limit for regular (nonovertime) hours, and OVR_FACTOR is the fraction by which overtime hours are to be increased (OVR_FACTOR represents the "half" in "time-and-a-half").

For each employee who works overtime, the hours worked must be increased by the overtime hours, hours - REG_LIMIT, multiplied by the fractional increase for overtime, OVR_FACTOR:

```
if (hours > REG_LIMIT)
    hours += OVR_FACTOR * (hours - REG_LIMIT);
```

Note that the if statement is necessary. If this calculation were carried out for someone who had not worked overtime, the value of hours - REG_LIMIT would be zero or negative. In the latter case, the worker would be penalized for working less than REG_LIMIT hours, which is not intended.

This program has a few other points of interest aside from the selection statement. The input data consists of the employee number, hours worked, and hourly rate for each employee. The end of the input data is signaled by a *sentinel value* consisting of an employee number of −1. The program produces a report consisting of the input data and the wages calculated for each worker. Thus the input

```
10372 42.3 7.85
11925 51.6 10.80
23945 30.7 8.25
-1
```

Listing 2-4

```c
/* File wages.c */

#include <stdlib.h>
#include <stdio.h>

#define REG_LIMIT    40.0   /* Maximum regular hours */
#define OVR_FACTOR   0.5    /* Fraction by which overtime
                               hours are to be increased */
#define SENTINEL     -1     /* Signals end of input data */

int main(void)
{
    int emp_no;
    double hours, rate, wages;

    printf("%-8s    %-5s    %-5s    %-6s\n\n",
            "Employee", "Hours", "Rate", "Wages");

    scanf("%d", &emp_no);
    while (emp_no != SENTINEL) {
        scanf("%lf%lf", &hours, &rate);
        printf("%8d    %5.1f    %5.2f    ",
                emp_no, hours, rate);
        if (hours > REG_LIMIT)
            hours += OVR_FACTOR * (hours - REG_LIMIT);
        wages = hours * rate;
        printf("%6.2f\n", wages);
        scanf("%d", &emp_no);
    }
    return EXIT_SUCCESS;
}
```

produces the following output:

Employee	Hours	Rate	Wages
10372	42.3	7.85	341.08
11925	51.6	10.80	619.92
23945	30.7	8.25	253.28

For each employee, the employee number must be read and tested, to see if it is the sentinel, *before* any other input or processing can be carried out for that employee. This leads to the following iteration for reading and processing employee data:

```
scanf("%d", &emp_no);        /* Get first employee No. */
while (emp_no != SENTINEL) {
   scanf("%lf%lf", &hours, &rate);
   /* Process one employee */
   scanf("%d", &emp_no);   /* Get next employee No. */
}
```

Note that the input data items can be arranged in lines as desired. Before reading a number, `scanf()` always skips whitespace, which includes newlines.

Redirection

Programs such as the wages program normally read their input from a disk file and send their output to a disk file or a printer. Later we will see how to specify such files from within a C program. For now, however, we can achieve the same end with *redirection*, which connects the standard input and output streams to specified files and devices. Redirection is a service of the operating system, and so its availability and the details of its use will vary. The following remarks apply to both MS-DOS and Unix, the operating systems most commonly used by students of C.

In the command line that runs a program, we can use the symbol < to designate the file or device from which input is to be read. For example, the command line

```
wages < datafile
```

runs the program `wages` with the standard input stream connected to the disk file `datafile`. The output from the program will appear on the user's display as usual.

Likewise, we can use > to designate the file or device to which output is to be sent. For example,

```
wages > report
```

runs `wages` with the standard output stream connected to the disk file `report`. The input data for the program is read from the user's keyboard, as usual.

Finally, we can combine the two forms of redirection. The command line

```
wages < datafile > report
```

causes `wages` to read its input from `datafile` and store its output in `report`.

Responding to Menu Selections

We now turn to the programs in Listings 2-5 and 2-6, which do the same job but make use of different selection statements (nested `if-else` statements in Listing 2-5, a `switch` statement in Listing 2-6). Each program displays a menu that offers to calculate the areas of various geometrical figures or to quit:

```
1. Compute Area of Rectangle
2. Compute Area of Triangle
3. Compute Area of Circle
4. Quit

Enter number of command:
```

If the user enters 1, 2, or 3, the program requests the necessary input data and prints the result of the corresponding calculation:

```
Enter number of command: 1
Length and width? 75 20
Area is 1500.0
```

The program then redisplays the menu and prompts for another command number. If the user enters 4, the program prints a final message and terminates:

```
Enter number of command: 4
Have a nice day!
```

If the user enters an invalid command number, the program prints an error message:

```
Enter number of command: 100
Invalid command--please try again
```

The menu and command prompt are then redisplayed.

A variable with a *true*-or-*false* value is known as a *flag*. In both programs, the flag `running` determines whether the program will dis-

Listing 2-5

```c
/* File areas1.c */

#include <stdlib.h>
#include <stdio.h>

void print_menu(void);

#define TRUE       1   /* Logical values */
#define FALSE      0

#define RECTANGLE  1   /* Command numbers */
#define TRIANGLE   2
#define CIRCLE     3
#define QUIT       4

#define PI         3.14159265

int main(void)
{
    int command;
    int running = TRUE;   /* flag */
    double length, width, base, height, radius, area;

    do {
        print_menu();
        scanf("%d", &command);
        if (command == RECTANGLE) {
            printf("Length and width? ");
            scanf("%lf%lf", &length, &width);
            area = length * width;
            printf("Area is %.1f\n", area);
        }
        else if (command == TRIANGLE) {
            printf("Base and height? ");
            scanf("%lf%lf", &base, &height);
            area = 0.5 * base * height;
            printf("Area is %.1f\n", area);
        }
        else if (command == CIRCLE) {
            printf("Radius? ");
            scanf("%lf", &radius);
```

(continued)

```c
        area = PI * radius * radius;
        printf("Area is %.1f\n", area);
    }
    else if (command == QUIT) {
        running = FALSE;
        printf("Have a nice day!\n");
    }
    else
        printf("Invalid command—please try
again\n");
    } while (running);
    return EXIT_SUCCESS;
}

void print_menu(void)
{
    printf("\n\n\n");
    printf("1.  Compute Area of Rectangle\n");
    printf("2.  Compute Area of Triangle\n");
    printf("3.  Compute Area of Circle\n");
    printf("4.  Quit\n\n");
    printf("Enter number of command: ");
}
```

play the menu again (the value of `running` is *true*) or terminate (the value of `running` is *false*). For convenience in assigning values to `running`, we define the constants TRUE as 1 and FALSE as 0.

Both programs define a function `print_menu()` to print the menu and the command prompt. Commands are read and processed while the value of `running` is *true*. Because `running` will be set to *false* by a command (command number 4), the value of `running` should be checked *after* each command is carried out. Therefore, we use a `do-while` statement to control the iteration:

```c
int command;
int running = TRUE;   /* flag */

do {
    print_menu();
    scanf("%d", &command);
    /* Process command */
} while (running);
```

Listing 2-6

```
/* File areas2.c */

#include <stdlib.h>
#include <stdio.h>

void print_menu(void);

#define TRUE        1   /* Logical values */
#define FALSE       0

#define RECTANGLE   1   /* Command numbers */
#define TRIANGLE    2
#define CIRCLE      3
#define QUIT        4

#define PI          3.14159265

int main(void)
{
    int command;
    int running = TRUE;  /* flag */
    double length, width, base, height, radius, area;

    do {
        print_menu();
        scanf("%d", &command);
        switch (command) {
        case RECTANGLE:
            printf("Length and width? ");
            scanf("%lf%lf", &length, &width);
            area = length * width;
            printf("Area is %.1f\n", area);
            break;
        case TRIANGLE:
            printf("Base and height? ");
            scanf("%lf%lf", &base, &height);
            area = 0.5 * base * height;
            printf("Area is %.1f\n", area);
            break;
```

(continued)

```
        case CIRCLE:
            printf("Radius? ");
            scanf("%lf", &radius);
            area = PI * radius * radius;
            printf("Area is %.1f\n", area);
            break;
        case QUIT:
            running = FALSE;
            printf("Have a nice day!\n");
            break;
        default:
            printf("Invalid command—please try
again\n");
            break;
        }
    } while (running);
    return EXIT_SUCCESS;
}

void print_menu(void)
{
    printf("\n\n\n");
    printf("1.  Compute Area of Rectangle\n");
    printf("2.  Compute Area of Triangle\n");
    printf("3.  Compute Area of Circle\n");
    printf("4.  Quit\n\n");
    printf("Enter number of command: ");
}
```

The commands are processed by the selection statements that are the object of the examples. To clarify the selection statements, we define constants RECTANGLE, TRIANGLE, CIRCLE, and QUIT to represent the corresponding command numbers. In Listing 2-5 the selection is handled by nested if-else statements arranged in the standard form discussed earlier. Note that the case of an invalid command number is handled by the final else part. In Listing 2-6 the selection is handled by a switch statement. Note that the statements for each case end with a break statement, and invalid command numbers are handled by the default case.

LOGICAL OPERATORS

The logical operators are && (logical AND), || (logical OR), and ! (logical NOT). Like the relational operators, the logical operators help us construct expressions representing conditions. The *logical* AND, OR, and NOT operators must be carefully distinguished from the *bitwise* AND, OR, and NOT operators. The bitwise operators are used not for representing conditions but for manipulating the individual bits that represent an integer value.

The operands of the logical operators and the values that the operators return both represent truth values. For the operands, a zero value represents *false* and a nonzero value represents *true*. The logical operators return 0 for *false* and 1 for *true*.

Appendix 2 shows the precedences and associativities of the logical operators. The ! operator, which is a prefix unary operator, has the same precedence and right-to-left associativity as other prefix unary operators, such as unary +, unary −, and prefix ++. The operators && and || associate from left to right and have relatively low precedences—lower than those of the arithmetic and relational operators, for example. The precedence of && is greater than that of ||.

The logical AND operator, &&, returns *true* only if both of its operands are *true*. If either operand is *false*, the operator returns *false*. For example,

```
(m > n) && (m < 0)
```

returns *true* only if the value of m is greater than the value of n *and* the value of m is less than zero.

Because && has lower precedence than the relational operators, we could omit the parentheses in the preceding expression:

```
m > n && m < 0
```

This version, however, seems somewhat harder to read than the original. Expressions with logical operators are another case in which optional parentheses often greatly improve the readability of an expression.

The logical OR operator, ||, returns *true* if either of its operands is *true* or if both of them are *true*. It returns *false* only if both its operands are *false*. For example,

```
(m == 3) || (n != 5)
```

yields *true* if the value of m is 3 *or* the value of n is not equal to 5 (or both). Again, the parentheses are optional.

The logical NOT operator, !, returns *true* when its operand is *false* and vice versa. For example,

```
!(m > 0 && n > 0)
```

yields *true* only if it is *not true* that the values of both m and n are greater than 0. In this case, the parentheses are *not* optional. Because of the high precedence of !, the expression to which it is applied must usually be enclosed in parentheses.

We can often reformulate an expression to avoid the ! operator. For example,

```
!(m > 0 && n > 0)
```

will be true only if the value of at least one of the variables is less than or equal to zero. Therefore the desired condition can also be expressed as

```
m <= 0 || n <= 0
```

Expressions generally become simpler and easier to understand when ! operators are eliminated.

Short-Circuit Evaluation

The operators && and || are additional examples of operators whose operands are evaluated in a particular order. The left operand is evaluated first, its side effects (if any) are carried out, before the right operand is evaluated.

What's more, it may not be necessary to evaluate the right operand at all. If the left operand of && is *false*, the operator returns *false*; and if the left operand of || is *true*, the operator returns *true*. In these cases the right operand is not evaluated. This process is known as *short-circuit evaluation*.

C programmers often rely on short-circuit evaluation to prevent an evaluation that would cause an error. For example, the library function sqrt() is not defined for negative arguments. However, the expression

```
(x >= 0.0) && (sqrt(x) < 30.0)
```

cannot cause an error. Because of short-circuit evaluation, the right operand will be evaluated only when the value of x is not negative.

Classifying Triangles

The program in Listing 2-7 classifies triangles as equilateral (three sides equal), isosceles (two sides equal), or scalene (no sides equal). The classification is performed by a function classify() that takes the

Listing 2-7

```
/* File triangle.c */
/* Classify triangles */

#include <stdlib.h>
#include <stdio.h>

int classify(double, double, double);

#define EQUILATERAL    1   /* Codes for classifications */
#define ISOSCELES      2
#define SCALENE        3

#define END_OF_DATA   0.0

int main(void)
{
   double s1, s2, s3;

   printf("Enter three sides (or 0 to stop): ");
   scanf("%lf", &s1);
   while (s1 != END_OF_DATA) {
      scanf("%lf%lf", &s2, &s3);
      switch (classify(s1, s2, s3)) {
      case EQUILATERAL:
         printf("Equilateral\n");
         break;
      case ISOSCELES:
         printf("Isosceles\n");
         break;
      case SCALENE:
         printf("Scalene\n");
         break;
      }
      printf("Enter three sides (or 0 to stop): ");
      scanf("%lf", &s1);
   }
   return EXIT_SUCCESS;
}
```

(*continued*)

```
/*  Return integer code for kind of triangle */

int classify(double s1, double s2, double s3)
{
   if ((s1 == s2) && (s2 == s3))
      return EQUILATERAL;
   else if ((s1 == s2) || (s2 == s3) || (s1 == s3))
      return ISOSCELES;
   else
      return SCALENE;
}
```

sides of a triangle as arguments and returns an integer code representing the classification. The three integer codes are represented by the macros EQUILATERAL, ISOSCELES, and SCALENE.

The function uses a multiway selection to check first for an equilateral triangle (which must satisfy the most restrictive condition) and then for an isosceles triangle. A triangle that is neither equilateral nor isosceles is classified as scalene.

The sides of the triangle are represented by the formal arguments s1, s2, and s3. The expression

```
(s1 == s2) && (s2 == s3)
```

tests for an equilateral triangle. At first thought we might write

```
(s1 == s2) && (s2 == s3) && (s1 == s3)
```

Why can the third parenthesized term be omitted?

To test for an isosceles triangle, we use

```
(s1 == s2) || (s2 == s3) || (s1 == s3)
```

Unlike the expression for the equilateral triangle, this expression cannot be simplified further (why?).

THE COMMA OPERATOR

We often need to evaluate a series of expressions sequentially—that is, one after the other. The normal way of doing this is to write a separate expression statement for each expression. Sometimes, however, we need to evaluate several expressions where only one expression is allowed. In such cases we turn to the comma operator, which allows us to write an expression whose subexpressions will be evaluated sequentially in left-to-right order.

When an expression of the form

exp-1, *exp-2*

is evaluated, *exp-1* is evaluated and its side effects are carried out, after which *exp-2* is evaluated and its side effects are carried out. The value of *exp-1* is discarded; the value of *exp-2* is returned as the value of the entire expression.

The comma operator has lower precedence than any other C operator. That means that any other operators can appear in *exp-1* and *exp-2* without requiring the expressions to be enclosed in parentheses.

The comma operator associates from left to right. This means that any series of expressions separated by operators will be evaluated in left-to-right order, as just described. For example, in

exp-1, *exp-2*, ..., *exp-n*

exp-1 is evaluated and its side effects are carried out, *exp-2* is evaluated and its side effects are carried out, and so on. The value of *exp-n* becomes the value of the entire expression. The values of the other *exp* subexpressions are discarded. Thus the expression

```
m = 5, n = 7, m*n
```

assigns 5 to m, assigns 7 to n, and yields the value 35, which is the value of the right-most expression, m*n.

A common use for the comma operator is to allow a `for` statement to initialize and increment more than one variable. The `for` statement format allows one expression for initializing a variable and one expression for incrementing a variable. Courtesy of the comma operator, however, each of those expressions can be made up of subexpressions that initialize or increment different variables. For example, the `for` statement

```
for (m = 1, n = 10; m <= 5; m++, n += 10)
    printf("%d  %2d\n", m, n);
```

prints

```
1   10
2   20
3   30
4   40
5   50
```

The initialization expression

```
m = 1, n = 10
```

initializes m to 1 and n to 10. After each execution of the controlled statement, the expression

```
m++, n += 10
```

increments m by 1 and n by 10.

Finally, we must distinguish comma operators from the commas in *comma-separated lists*—lists whose elements are separated by commas. We have encountered examples of comma-separated lists in declarations:

```
int m, n, p;
```

in function calls:

```
printf("%d  %2d\n", m, n);
```

and in the corresponding function declarations. Commas in a comma-separated list act as punctuation marks, *not* comma operators. A comma is interpreted as a comma operator only if it cannot be interpreted as a punctuation mark in a comma-separated list. In particular, the commas separating the actual arguments of a function are not comma operators. Expressions representing actual arguments can be evaluated in any order, rather than in the left-to-right order that would be required if the commas were comma operators.

EXERCISES

2-1. According to legend, the inventor of chess was asked by the king to name his own reward. "All I ask," said the inventor, "is one grain of wheat for the first square of my chessboard, two grains for the second square, four grains for the third, and so on for all 64 squares, doubling the number of grains for each square." How many grains of wheat did the inventor request? *Hints:* Use type double for the number of grains; the result is too large for any of the integer types. For printing the result, you may wish to use the format specifier e, which is similar to f except that e prints the result in exponential notation.

2-2. The factorial of 0 is 1, and the factorial of any integer greater than 0 is the product of all integers from 1 through the integer in question. Write a function

```
int factorial(int n);
```

that returns the factorial of n. Write a program that uses the function to print a short table of factorials. *Hints:* Initialize an integer variable to 1, and use `*=` to multiply the value of the variable by each of the integers from 1 through n. In implementations for which the largest `int` value is 32,767, you will only be able to compute the factorials of 0 through 7 (the factorial of 8 is 40,320).

2-3. The numbers in the following sequence, which have important applications in computer science, are called the *Fibonacci numbers*:

0, 1, 1, 2, 3, 5, 8, 13, 21, ...

After the first two numbers, each number in the sequence is the sum of the two preceding numbers. This is the same rule used to solve Fibonacci's rabbit problem, from which the numbers take their name.

Suppose that the terms of the sequence are numbered starting with 0, so that term 0 is 0, terms 1 and 2 are 1, term 3 is 2, and so on. Define a function

```
int fibonacci(int n);
```

that returns term n of the sequence. Write a program that uses the function to print a short table of Fibonacci numbers. *Hints:* The computations are similar to those for the rabbit problem. A useful trick is to assume that the terms −1 and 1 *precede* term 0 of the sequence. This allows terms 0 and 1 to be computed according to the same rule used for the remaining terms.

2-4. Write a program to print one of the following patterns:

```
* * * * *    * * * * *          *                *
*       *    * * * * *        * * *            * * *
*       *    * * * * *      * * * * *        * * * * *
*       *    * * * * *    * * * * * * *        * * *
* * * * *    * * * * *  * * * * * * * * *        *
```

The program should print the following menu and prompt:

```
1. Print Box
2. Print Block
3. Print Triangle
4. Print Diamond
5. Quit

Enter number of command:
```

Depending on the number entered, the program should either print the designated pattern or terminate. After printing a pattern, the program should again print the menu and prompt. If the user enters a number outside the range 1–5, the program should print an error message followed by another menu and prompt.

2-5. A machine part in the shape of a cylinder comes in two different sizes. For each size, the length and diameter of the cylinder must lie within certain ranges, as follows:

Size 1:	*Size 2:*
length: 5.43–5.58 cm	length: 12.13–12.27 cm
diameter: 1.21–1.34 cm	diameter: 1.05–1.09 cm

Write a program to check the lengths and diameters of parts, which may be of either size. The program should read the lengths and diameters from a file. For each part, the program should print the length and diameter of the cylinder and print "accept" if the part satisfies the criteria for either size. If a part does not meet the criteria for either size, the program should print "reject." Use a single logical expression to test whether a part of either size should be accepted or rejected.

3 Types and Conversions

S O FAR WE have used only two types, `int` and `double`. Now it is time to consider all of C's numerous arithmetic types as well as the rules by which values are converted from one arithmetic type to another. Also, we will update our knowledge of `scanf()` and `printf()` format strings so that we can input and output values of any arithmetic type.

BITS, BYTES, AND ADDRESSES

Some features of C reflect the memory organization of the computer on which the language was first implemented. Fortunately for the popularity of C, this *byte-oriented* memory organization has become a de facto industry standard and is now found on the most popular mainframes, minicomputers, and microcomputers. A brief look at byte-oriented memory organization will help us understand a number of otherwise-mysterious features of C.

Byte-Oriented Memory

A computer memory can only store 0s and 1s, which are known as *bits*. Data items are represented by *binary codes*, each consisting of a certain number of bits. To simplify storing and retrieving such data items, the bits of memory are organized into *memory locations*, each of which can be designated by an *address*.

In a byte-oriented memory, the smallest-size memory location contains eight bits,* or one *byte*. Larger memory locations are formed by combining adjacent bytes. Typical memory-location sizes are one byte (8 bits), two bytes (16 bits), four bytes (32 bits), and eight bytes (64 bits).

---

*The C standard allows a byte to be larger (but not smaller) than eight bits. This possibility will be rarely encountered, however: eight-bit bytes are the norm.

Figure 3-1

A segment of byte-oriented memory. Note that each byte has its
own unique address. The addresses
are shown in decimal notation here,
although they are stored in binary
notation in the computer.

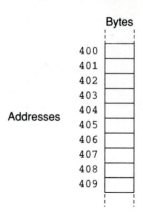

Addresses

Each byte has a unique address. The address of a multibyte location is the address of its first byte. Schemes for assigning addresses
vary among computers and even among different operating modes of
the same computer. In examples, we will assume the simplest
scheme, in which the first byte of memory has address 0, the second
byte has address 1, the third has address 2, and so on. Because of variations in addressing schemes, however, it is unwise to assume anything about the nature of an address.

Figure 3-1 shows a segment of a byte-oriented memory; note that
each byte has a unique address. Figure 3-2 shows how this memory
can be used to store data items of several different sizes. Note that
the address of each data item is the address of its first byte.

Alignment

In Figure 3-2, the addresses of two-byte data items are multiples
of 2, the addresses of four-byte data items are multiples of 4, and so
on. Data items that satisfy this restriction are said to be *aligned*. Many
computers can access memory faster if the data items are aligned. As
Figure 3-2 illustrates, we may have to leave unused bytes between
some data items to achieve alignment. These unused bytes can make
our data occupy more memory that we might otherwise expect.

Byte Order

Computers vary as to the order in which the bytes of a data item
are stored in successive memory locations. We normally think of a
binary code as written out from left to right:

01110001 11110000 00101101 00000101
(big end)   (little end)

Figure 3-2
How adjacent bytes can be combined to form larger memory locations. The address of each location is the address of its first byte. Shading indicates unused bytes that are needed for alignment, which requires that the address of a two-byte location be a multiple of 2, and the address of a four-byte location be a multiple of 4.

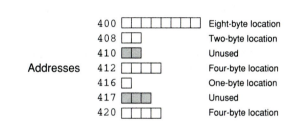

Addresses

400		Eight-byte location
408		Two-byte location
410		Unused
412		Four-byte location
416		One-byte location
417		Unused
420		Four-byte location

We can think of the left end (which holds the most significant digits of a numerical value) as the "big end," and the right end (which holds the least significant digits) as the "little end." A computer that stores the bytes in left-to-right order (big end first) is called "big endian":

```
01110001    (big end)
11110000
00101101
00000101    (little end)
```

A computer that stores the bytes in right-to-left order (little end first) is called "little endian":

```
00000101    (little end)
00101101
11110000
01110001    (big end)
```

For example, microprocessors in the Intel 80x86 family are little-endian, and those in the Motorola 680x0 family are big-endian. Programmers must not assume a particular byte order if the program is to work on both little-endian and big-endian machines.

Signed and Unsigned Integers

With n bits we can represent 2^n distinct values. For example, with three bits we can represent 2^3, or eight, values with the eight binary codes 000, 001, 010, 011, 100, 101, 110, and 111. Thus with one byte we can represent 2^8, or 256, values, with two bytes we can represent 2^{16}, or 65,536, values, and so on.

	BYTES	SIGNED RANGE	UNSIGNED RANGE
Table 3-1	1	−128 to 127	0 to 255
Integer Ranges for Common	2	−32,768 to 32,767	0 to 65,535
Memory-Location Sizes	4	−2,147,483,648 to 2,147,483,647	0 to 4,294,967,295

A memory location can hold either *unsigned integers* (positive values only) or *signed integers* (both positive and negative values). For unsigned integers, the values that can be stored in an *n*-bit location range from 0 to $2n - 1$. Thus one byte allows us to represent unsigned integers from 0 to 255, two bytes provide a range of 0 to 65,535, and so on.

We will assume that signed integers are represented using the *twos-complement system* (which is described in detail in many introductory computing books). Although not universal, this representation is overwhelmingly the most popular on modern computers.

The twos-complement system uses half the available binary codes for positive integers and half for negative integers. With one byte, for example, 128 codes (half of the 256 available) are used for positive integers and the remaining 128 are used for negative integers. We can thus represent negative integers in the range −128 to −1 and positive integers in the range 0 to 127. Likewise, with two bytes we have 32,768 negative integers and 32,768 positive integers. The negative integers range from −32,768 to −1 and the positive integers from 0 to 32,767. Table 3-1 summarizes the ranges of signed and unsigned values for the memory-location sizes most commonly used for integers.

Correspondence Between Signed and Unsigned Values

It is possible for the binary code representing a signed integer to be interpreted as representing an unsigned number, or vice versa. In C, we say that the signed integer has been converted to the corresponding unsigned type (or vice versa). Such conversions are easy to specify in C, so easy in fact that they can take place inadvertently if the programmer is not careful. More will be said about type conversions later in the chapter. For now, we concentrate on what can happen if signed or unsigned interpretation of an integer code is changed (perhaps inadvertently).

Let's use one-byte integers as an example. The correspondence between signed and unsigned values is as follows:

Unsigned	0 to 127	128 to 255
Signed	0 to 127	−128 to −1

Signed and unsigned integers in the range 0 to 127 are represented by the same binary codes; a conversion between signed and unsigned (in either direction) does not change the integer values. On the other hand, unsigned integers in the range 128 to 255 are represented by the same codes as signed integers in the range −128 to −1. For values in these ranges, a conversion from unsigned to signed will change a negative number into a positive number, and vice versa. For example, an unsigned 128 would be converted to a signed −128, and a signed −1 would be converted to an unsigned 255. If not anticipated, such conversions will surely have an adverse effect on our calculations.

BASIC ARITHMETIC TYPES

From the preceding we see that C needs a good supply of arithmetic types to accommodate different-size memory locations and to provide signed and unsigned versions of each integer type.[*] We begin with the *basic* arithmetic types, which are those whose definitions are built into the language. There are 12 basic arithmetic types —nine integer types and three floating types.

Basic Integer Types

If we disregard the signed/unsigned distinction for the moment, then we have four basic integer types: `char`, `short`, `int`, and `long`. As its name suggests, type `char` is often used for characters, which are represented in C by integer codes. The names of types `short` and `long` are abbreviations of `short int` and `long int`; `int` can be omitted from a type name when it is preceded by a descriptive keyword such as `short` or `long`.

The *size* of a type is the number of bytes required to store a value of that type. The following sizes, although not universal, are in widespread use on popular computers:

Type	Bytes
char	1
short	2
int	2 or 4
long	4

Type `char` always uses one byte, which is just large enough to hold characters represented by standard codes such as ASCII and EBCDIC. Type `int` is the integer size for which arithmetic and

---

[*]The integer types are also known as *integral types*; in fact, the ANSI standard uses the latter term.

other operations are most efficient. Thus `int` uses two bytes on a 16-bit computer (which favors operations on 16 bits) and four bytes on a 32-bit computer.

We can use the keyword `signed` or `unsigned` to specify that a type has signed or unsigned values. Thus `signed char`, `signed short`, `signed int`, and `signed long` are signed types, and `unsigned char`, `unsigned short`, `unsigned int`, and `unsigned long` are unsigned types. As usual, we can omit `int` when it is preceded by a descriptive keyword, so `signed int` can be abbreviated to `signed`, and `unsigned int` can be abbreviated to `unsigned`.

Types `short`, `int`, and `long` are the same as `signed short`, `signed int`, and `signed long`. The keyword `signed` has no effect for these types and so is usually omitted. Type `char` can be either signed or unsigned, depending on whether the computer in question treats character codes as signed or unsigned integers. Therefore, `char`, `signed char`, and `unsigned char` are three distinct types. If you want to insist on either signed or unsigned character codes, use `signed char` or `unsigned char`. If you are willing to accept the default for the system on which the program is run, use type `char`. For numerical values that are not character codes, it is probably best to specify either `signed char` or `unsigned char`.

Table 3-2 summarizes all nine basic integer types. Each line shows signed and unsigned versions types of the same size; typical sizes are given in the left-most column. Each type is designated in the simplest possible way. For example, we write `signed int` as `int`, `unsigned int` as `unsigned`, `unsigned long int` as `unsigned long`, and so on.

Arithmetic and other integer operations are carried out on values of only four types: `int`, `unsigned int`, `long`, `unsigned long`. When a value of another integer type, such as `char` or `short`, appears in an expression, it is converted to `int` or `unsigned int` before any operation on it is carried out (details of conversions are discussed later). The values of all expressions, includ-

	BYTES	TYPES		
Table 3-2 *Basic Integer Types*	1	`char`	`unsigned char`	`signed char`
	2	`short`	`unsigned short`	
	2 or 4	`int`	`unsigned`	
	4	`long`	`unsigned long`	

ing constants, belong to one of these four types. The reason is that some computers do not provide instructions for manipulating values of types smaller than `int`. Because not all computers can carry out such operations efficiently, it is not practical to support them in C.

Integer Constants

We already know that integers can be represented by decimal constants such as 23 and 1000. We still need to see, however, how the compiler chooses the type of an integer constant, and how we can influence that choice if the default is not satisfactory. Also, we will look briefly at nondecimal notation, which is better suited than decimal notation for representing nonnumeric binary codes.

Nondecimal Notation

The integer types are used not only for numerical values but also for arbitrary binary codes that have nothing to do with numbers. Decimal notation is not well suited for such codes because there is no obvious correspondence between the decimal digits and the corresponding bits. On the other hand, writing out all the bits is confusing: a sequence of 16 or 32 bits is hard to read, write, or remember.

For conveniently representing binary codes, the computer industry makes use of two nondecimal notations: octal notation, which uses eight digits, and hexadecimal notation, which uses 16. Originally, C offered only octal notation, which some C programmers still prefer. Nowadays, however, hexadecimal notation is far more widely used in the industry.

Each digit in an octal number represents a group of three bits, as follows:

0	1	2	3	4	5	6	7
000	001	010	011	100	101	110	111

For example, the octal number 315 represents the binary code 011001010, the octal number 3214 represents the binary code 011010001100, and so on.

In C, an octal constant is signaled by a leading 0. For example, 315 is a decimal constant but 0315 is an octal constant; 3214 is a decimal constant but 03214 is an octal constant, and so on. When writing decimal constants, we must be careful not to use a leading zero, which would cause the constant to be misinterpreted as an octal number.

In hexadecimal notation, each digit represents a group of four bits, as follows:

0	1	2	3	4	5	6	7
0000	0001	0010	0011	0100	0101	0110	0111

8	9	a	b	c	d	e	f
1000	1001	1010	1011	1100	1101	1110	1111

For example, the hexadecimal number `2f` represents the binary code 00101111, and the hexadecimal number `abcd` represents the binary code 1010101111001101. Digits `a` through `f` can be either upper- or lowercase; C programmers seem to prefer the latter.

In C, a hexadecimal constant is signaled by a leading `0x`. Thus `0x2f` and `0xabcd` are hexadecimal constants in C. Likewise, `725` is a decimal constant, `0725` is an octal constant, and `0x725` is a hexadecimal constant.

Determining the Type of a Constant

To determine the type of an integer constant, we consider a sequence of possible types and choose the first type whose range of values includes the value of the constant. Because constants are provided only for types `int` and larger, only those types are included in the sequence. Because constants in C are always positive, only the range of positive values need be considered for a signed type. The sequence of types is based on the following, which may be modified by omitting one or more types:

```
int   unsigned   long   unsigned long
```

For nondecimal constants, this sequence is used in its entirety. Thus, assuming two-byte `int`s and four-byte `long`s, `0x7fff` has type `int`, `0xffff` has type `unsigned`, `0x7fffffff` has type `long`, and `0xffffffff` has type unsigned long.[*]

For decimal constants, the sequence is modified by omitting `unsigned`:

```
int   long   unsigned long
```

The sequence now favors the signed types `int` and `long`, turning to an unsigned type only as a last resort. This is reasonable, because decimal constants are frequently used to represent signed integers.

[*]Here's some help for those new to integer representations and hexadecimal notation. For type `int`, the binary codes for positive integers range from `0x0000` through `0x7fff`; the remaining codes—`0x8000` through `0xffff`—represent negative integers and so are not considered. For type `unsigned`, all possible codes, `0x0000` through `0xffff`, represent positive integers. Similar remarks apply to `long` and `unsigned long`.

For example (again assuming two-byte `ints` and four-byte `longs`), `32767` has type `int`, `2147483647` has type `long`, and `4294967295` has type `unsigned long`. (Again, we have used the largest value of each type as our example.)

Suffixes

If we are not satisfied with these typing rules, we can modify them by using the suffixes `U` (unsigned), `L` (long), and `UL` (unsigned long). (The suffixes can also be lowercase; we suggest avoiding the lowercase ell, which is easily confused with the numeral one.) Each suffix specifies a sequence of types to be used in determining the type of the constant. When suffixes are used, the sequence of types is the same for decimal and nondecimal constants.

For suffix `U`, we use a sequence containing only unsigned types:

```
unsigned   unsigned long
```

For example, `25U` has type `unsigned` and `70000U` has type `unsigned long`. If the `U` were not present, these constants would have types `int` and `long`, respectively.

For suffix `L`, we use a sequence containing only the signed and unsigned versions of type `long`:

```
long   unsigned long
```

For example, `30L` has type `long` and `3000000000L` has type `unsigned long`. If the `L` suffix were not present, `30` would have type `int` but `3000000000` would still have type `unsigned long`.

For suffix `UL`, the sequence contains only one type, `unsigned long`. Thus `5UL`, `40000UL`, and `3000000000UL` all have type `unsigned long`. If the `UL` suffix were omitted, `5` would have type `int` and `40000` would have type `long`.

Suffixes are commonly used to force a constant with a small numerical value to belong to a large type. For example, `0`, `0U`, `0L`, and `0UL` represent the zero values of, respectively, types `int`, `unsigned`, `long`, and `unsigned long`.

Character Constants

Characters are represented by integer codes that can belong to any of the integer types and can be represented by any of the decimal or nondecimal notations discussed so far. However, character constants—integer constants specifically intended for representing characters—save us the trouble of looking up the integer codes and make our programs independent of any particular coding scheme (such as ASCII or EBCDIC).

A character constant consists of a character or escape sequence enclosed in single quotation marks (apostrophes):

```
'A'     'z'     '5'     '$'       '\n'
```

The value of a character constant is the integer code for the character. The type of this value is `int` (not `char`), because (for the reasons discussed earlier) constants are provided only for `int` and larger types. Values of type `int` and larger types are easily converted to type `char` when necessary.

Escape Sequences

Table 3-3 shows all of the escape sequences, which can be used in both string literals and character constants. The first four escape sequences listed are used to represent certain characters in contexts where they would otherwise be invalid. For example, because quotation marks delimit a string literal, they cannot occur inside the delimited string. Thus

```
"Paris is a city; "Paris" is a word."
```

is invalid because the first internal quotation mark would terminate the string literal. However, the escape sequence for a double quotation mark can be used without difficulty:

```
"Paris is a city; \"Paris\" is a word."
```

Table 3-3	\"	double quotation mark
Escape Sequences	\'	single quotation mark
	\\	backslash
	\?	question mark
	\a	alert (bell or beep)
	\b	backspace
	\f	form feed (new page)
	\n	newline
	\r	carriage return
	\t	horizontal tab
	\v	vertical tab
	\ddd	character represented by octal code
	\xhhh	character represented by hexadecimal code

This string literal is valid, and the string will be stored with each \" replaced by ".

Likewise, the single quotation mark must be represented by \' inside a character constant, which is delimited by single quotation marks. Thus the character constant for a single quotation mark is \' enclosed in single quotation marks:

```
'\''
```

Because \ introduces escape sequences, we must use the escape sequence \\ when we want a backslash to be treated as just another character. For example, the character constant for \ is

```
'\\'
```

and the MS-DOS path name

```
\QC\INCLUDE\STDIO.H
```

is represented by the string literal

```
"\\QC\\INCLUDE\\STDIO.H"
```

MS-DOS users must remember to "double the backslashes" when writing string literals representing path names.

Explaining the need for \? requires a brief digression. Some characters used in C programs are not available on all computers, particularly computers of older design and those used in non-English-speaking countries. Therefore, C allows such characters to be represented by three-letter sequences called *trigraphs*, as shown in Table 3-4. Although most of us will never need to use trigraphs, we must nonetheless take care not to use them inadvertently. For example, a compiler that processes trigraphs will treat

```
"The child said 'What??' when I spoke to him."
```

Table 3-4	CHARACTER	TRIGRAPH
Representations of	[	??(
Characters by Trigraphs	\	??/
	]	??)
	^	??'
	{	??<
	|	??!
	}	??>
	~	??-
	#	??=

as representing

```
The child said 'What^ when I spoke to him.
```

If we represent the second question mark by an escape sequence, the backslash will break up the `??'` trigraph. Thus

```
"The child said 'What?\?' when I spoke to him."
```

represents the string

```
The child said 'What??' when I spoke to him.
```

The escape sequences `\a` through `\v` represent common control characters such as alert (often called *bell*), backspace, newline, and horizontal or vertical tab.

The final two escape sequences in Table 3–3 allow characters to be represented by octal or hexadecimal codes. In the table, *ddd* stands for *one to three* octal digits and *hhh* stands for *any number of* hexadecimal digits. For example, `\33` and `\x1b` both represent the ASCII Esc character, whose code is 33 in octal and 1b in hexadecimal.

Note that `'\33'` has the same type and value as `033`, and `'\x1b'` has the same type and value as `0x1b`. Using the character constant, however, makes it clear that the constant represents a character code, which would not be clear if an integer constant were used. Even clearer is to define a macro that represents the character constant by an appropriate name:

```
#define ASCII_ESC    '\x1b'
```

In strings, there is the danger that characters following an octal or hexadecimal escape sequence inadvertently will be included in the sequence. This is most easily avoided for octal sequences, which allow a maximum of three digits. If we write `\33` as `\033`, we can be sure that no additional digits will inadvertently be added to the escape sequence. For example, in

```
"1234567\0331234567"
```

the escape sequence includes only the three digits following the backslash.

The problem is trickier in hexadecimal, because any number of hexadecimal digits are allowed and because letters `a` through `f` are allowed as hexadecimal digits. This problem is best solved with *string concatenation*, whereby a series of string literals separated by whitespace are concatenated (joined) to represent a single string. For example,

```
printf("to" "get"
       "her");
```

prints `together`, because the three string literals are concatenated. Note carefully that the string literals to be concatenated are separated only by whitespace, not commas.

Now, in

```
"abcdef\x1babcdef"
```

all the characters following the backslash are included in the character constant. But if we use string concatenation

```
"abcdef\x1b" "abcdef"
```

the escape sequence will consist only of `\x1b`.

Multibyte Characters

With one byte we can represent at most 255 characters. This number is sufficient for Western languages but not for most oriental languages, which can have many thousands of characters. To accommodate oriental languages, C provides for *multibyte characters*, each of which is represented by more than one byte.

Each multibyte character can also be represented by an integer code, known as a *wide-character code*. Header file `stdlib.h` defines `wchar_t` as the integer type for wide-character codes.[*] Thus

```
wchar_t wch;
```

declares `wch` as an integer variable that can hold a wide character code.

A prefix L indicates that a character constant represents a multibyte character and yields a wide-character code:

```
L'm'
```

Here, m stands for a multibyte character, which in reality would probably be a foreign-language character. Such a constant yields an integer value that can be assigned to a variable of type `wchar_t`:

```
wch = L'm';
```

Likewise, a prefix L indicates indicates that a string literal represents a string of multibyte characters:

```
L"mnopqrst"
```

Here, m, n, etc., stand for multibyte characters.

[*]Here, `wchar_t` is not a new type but another name for an existing integer type. We will see shortly how such "typedef names" are defined.

	Type	Bytes Required	Significant Digits	Exponent Range
Table 3-5	float	4	7	–37 to 38
Properties of Floating-Point	double	8	15	–307 to 308
Representations	long double	10	19	–4931 to 4932

Because few readers will have any need for multibyte characters, and because compilers sold in Western countries often do not implement them, multibyte characters will not be discussed further in this book.

Floating Types

Most computers provide two or three sizes of floating-point numbers, which are designated as *single precision*, *double precision*, and (where available) *extended precision*. The corresponding C types are float, double, and long double.

Because of their greater complexity, floating-point representations are less standardized than integer representations and are harder to characterize. Several properties of interest are the number of bytes required, the number of significant digits that can be represented, and the range of exponents allowed in exponential notation. Table 3-5 gives typical values of these properties for the three floating types. The properties given for float and double are roughly typical of many implementations, with the greatest variation being in the exponent range. The properties of long double vary considerably, so the table entry represents just one possible way of implementing this type. When extended precision is not available, long double has the same properties as double, although the two types are still considered distinct in C.

Floating constants such as 3.1416 and 7.5e-20 represent values of type double. As with integers, we can use suffixes to specify other types. The suffix F (or f) specifies float, and L (or l) specifies long double. For example, 3.1416F and 7.5e-20F represent values of type float, whereas 3.1416L and 7.5e-20L represent values of type long double.

DEFINING AND NAMING TYPES

We now turn from the basic, or predefined, arithmetic types to integer types defined and named by the programmer. After finishing this section we will have been introduced to all the integer types, although in one case (bitfields) the introduction will be brief and preliminary.

Type Definitions

In C, a type definition is best thought of as a *type-name* definition, in that it defines a name for a type that is specified by other means. The type to be named can be specified by an existing name or by a construction that describes the type. If the type is specified by an existing name, the newly defined name and the existing one become synonyms, both referring to the same type. Type definitions begin with the keyword `typedef`, and the names that they define are called *typedef names*.

A type definition has the same form as a variable declaration except that (1) it begins with `typedef` and (2) it defines a type name instead of declaring a variable. For example, the declaration

```
int count;
```

declares a variable `count` with type `int`. In contrast, the type definition

```
typedef int whole_num;
```

defines `whole_num` as a synonym for `int`. Because name `whole_num` and `int` are now interchangeable, we can declare `count` as follows:

```
whole_num count;
```

This declaration of `count` is equivalent in every respect to the preceding one.

We can use `typedef` to provide a one-word name for a type that is specified in a more complex manner. For example,

```
typedef unsigned long word;
```

defines the typedef name `word` as a synonym for `unsigned long`. The declaration

```
word size;
```

declares `size` as a variable of type `word`, which is the same as type `unsigned long`.

Type `size_t` and the `sizeof` Operator

A C implementation defines a number of typedef names in header files. Each typedef name corresponds to a particular purpose that a type can serve. Because the type definitions can vary from implementation to implementation, a particular purpose can be served by different types in different implementations, as might be required by differences in computer hardware.

For example, `size_t` is an unsigned integer type used to represent the number of bytes in a region of memory. Depending on the computer hardware, type `unsigned` or `unsigned long` might reasonably be used for this job. The typedef name `size_t` is defined in several header files, including `stdlib.h`. If these header files contain the definition

```
typedef unsigned size_t;
```

then type `unsigned int` will be used to represent the number of bytes in a region of memory. If the definition is

```
typedef unsigned long size_t;
```

then type `unsigned long` will be used for this purpose.

Now suppose we declare

```
size_t byte_count;
```

We do not know if `byte_count` is an `unsigned` or an `unsigned long` variable, but we do know that it is large enough to hold the number of bytes in any region of memory.

C has a prefix unary operator, `sizeof`, which returns the number of bytes required to store a value of a particular type. The type can be specified by any expression; the type of value returned by the expression is the type to which `sizeof` is applied. The number of bytes is returned as a value of type `size_t`.

For example, the expression

```
sizeof 100
```

yields the number of bytes for an `int` value, and

```
sizeof 3.1416
```

yields the number of bytes for a `double` value. If we declare

```
unsigned long n;
size_t byte_count;
```

then

```
byte_count = sizeof n;
```

assigns `byte_count` the number of bytes in an `unsigned long` value, and

```
byte_count = sizeof byte_count;
```

assigns `byte_count` the number of bytes needed to store a memory size.

The `sizeof` operator can be applied directly to a type rather than an expression, but the type must be enclosed in parentheses. Thus

```
sizeof(unsigned long)
```

yields the size of an `unsigned long` value, and

```
sizeof(size_t)
```

yields the number of bytes needed to store a memory size.

Note that no harm is done if parentheses are also used when `sizeof` is applied to constants and variables:

```
sizeof(100)
sizeof(n)
```

For uniformity, many programmers prefer always to put parentheses around the item to which `sizeof` is applied.

Enumerated Types

An *enumeration* specifies an integer type and defines constants to represent values of the type. The constants are called *enumeration constants* and (like character constants) have type `int`. For example, the enumeration

```
enum {RED, GREEN, BLUE}
```

specifies an enumerated type whose values can be represented by the enumeration constants RED, GREEN, and BLUE. If we do not specify otherwise, the constants are given successive integer values starting with 0. Thus the values of RED, GREEN, and BLUE are, respectively, 0, 1, and 2.

We can use an enumeration to declare variables with the enumerated type. For example,

```
enum {RED, GREEN, BLUE} c, d;
```

declares `c` and `d` as variables of the type specified by the enumeration. We can assign values to the variables with statements such as

```
c = RED;
d = BLUE;
```

We can test the values of the variables with expressions such as

```
(c == RED) && (d != BLUE)
```

The assignment operators convert the values of the enumeration constants from type `int` to the enumeration type. When values of an enumeration type appear in an expression (such as the logical expression just shown), the values are converted to type `int`.

We can specify any `int` values for the enumeration constants. For example,

```
enum {RED = 100, GREEN = 30, BLUE = 1000} c, d;
```

defines enumeration constants with the specified values and declares c and d with an integer type whose range of values includes all three constants.

We often need to refer to an enumeration by name from elsewhere in the program. We can do this in two ways, using either tags or (the preferred way) typedef names. The keyword `enum` can be followed by an optional identifier called a *tag*, which can be used to refer back to the enumeration. For example,

```
enum color {RED, GREEN, BLUE} c, d;
```

defines the tag `color` and the enumeration constants, and declares the variables c and d. If, further on in the program, we need to declare e and f with the same enumerated type, we can write

```
enum color e, f;
```

Here, `enum color` is an abbreviated form of the complete enumeration; when the abbreviated form is encountered, the compiler looks up the complete enumeration and uses it to declare the variables.

What is usually a better method of referring to enumerations is to define a typedef name for the enumerated type. Unlike tags, typedef names are on the same footing with other type names, such as `int` and `float`. Recalling that a type definition has the same structure as a variable declaration, we define `color_t` as follows:

```
typedef enum {RED, GREEN, BLUE} color_t;
```

The typedef name `color_t` refers to the enumerated type specified by the enumeration. We can use `color_t` just like any other type name to declare variables of the enumerated type:

```
color_t c, d;
color_t e;
color_t f;
```

Figure 3-3

This 16-bit value contains three bitfields: (1) the left-most three bits; (2) the middle eight bits; and (3) the right-most five bits.

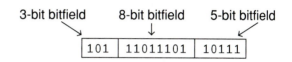

Bitfields

Although we are not yet ready to discuss bitfields in depth, they are introduced briefly here for completeness and because they are mentioned in the upcoming section on type conversions.

A *bitfield* is a sequence of adjacent bits within a larger integer value. For example, Figure 3-3 illustrates three bitfields within a 16-bit value: (1) the left-most three bits; (2) the middle eight bits; and (3) the right-most five bits. The contents of a bitfield can be regarded as representing either a signed or an unsigned integer. Accordingly, there are three kinds of bitfields: *plain*, *signed*, and *unsigned*. As with type `char`, plain bitfields contain either signed or unsigned values, depending on the implementation.

When a bitfield occurs in an expression, it is converted to type `int` or `unsigned int` before any operations are carried out. The details of this and many other type conversions are the subject of the next section.

TYPE CONVERSIONS

In everyday arithmetic we deal with numerical values that are independent of computer representations and of computer-inspired distinctions such as integer vs. floating-point. Such a numerical value can generally be represented by values drawn from a number of C types. For example, the numerical value 5 can be represented by values from all nine basic integer types, all three floating types, and suitably defined enumeration types and bitfields.

Because there are so many ways to represent a given numerical value, we frequently need to change from one representation to another. That is, we need to convert a C value from one type to another while (hopefully) preserving the underlying numerical value. C performs many such conversions automatically while evaluating expressions and carrying out assignments. Unfortunately, it is left up to us to make sure that the conversions are harmless—that they do indeed preserve underlying numerical values.

Promotions

Converting an integer value to a larger type—one that uses more bits to represent a value—is always harmless. We already know that such a conversion is carried out automatically whenever an integer value of a type smaller than `int` appears in an expression. We say that the conversion *promotes* the type of the value.

Types smaller than `int` are promoted to `int` or `unsigned` according to the following rules. Enumerated types are promoted to `int`, as are types that are definitely signed (`signed char`, `short`, signed bitfields). Types that are definitely unsigned (`unsigned char`, `unsigned short`, unsigned bitfields) and types that could be unsigned (`char`, plain bitfields) are promoted to type `int` if the numerical value in question can be represented as an `int` value. If it cannot be, the type is promoted to `unsigned`.

Balancing

The binary operations provided by the computer hardware apply to two values of the same type and yield a result of that type. For example, one operation might multiply two `int` values to get an `int` result, another might multiply two `unsigned long` values to get an `unsigned long` result, and so on. On the other hand, C allows mixed-mode expressions in which an operator can be applied to values of different types. The `*` operator, for example, might be applied to an `int` and a `long` value, to a `long` and a `double` value, and so on.

When a binary operator is applied to operands of different types, the type of one of the operands is chosen for carrying out the operation and expressing the result. The other operand must be converted to the chosen type so that the machine operation can be applied to operands of the same type. Choosing the type for carrying out an operation is called *balancing*, and the type chosen is called the *balanced type*. The rules for balancing are designed to favor safe conversions—those that do not change underlying numerical values.

To begin with, any promotions are carried out before balancing. Therefore, balancing need deal only with the integer types `int`, `unsigned`, `long`, and `unsigned long` and with the three floating types. Of the two operand types, the balanced type is the one that occurs further down in the following list:

```
int
unsigned              (See exception discussed in the next
long                  paragraph for types unsigned and long.)
unsigned long
float
double
long double
```

For example, if the operand types are long and double, the balanced type is double, and the long operand must be converted to double. Likewise, the balanced type for the expression

    25U + 3.5F

is float; the left operand must be converted to 25.0F and the result is 28.5F.

There is an exception when type long cannot represent all the values of type unsigned. (This is true, for example, when unsigned and long have the same size.) For implementations affected by the exception, the balanced type for unsigned and long operands is unsigned long rather than long. Both the unsigned and the long operands are converted to unsigned long.

Although balancing favors safe conversions, a couple of problems can arise. First, balancing can convert a signed operand to the corresponding unsigned type, which is safe if the signed value is positive. If the signed value is negative, however, it will be converted to a large positive number, with a likely adverse affect on the calculation. Avoid mixing signed and unsigned types unless you can guarantee that the signed values will always be positive. Second, a loss of precision is possible when an integer is converted to a floating-point number. For example, types long and unsigned long may contain 10-digit numbers, whereas the precision of type float may be limited to six significant digits.

Assignment and Initialization

When initializing a variable or assigning it a value, C tries to convert the type of the value to the type of the variable. Assignment and initialization can convert from any arithmetic type to any other arithmetic type. Not all such conversions are safe, however. Some conversions can drastically change numerical values, and some can cause the program to terminate with a run-time error.

The conversion will be safe if the value to be assigned can be represented in the type of the variable. For example, in

```
unsigned char c;
c = 200;
```

the `int` value 200 must be converted to `unsigned char` before it can be assigned to `c`. This conversion is safe, because values of `unsigned char` range from 0 to 255. On the other hand,

```
c = 1000;
```

is not safe, because 1000 cannot be represented in type `unsigned char`. Specifically, the code for 1000 has 10 bits, whereas `c` can hold only eight bits. Therefore, the left-most two bits of the `int` value are discarded, and only the remaining eight bits are stored. Those eight bits happen to represent 232, which is the value stored in `c`.

When converting from a larger floating type to a smaller, two problems can occur. First, the value of the larger type may have more significant digits than can be represented in the smaller type. The conversion will reduce the precision with which the value is represented but will not drastically change its value. Second, the value of the larger type may have an exponent that cannot be represented in the smaller type. This problem causes the program to terminate with a run-time error.

When a floating-point number is converted to an integer, the digits to the left of the decimal point are retained unchanged and those to the right are discarded. This conversion is often performed deliberately for the purpose of truncating the floating-point value. The integer part of the floating-point number must lie in the range of values allowed for the target integer type. If it does not, the program will terminate with a run-time error.

Conversions between integer types never cause run-time errors, even if a conversion drastically changes the numerical value of an integer. As our example indicated, an integer is converted from a larger to a smaller type by discarding bits from left to right. An unsigned integer is stored with leading zeros filling unused bit positions:

```
0000000011010011
```

The numerical value of an unsigned integer will not change if only leading zeros are discarded. Thus the preceding 16-bit value can be safely converted to eight bits:

```
11010011
```

This is because the conversion discards only leading zeros. On the other hand, the value of

```
0000000100101001
```

changes if the code is converted to eight bits:

```
00101001
```

The conversion discards a bit that is not a leading zero.

In the twos-complement system, a signed number is stored with a *sign bit* that is 0 for a positive number and 1 for a negative number. Unused bit positions are filled with copies of the sign bit:

```
0000000001110101   (positive integer)
1111111110111011   (negative integer)
```

A conversion to a smaller type is safe if only *extra* copies of the sign bit are discarded. We must not discard all copies of the sign bit, however, because that would leave no sign bit for the converted value.

For example, both of the preceding values can be converted to eight bits:

```
01110101   (positive integer)
10111011   (negative integer)
```

Note that, in each case, one copy of the sign bit was retained as the sign bit of the converted value. On the other hand, the value of

```
1111111011011110
```

changes if the code is converted to eight bits:

```
11011110
```

The conversion discards one bit that is not a copy of the sign bit.

Passing Arguments to Functions

When a function is called, the actual arguments are evaluated, and (if necessary) their values are converted to the types of the formal arguments (as given in the function declaration). The conversion process is the same as for assignment. For example, given the declaration

```
void f(long);
```

the call

```
f(25);
```

is valid and safe. The actual argument, 25, will be converted from int to long before being passed to the function. Now suppose that the function

```
void g(int);
```

is called with

```
g(1000000L);
```

This call is also valid but may be unsafe. The long argument will be converted to type int, but its numerical value may be changed in the process.

In functions that can be called with varying numbers of arguments, such as printf() and scanf(), the types of the optional arguments cannot be declared. For example, printf() is declared in stdio.h as follows:

```
int printf(const char *, ...);
```

The first formal argument (whose declaration we will not try to decipher at the moment) corresponds to the required format string. The three dots indicate that other, optional arguments are possible, but say nothing about their number or types.

Promotions are carried out for optional arguments, but no other conversions can be performed because the target types are not known. Aside from promotions, it is up to the programmer to make sure that each optional actual argument has the type required by the function. For example, if x is a float variable, the call

```
printf("%f", x);
```

will not work properly. The compiler (which knows nothing about the meaning of format strings) has no way of knowing that the function expects a double value for its second argument. The float argument, together with adjacent memory bytes containing who knows what, will be misinterpreted as a double value, preventing the function call from working as expected.

Type Casts

All conversions discussed so far take place automatically, without so much as a by-your-leave to the programmer. In contrast, type casts allow us to request conversions explicitly wherever they may be needed. A *type cast* is an operator formed by enclosing a type designation in parentheses, as in (int), (size_t), and (unsigned long). The type cast is a prefix unary operator with the same precedence as other prefix unary operators, such as unary + and unary -. The effect of the type cast is to convert its operand to the specified type (if possible). The conversions are carried out the same as for assignment, so inappropriate type casts can change numerical values or cause run-time errors.

For example, the previous incorrect attempt to print the value of a `float` variable `x`,

```
printf("%f", x);
```

can be corrected with a type cast:

```
printf("%f", (double)x);
```

The value of the expression

```
(double)x
```

is the value of `x` converted to type `double`. The function call now works properly because the second argument has type `double`, the type that the format string told `printf()` to expect. This example is a practical one: there is no conversion specification for printing `float` values, so a float value must be converted to another type, normally `double`, in order to be printed.

Type casts can clarify an expression by explicitly indicating type conversions that might otherwise be overlooked. For example, if `x` and `n` are declared by

```
double x;
long n;
```

then

```
n = x + 0.5;
```

assigns `n` the value of `x` rounded to the nearest integer. Someone reading the program might miss the significance of this statement because the crucial operation of converting a floating-point value to an integer is not explicitly indicated. The equivalent statement

```
n = (long)(x + 0.5);
```

emphasizes the type conversion.

MORE ABOUT FORMAT STRINGS

Our previous discussion of format strings must be expanded to include the many additional types introduced in this chapter. In the following, we will distinguish between a *conversion specifier* (a letter designating a conversion, such as d, f, or s) and a *conversion speci-fication* (a complete specification of a conversion, such as %8d, %6.3f, or %-10s). A conversion specification begins with a per-cent sign and ends with a conversion specifier.

Most of our discussion will focus on printf(), which gener-ally uses the more complex format strings. A short discussion will then suffice to explain how format strings for scanf() differ from those for printf().

Flags for printf()

The percent sign of a conversion specification can be followed by one or more *flags* specifying additional details of the conversion, as shown in Table 3-6. For example, the statements

```
printf("%08d\n", 125);
printf("%+08d\n", 125);
printf("% 08d\n", 125);
```

(0, +, and the space are flags) print

```
00000125
+0000125
 0000125
```

Likewise,

```
printf("%8.0f", 125.0);
printf("%#8.0f", 125.0);
```

print

```
     125
     125.
```

Table 3-6	−	Left-justify printed value.
Flags for printf()	+	Print a plus sign before positive signed numbers.
	space	Print a space before positive signed numbers. This flag has no effect if a + flag is also present.
	#	Print octal and hexadecimal numbers in C format (leading 0, 0x, or 0X). Print a floating-point number with a decimal point even if no digits are to be printed to the right of the decimal point.
	0	When right-justifying a value in a field, use leading zeros rather than leading spaces as padding. Any sign or base indication (such as +, 0, or 0x) precedes the leading zeros. This flag has no effect if a − flag is also present.

Field Width and Precision

The flags, if any, can be followed by an optional field width and precision, as in `%#8.0f`. The precision, if present, is preceded by a decimal point. The meaning of the precision depends on the type being converted. For integer types, the precision is the *minimum* number of digits that will be printed; integers with fewer than the minimum number of digits are padded with leading zeros. For strings, the precision is the *maximum* number of characters that will be printed. Thus, the statements

```
printf("%.4d\n", 1);
printf("%.4s\n", "computer");
```

print

```
0001
comp
```

For floating types, the meaning of the precision depends on the conversion specifier. If the conversion specifier is e, E, or f, the precision specifies the number of digits to the right of the decimal point. If the conversion specifier is g or G, the precision specifies the maximum number of significant digits. (These conversion specifiers will be discussed further shortly.)

Replacing the field width or precision with an asterisk allows the corresponding parameter to be supplied as an `int` argument to `printf()`. For example, `%*.*f` prints a `double` value using a field width and precision supplied as integer arguments. Field width and precision arguments (in that order if both are present) immediately precede the value to be printed. For example, if `width` and `precision` are integer variables, then

```
printf("%*.*f", width, precision, 3.1416);
```

prints `3.1416`, with the field width and precision given by the values of `width` and `precision`.

Printing Characters

The conversion specifier c prints a single character. The corresponding argument, which has type `int`, gives the numerical code for the character; `printf()` sends this code to the output device, which displays or prints the corresponding graphic. The argument can also have type char, signed char, or unsigned char; such arguments will be promoted to int before being passed to printf().

For example,

```
printf("%c%c%c", 'A', 'B', 'C');
```

prints

ABC

We could also use integer constants to specify the character codes:

```
printf("%c%c%c", 65, 66, 67);
```

Assuming the ASCII code, this statement will also print ABC.

Now suppose we write

```
char ch;
ch = 'A';
printf("%c", ch);
```

The assignment converts the int code 'A' to type char and stores it in ch. When ch is used as an argument, its value is promoted to type int and passed to printf(), causing A to be printed.

There is a special conversion specification, %%, for printing the character %. Because a % in a format string introduces a conversion specification, we cannot use % as a *literal character*—a character that is not part of a conversion specification and therefore is to be printed unchanged. To print %, we must use the conversion specification %%. For example,

```
printf("Are you 100%% sure?\n");
```

prints

Are you 100% sure?

and

```
printf("You got %d%% correct\n", 75);
```

prints

You got 75% correct

Note that there is no argument corresponding to the conversion specification %%.

Printing Integers

The conversion specifiers for types int and unsigned are given in Table 3-7. An int value can be printed in decimal notation using either d (for decimal) or i (for int) as a conversion

Table 3-7

Conversion Specifiers for Types
int *and* unsigned

Conversion Specifier	Argument Type	Notation
d, i	int	decimal
u	unsigned	decimal
o	unsigned	octal
x, X	unsigned	hexadecimal

specifier; most C programmers use d. An unsigned value can be printed in decimal notation (using u), octal notation (using o), or hexadecimal notation (using x or X). For x, the hexadecimal digits a through f and the x in the prefix 0x are printed in lowercase letters; for X, uppercase letters are used. The prefix 0 for octal and 0x or 0X for hexadecimal are printed only if the # flag is present.

The conversion specifiers in Table 3-7 are adapted to other integer types by preceding them with h (for types short and unsigned short) or l (for types long and unsigned long). All other properties of a conversion specifier, such as whether the type is signed or unsigned and what notation will be used for printing, remain unchanged. For example, we use ld to print a long value, lu to print an unsigned long value in decimal notation, lx to print an unsigned long value in hexadecimal notation, and so on.

Values of types short and unsigned short are promoted before being passed as arguments. Type short is always promoted to int, but it is implementation dependent whether unsigned short will be promoted to int or unsigned int. These promotions are taken into account by printf(). When the h prefix is used, printf() expects the corresponding argument to have the type to which short or unsigned short is promoted.

Here are a couple of examples. The following code prints 1,000,000 in decimal, octal, and hexadecimal notation:

```
unsigned long n;
n = 1000000;
printf("%lu  %lo  %#lx\n", n, n, n);
```

The printout is

```
1000000  3641100  0xf4240
```

Note that the hexadecimal version is printed with the prefix 0x and uses lowercase letters throughout. The octal version is not preceded by a leading zero, because the # flag was not used.

The following code prints 100 three times:

```
short p = 100;
int q = 100;
long r = 100;
printf("%hd  %d  %ld\n", p, q, r);
```

The numerical value 100 is printed first as a value of type `short`, then as a value of type `int`, and finally as a value of type `long`.

Printing Floating-Point Numbers

The conversion specifiers used to print values of type `double` are given in Table 3-8. Corresponding uppercase and lowercase conversion specifiers are identical except that an uppercase specifier causes E to be used in exponential notation (as in 3.5E-005) and a lowercase specifier causes e to be used (as in 3.5e-005). For the e, E, and f specifiers, the precision gives the number of digits to the right of the decimal point; for g and G it gives the maximum number of significant digits.

For g and G, a value is printed in fixed-point notation unless (1) there would be more than three zeros between the decimal point and the first significant digit (as in 0.00005) or (2) the number of digits to the left of the decimal point would exceed the specified precision. In either of these cases, exponential notation is used. For example, the statements

```
printf("%.6g\n", .00005);
printf("%.6g\n", .0005);
printf("%.6g\n", 654321.0);
printf("%.6g\n", 7654321.0);
```

print

```
5e-005
0.0005
654321
7.65432e+006
```

As mentioned earlier, there are no conversion specifiers for printing `float` values; we can print a `float` value by converting it to `double` with a type cast. The prefix L causes the conversion specifiers in Table 3-8 to apply to type `long double`. For example, Le prints a `long double` value in exponential notation, Lf prints a `long double` value in fixed-point notation, and so on.

	CONVERSION SPECIFIER	NOTATION
Table 3-8	e, E	Exponential
Conversion Specifiers for Type	f	Fixed point
`double`	g, G	Either exponential or fixed point, depending on value

Format Strings for `scanf()`

For `scanf()`, a conversion specification gives the format of a value to be read; the corresponding argument gives the address of the variable in which the value is to be stored. In contrast to `printf()`, no promotions or conversions with type casts are possible; therefore, the type of each variable must match exactly the type of the value to be stored in it.

Literal characters in a `scanf()` format string are matched with corresponding characters in the input. Input characters that match literal characters are read and discarded. If a literal character (other than a space) fails to match the corresponding input character, `scanf()` returns immediately without reading any more input or storing any more values. For example, the `scanf()` call

```
scanf("***$%lf", &x);
```

requires that the input begin with the characters `***$`. Thus

```
***$25.99
```

is acceptable, but

```
**$$25.99
```

will cause `scanf()` to return before the number is read and stored. In analogy with `printf()`, the `scanf()` conversion specification `%%` matches a `%` character in the input.

A literal space character matches zero or more whitespace characters. Thus, a space in the format string causes `scanf()` to skip whitespace until a non-whitespace character is encountered. Because a literal space can match zero input characters, the match always succeeds, and the space cannot cause `scanf()` to return prematurely. For example, the call

```
scanf("Amount is $%lf", &x);
```

will accept as valid input both

```
Amountis$49.99
```

and

```
Amount
          is
               $49.99
```

Most `scanf()` conversion specifications, including all those that read numbers, automatically skip whitespace before reading a value. Thus in the preceding example, we could also have whitespace between $ and `49.99`. The conversion specification `%lf` would skip this whitespace before reading the number.

In place of all the `printf()` flags, `scanf()` allows an optional `*` to follow the `%` that introduces a conversion specification. When the `*` is present, the value read by the specification is discarded rather than stored in a variable. There is no corresponding argument for such a specification. For example,

```
scanf("%*d%lf", &x);
```

reads and discards an `int` value, then reads a `double` value into `x`.

Only a field width (no precision) is allowed in a `scanf()` conversion specification. When present, the field width specifies the maximum number of characters to be read. The field width does not include any whitespace that is skipped before beginning to read the input value.

The conversion specifiers for integer types are the same for `scanf()` and `printf()`. For example, `%u` reads an `unsigned` value in decimal notation, `%o` reads an `unsigned` value in octal notation, and `%x` or `%X` (the two are equivalent for input) reads an `unsigned` value in hexadecimal notation. Each value must be stored in a variable of the correct type. For example, a value read with `%hd` must be stored in a `short` variable, a value read with `%d` must be stored in an `int` variable, and a value read with `%ld` must be stored in a `long` variable.

For floating-point input, the conversion specifiers e, E, f, g, and G are all equivalent. All read floating-point numbers in either fixed-point or exponential format. The e in exponential format can be either uppercase or lowercase.

We recall that `printf()` provides no conversion specifiers for type `float`; `float` values must be converted to type `double` for printing. Because no such conversion is possible with `scanf()`, the conversion specifiers have to be redefined to handle type `float`. Therefore, the unprefixed conversion specifiers e, E, f, and so on, read `float` (not `double`) values. The prefix l is used for type double and the prefix L for type `long double`. For example, the following code reads a `float` value, a `double` value, and a `long double` value:

```
float x;
double y;
long double z;

scanf("%f%lf%Lf", &x, &y, &z);
```

The conversion specification `%c` reads the next input character and stores it in a `char` variable. Unlike the numeric conversion specifiers, `%c` does not skip whitespace before reading a character. If we want to skip whitespace, we must precede `%c` with a literal space character. For example,

```
scanf("%c", &ch);
```

reads the next input character (whitespace or not) and stores it in the `char` variable ch. In contrast,

```
scanf(" %c", &ch);
```

skips any whitespace, then reads a non-whitespace character.

EXAMPLE PROGRAMS

We now look at several programs that illustrate some of the types and conversion specifiers introduced in this chapter. To avoid the need for lengthy explanations, these programs are based on Exercises 2-1, 2-2, and 2-4. Please see these exercises for a complete statement of the problem solved by each program.

Exercise 2-1 asks for a program to compute the requested number of grains of wheat, using type `double` for the computation. Unfortunately, the desired result turns out to have 20 significant digits, too many for type `double`, so that a `double` result is necessarily approximate. For some implementations, however, the result can be represented accurately as a `long double` value. When this is true, the program in Listing 3-1 will compute the result accurate to the last grain of wheat.

In Listing 3-1, in the declaration

```
long double total = 0,
            this_square = 1;
```

the `int` values 0 and 1 are converted to `long double` before being used to initialize total and this_square. In the statement

Listing 3-1

```
/* File grains.c */
/* Compute number of grains of wheat
   requested by inventor of chess    */

#include <stdio.h>
#include <stdlib.h>

int main(void)
{
   long double total = 0,
               this_square = 1;
   int sq_num;

   for (sq_num = 1; sq_num <= 64; sq_num++) {
      total += this_square;
      this_square *= 2;
   }
   printf("Grains requested: %.0Lf (%.2Lg)\n",
          total, total);
   return EXIT_SUCCESS;
}
```

```
   this_square *= 2;
```

the `int` value 2 is converted to `long double`. The computation is done in `long double`, and a `long double` result is stored in `this_square`.

We wish to print the result in two forms: an exact result in conventional notation, and an easier-to-read approximate result in exponential notation:

```
Grains requested: 18446744073709551615 (1.8e+019)
```

For the exact result we use the conversion specification `%.0Lf`; the `.0` specifies that no decimal places will be printed. For the approximate result we use `%.2Lg`; the `.2` specifies that the result will be printed with two significant figures.

The program in Listing 3-2 computes factorials of 0 through 12 using a function `factorial()` that takes an `unsigned` argument and returns an `unsigned long` result. (The factorial of 13 is too large for `unsigned long`.) In the declaration

Listing 3-2

```
/* File factrls.c */
/* Compute table of factorials */

#include <stdio.h>
#include <stdlib.h>

unsigned long factorial(unsigned n);

int main(void)
{
   unsigned i;

   printf("%-6s    %-9s\n\n", "Number", "Factorial");
   for (i = 0; i <= 12; i++)
      printf("%6u      %9lu\n", i, factorial(i));
   return EXIT_SUCCESS;
}

/* Compute factorial of unsigned integer */

unsigned long factorial(unsigned n)
{
   unsigned i;
   unsigned long product = 1;

   for (i = 1; i <= n; i++)
      product *= i;
   return product;
}
```

```
          unsigned long product = 1;
```

the int 1 is converted to unsigned long. In the statement

```
      product *= i;
```

the value of i is converted from unsigned to unsigned long. The multiplication is done in unsigned long, and an unsigned long result is assigned to product. In main(), we use %6u to print an unsigned value in a six-character field and %9lu to print an unsigned long value in a nine-character field.

The program requested in Exercise 2-4 asks the user to make a selection from a menu to get a figure printed or to exit the program. As described in the exercise, the menu is a numbered list and the user's selection is entered as an `int` value. Listing 3-3 shows an alternate version in which the selection is entered as a character and the menu can be displayed more compactly:

```
Select Box, bLock, Triangle, Diamond, or Quit
Enter letter for selection:
```

To make a selection, the user responds with the corresponding capitalized letter. The letter may be either upper- or lowercase.

The figures are printed by functions `print_box()`, `print_block()`, `print_triangle()`, and `print_diamond()`. Listing 3-3 does not show the definitions of these functions, the details of which are not relevant to our present discussion. The necessary definitions could be placed at the end of Listing 3-3, or they could be placed in another source file (in which case Listing 3-3 could be compiled as is).

Many languages provide a type (often called `Boolean`) for logical values. C does not, but we can define our own type `Boolean` as an enumerated type:

```
typedef enum {FALSE, TRUE} Boolean;
```

The values of `FALSE` and `TRUE` are 0 and 1, respectively. We use type `Boolean` to declare the flag `running`:

```
Boolean running = TRUE;
```

The value of `running` remains `TRUE` as long as the program is to continue accepting selections and printing figures. When the user elects to exit the program, `running` is set to `FALSE`.

The character entered by the user is stored in the `char` variable `selection`. The following code displays the menu and inputs the user's selection:

```
printf("\nSelect Box, bLock, Triangle, "
        "Diamond, or Quit\n");
printf("Enter letter for selection: ");
scanf(" %c", &selection);
```

Note that the first call to `printf()` uses string concatenation; the two string literals are joined to form a single string.

In `" %c"`, the space causes `scanf()` to skip whitespace before reading the value of `selection`. If the space were not present,

Listing 3-3

```
/* File figures.c */
/* Print figure selected from menu */

#include <stdio.h>
#include <stdlib.h>

void print_box(void);          /* Definitions not shown */
void print_block(void);
void print_triangle(void);
void print_diamond(void);

typedef enum {FALSE, TRUE} Boolean;

int main(void)
{
   char selection;
   Boolean running = TRUE;

   do {
      printf("\nSelect Box, bLock, Triangle, "
             "Diamond, or Quit\n");
      printf("Enter letter for selection: ");
      scanf(" %c", &selection);
      switch (selection) {
      case 'b':
      case 'B':
         print_box();
         break;
      case 'l':
      case 'L':
         print_block();
         break;
      case 't':
      case 'T':
         print_triangle();
         break;
      case 'd':
      case 'D':
         print_diamond();
         break;
```

(continued)

```
            case 'q':
            case 'Q':
                running = FALSE;
                break;
            default:
                printf("Invalid selection\n");
                printf("Please try again\n");
                break;
        }
    } while (running);
    return EXIT_SUCCESS;
}
```

---

scanf() would read the newline at the end of the preceding line of input, and the program would not work properly.

The switch statement converts the value of selection to type int and jumps to the corresponding case label. (The case labels are defined with character constants, which yield int values.) Note that a given group of statements can have more than one case label. For example, a selection of either b or B will cause the statements for printing a box to be executed.

Selecting q or Q causes running to be set to FALSE. The do statement accepts selections and prints figures as long as the value of running is TRUE. When the value of running is set to FALSE, the do statement terminates and the return statement terminates the program.

EXERCISES

3-1. Standard C implementations provide a header file, limits.h, that defines macros giving the range of values allowed for each integer type. For example, int values range from INT_MIN to INT_MAX, and unsigned values range from 0 to UINT_MAX. The following shows the macros that apply to the signed and unsigned versions of each type:

char	CHAR_MIN	CHAR_MAX	
signed/unsigned char	SCHAR_MIN	SCHAR_MAX	UCHAR_MAX
short	SHRT_MIN	SHRT_MAX	USHRT_MAX
int	INT_MIN	INT_MAX	UINT_MAX
long	LONG_MIN	LONG_MAX	ULONG_MAX

Write a program to print the range of values for each integer type. The types shown for the constants are the types of the corresponding values *after* any promotions have been applied. For example, LONG_MIN and LONG_MAX have type long, and ULONG_MAX has type unsigned long. But the type of CHAR_MIN and CHAR_MAX is int, the type to which char values are promoted.

3-2. The header file float.h defines macros giving various facts about the floating types. For example, FLT_DIG gives the number of decimal digits of precision for type float, while FLT_MIN_10_EXP and FLT_MAX_10_EXP give the range of decimal exponents allowed. The following shows the corresponding macros for each floating type:

```
float         FLT_DIG     FLT_MIN_10_EXP     FLT_MAX_10_EXP
double        DBL_DIG     DBL_MIN_10_EXP     DBL_MAX_10_EXP
long double   LDBL_DIG    LDBL_MIN_10_EXP    LDBL_MAX_10_EXP
```

Write a program to print the precision and exponent range for each floating type. For most implementations, all these constants will represent int values.

3-3. Write a version of the program in Listing 3-2 in which factorial() takes an unsigned argument but computes and returns the factorial as a value of type long double. Modify the program so that the user can specify the range of numbers whose factorials will be printed.

3-4. Modify the program of Exercise 2-3 to use type unsigned long for Fibonacci numbers.

3-5. Write a program to accept unsigned integers in decimal, octal, or hexadecimal notation and to display each in all three notations. Octal and hexadecimal numbers are entered and displayed in C notation (leading 0, 0x, or 0X), as in the following sample dialog:

```
Value to convert (0 to terminate)? 1000
1000      01750      0x3e8
Value to convert (0 to terminate)? 0X64
100       0144       0x64
Value to convert (0 to terminate)? 01000
512       01000      0x200
Value to convert (0 to terminate)? 0
```

4 Arrays and Pointers

We now turn to two of the central concepts of C: arrays and pointers. Arrays provide means for allocating and accessing memory. Pointers provide means for accessing memory that has been allocated by other means, often as an array. The two concepts are thoroughly intertwined in C, so that it is difficult to discuss one without the other.

Also, this chapter provides additional information on the use of identifiers and variables in C. We begin by seeing how the traditional concept of a variable is split into two C concepts: lvalues and objects.

LVALUES AND OBJECTS

Although the term *variable* is widely used to refer to a named memory location, it is not part of the standard terminology of C. Instead, C employs its own somewhat eccentric terminology for referring to memory locations and their names.

A region of memory in which data is stored is called an *object*.* Normally, an object occupies a sequence of one or more contiguous bytes. An exception is a bitfield, which may occupy only part of its first and last bytes. A C object is the same as what we have, so far, referred to somewhat loosely as a "memory location."

A programming-language expression that names an object is called an *lvalue*. The only lvalues we have encountered in C so far are variable names, such as `discount` and `interest`. From other languages, however, readers will be familiar with subscripted

*This use of the word *object* differs from its use in object-oriented programming.

array names, such as `list[5]` and `table[i+j]`, which are lvalues that designate array elements.

A *modifiable lvalue* is one that allows us to assign a new value to the designated object. In contrast, we are forbidden to assign a new value of an object accessed via a nonmodifiable lvalue. Note than a single object can be designated by several different lvalues, some modifiable and some not. We can change the value of the object if we access it via a modifiable lvalue but not if we access it via a nonmodifiable lvalue. The left operand of an assignment operator (such as = or +=) must be a modifiable lvalue, as must an operand of ++ or --.

What we have called a *variable* so far is, in C terminology, an object designated by a modifiable lvalue. Like most C programmers, we will continue to use the term *variable* where it is applicable. In our study of arrays and pointers, however, we will frequently need to consider lvalues and objects separately.

THE QUALIFIERS const AND volatile

A declaration such as

```
int n;
```

declares n as a modifiable lvalue. The value of n can, as we know, be changed with the assignment, increment, and decrement operators.

When the qualifier `const` is present, as in the declaration

```
const int n;
```

n is declared as a nonmodifiable lvalue. We cannot assign a new value to n or change its value with an increment or decrement operator. We can, however, give n an initial value when it is declared:

```
const int n = 100;
```

The `const` qualifier prevents the program from attempting to change the value of the declared object. For example, the object might reside in read-only memory, so that any attempt to change its value will fail. Or we may simply wish to deny a certain part of the program the right to change the value. Later in the chapter we will encounter the most common use of `const`, which prevents a function from changing the value of an object accessed via a pointer.

The `const` qualifier is *not* generally used to define a name for a numerical constant:

```
const double PI = 3.14159265;
```

That purpose is usually accomplished with a macro:

```
#define PI   3.14159625
```

The `volatile` qualifier states that the value of an object can be changed by some other hardware or software component, such as a peripheral-device controller or an interrupt-service routine. Any time the program needs the value of a volatile object, it must fetch a fresh value from memory, because any value fetched previously may now be out of date. For example, we can use `volatile` to declare a printer-status location, whose contents are changed by hardware or software to reflect the current status of the printer:

```
volatile unsigned int printer_status;
```

Both `const` and `volatile` can be used in the same declaration:

```
const volatile unsigned long clock_tick;
```

The `const` qualifier states that the program cannot change the value of `clock_tick`. The `volatile` qualifier states that some other hardware or software component can do so.

ONE-DIMENSIONAL ARRAYS

Abstractly, a (one-dimensional) array is a series of objects, all of which have the same type; these objects are the *elements* of the array. Concretely, an array is a block of memory made up of memory locations of a fixed size. In many implementations, for example, a `char` array is a block of adjacent bytes, a `short` array is a block of adjacent two-byte locations, a `long` array is a block of adjacent four-byte locations, and so on.

As in many other languages, we declare an array in C by giving the name of the array and the type and number of elements. For example,

```
int a[5];
```

declares a as an array of five `int` objects. Likewise,

```
long double x[100];
```

declares x as an array of 100 `long double` objects.

We can initialize an array when it is declared by listing the initial values for its elements, as follows:

```
int a[5] = {75, 25, 100, -45, 60};
```

Figure 4-1

The array a *has five elements, whose subscripts range from 0 to 4. The individual elements are named by* a[0], a[1], a[2], *and so on.*

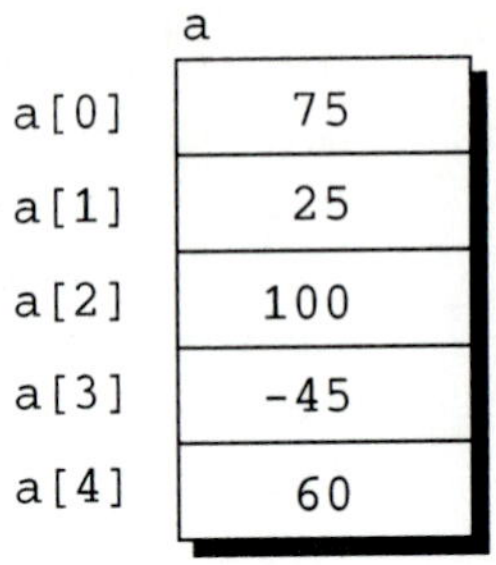

This array is illustrated in Figure 4-1. If the number of initial values given is less than the number of elements in the array, the remaining elements are initialized to zero. Thus

```
int b[5] = {75, 25};
```

is equivalent to

```
int b[5] = {75, 25, 0, 0, 0};
```

If we do not specify the number of elements for an initialized array, the number of initial values supplied determines the number of elements. Thus

```
int a[] = {75, 25, 100, -45, 60};
```

declares a as an array of five elements.

As illustrated in Figure 4-1, the elements of the array a are designated by a[0], a[1], a[2], a[3], and a[4]. The integers in brackets are *subscripts* and range from 0 through one less than the number of elements in the array. Thus if an array has 10 elements, the subscripts range from 0 through 9; if the array has 50 elements, the subscripts range from 0 through 49.

Subscripted array names are modifiable* lvalues that can be used just like variable names, such as discount and interest. For example,

*The lvalues are modifiable unless the array elements have been declared constant with const. For example, if we declare a by
    const int a[5];
then a[0], a[1], and so on are nonmodifiable lvalues whose values cannot be changed by the assignment, increment, or decrement operators.

```
a[2] = 5;
```

assigns 5 to element 2 (the third element) of a,

```
n = a[i] - a[j];
```

sets n to the difference of elements i and j, and

```
a[2*i - j]++;
```

increments the value of element 2*i - j.

In C, a subscript enclosed in brackets (such as [3] or [i]) is considered to be an operator applied to the array name. The *subscript operator*, designated by [] in Appendix 2, is a postfix unary operator. It has the highest possible precedence, and it associates from left to right.

Constants represented by macros are frequently used in declaring and manipulating arrays. For example, if COUNT is defined by

```
#define COUNT   1000
```

then

```
int c[COUNT];
```

declares c as an array of 1000 int objects.

Subscripts for c range from 0 through COUNT - 1. A for statement for processing all the elements of c has the form

```
for (i = 0; i < COUNT; i++) {
   /* Process element c[i] */
}
```

Because the less-than sign, < (rather than the less-than-or-equal-to sign, <=), is used, the values of i will range from 0 through COUNT - 1. For example,

```
for (i = 0; i < COUNT; i++)
   c[i] = 50;
```

set all the elements of c to 50.

Expressions such as c[i++] and c[i--] are frequently used in array processing. After the current value of i is used as an array subscript, the value of i is incremented or decremented; thus the next time i is used as a subscript it will refer to the next (for ++) or previous (for --) array element.

For example,

```
c[i++] = 50;
```

assigns 50 to `c[i]` and increments the value of `i`; if the statement is executed repeatedly, 50 will be assigned to successive elements of `c`. Thus

```
i = 101;
for (n = 1; n <= 10; n++)
    c[i++] = 50;
```

assign 50 to elements 101 through 110 of `c`.

On the other hand, beware of pitfalls such as

```
b[i] = a[i++];  /* effect is unpredictable */
```

Because we cannot say when side effects will take place during the evaluation of an expression, we do not know if the value of `i` will be incremented before or after it is used as a subscript of `b`. A variable that is incremented or decremented should be accessed only via the value returned by the increment or decrement operator. If we must access the variable more than once, the incrementation or decrementation should be done in a separate statement:

```
b[i] = a[i];
i++;
```

Array Names

We can apply the `sizeof` operator to an array name to determine the number of bytes in the array. For example, if `a` is an array of five `int` objects, and an `int` object occupies two bytes, then `sizeof a` will yield 10 as the number of bytes in `a`.

When an array name is used where a value is expected, the name is converted to the address of the first element of the array. This conversion, as we will see, provides the all-important connection between pointers (which are addresses) and arrays.

We can apply the address operator to an array name; the value of `&a` is the address of the array, which is equal to the address of its first element. Although the address of the array and the address of its first element are numerically equal, C distinguishes them by giving them different types.

An unsubscripted array name is a *nonmodifiable* lvalue—it behaves like a constant representing the address of the first array element. This means that we cannot use the array name to assign a value to an entire array. The attempt

```
b = a;  /* invalid */
```

(which would be valid in Pascal) is invalid in C for two reasons. First, b is not a modifiable lvalue and so cannot be used as the left operand of an assignment operator. Second, because a is used where a value is expected, it yields the address of the first element of a rather than an array value (as it would in some other languages). To assign the value of array a to array b in C, we must assign the value of each element a[i] to the corresponding element b[i]:

```
for (i = 0; i < 5; i++)
    b[i] = a[i];
```

POINTERS

A *pointer* is the address of an object *of a particular type*. We need to specify the type, because an address, by itself, just locates the first byte of an object. The type is necessary to determine the size of the object and the meaning of the bits stored in it. Therefore, the type of a pointer specifies the type of the target object—the object designated by the address. Typical pointer types are pointer-to-int, pointer-to-long, pointer-to-double, and so on.

The Indirection Operator

If p is a variable with type pointer-to-int, the value of p is the address of an int object. As shown in Figure 4-2, we diagram a pointer as an arrow extending from inside the pointer variable p to the target object. The *indirection operator*, *, enables us to refer to the target object: if p is a pointer variable, then *p is an lvalue that names the object pointed to by p. We can use *p in the same ways as other lvalues, such as interest and a[3]. If the target object has not been declared as constant, then *p is a modifiable lvalue and its value (that is, the value of the target object) can be changed by the assignment, increment, and decrement operators.

Figure 4-2
*We diagram a pointer as an arrow extended from inside the pointer variable p to the target object. We use the lvalue *p to designate the object pointed to by the value of p.*

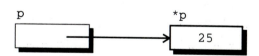

The indirection operator is a prefix unary operator and has the same precedence and right-to-left associativity as other prefix unary operators, such as unary + and unary –. The unary indirection operator can be distinguished from the binary multiplication operator because the indirection operator is applied to only one operand whereas the multiplication operator is always applied to two operands.

In the situation diagrammed in Figure 4-2, `*p` behaves like an `int` variable with value 25. For example,

```
printf("%d", *p);
```

prints the value 25, and

```
n = *p + 10;
```

assigns 35 to n. If `*p` has not been declared constant, then

```
*p = 20;
```

assigns 20 to the target object,

```
*p += 7;
```

adds 7 to the value of the target object, and

```
(*p)++;
```

increments the value of the target object. The parentheses are necessary because ++ has higher precedence than `*`.

We declare a pointer variable by giving the type of the target object. For example,

```
int *p;
double *q;
```

declare p with type pointer-to-`int` and q with type pointer-to-`double`. Note that merely declaring a pointer variable does *not* make it point to any particular object. We must not attempt to apply the indirection operator to a pointer variable until the variable has been assigned the address of a valid object.

Using the Address-Of Operator

We can use the address-of operator to compute the address of any object designated by an lvalue. Such addresses have pointer types and can be used to initialize and assign values to pointers. For example, if we declare

```
int n = 100;
double x = 3.5;
```

then &n has type pointer-to-int and &x has type pointer-to-double. If we now declare

```
int *p = &n;
```

then p is initialized to point to n. Thus *p and n name the same object (they are said to be *aliases*); both have the value 100, and an assignment to one will also change the value of the other. Note that, despite the appearance of the declaration, the address &n is assigned to the pointer variable p, not to the target object *p.

If we declare

```
double *q;
```

then q does not point to a valid object. This can be remedied with the assignment

```
q = &x;
```

Now q points to the object named by x, *q and x both have the value 3.5, and

```
*q = 7.9;
```

changes the value of both *q and x to 7.9.

Using const *in Pointer Declarations*

In a declaration for a pointer variable, const can be used in two different places, with two correspondingly different meanings. If const is placed at the beginning of the declaration, the *target object* is declared constant. For example, if we declare

```
const int *p;
```

then the value of the target object *p cannot be changed with the assignment, increment, and decrement operators. Thus statements such as

```
*p = 100;
```

and

```
(*p)--
```

are invalid. No such restrictions apply to the pointer variable p, however. If m and n are integer variables, then statements such as

```
p = &m;
```

and

```
p = &n;
```

are valid and cause p to point to different objects.

On the other hand, if `const` immediately precedes the pointer variable, the situation is reversed: the value of p is constant but that of *p can be freely changed. For example, if we declare

```
int *const p = &m;
```

then p will retain its initial value of &m. Assignments such as

```
p = &n;
```

are not allowed. On the other hand, we can freely assign to, increment, and decrement *p:

```
*p = 25;
*p += 3;
(*p)++;
```

Pointers and Arrays

We can use the name of an array to initialize a pointer to the address of the first element of the array. For example, after

```
int list[100];
int *p = list;
int *q;
q = list;
```

both p and q point to the first element of list. Although we will often think of p and q as pointers to the entire array, C treats them as pointers to just one of the `int` elements (element 0). Thus p and q have type pointer-to-`int`, which is appropriate for pointers to `int` objects.

The array name `list` and the pointer p play similar roles, in that the value of either is a pointer to `list[0]`. C exploits this similarity by allowing the subscript operator to be applied to pointers as well as array names. Thus we can use either `list[i]` or `p[i]` to refer to element i of the array (`list[i]` and `p[i]` are aliases). In fact, C defines the subscript operator *only* for pointers. In `list[i]`, the array name is converted to a pointer before the subscript operator is applied. For example, code for adding up the elements of `list` can be written as either

```
sum = 0;
for (i = 0; i < 100; i++)
    sum += list[i];
```

Figure 4-3

*Pointer p points to the first element of array a. The elements of a can be designated either a[0] to a[4] or p[0] to p[4]. The first element of a has three equivalent designations: a[0], p[0], and *p.*

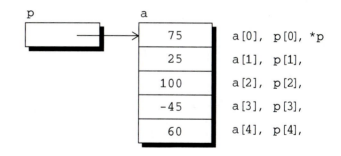

or

```
sum = 0;
for (i = 0; i < 100; i++)
    sum += p[i];
```

Figure 4-3 shows a pointer variable p pointing to the first element of a five-element int array, a. The elements of a can be designated by either a[0] to a[4] or p[0] to p[4]. The first element of the array has three equivalent designations (aliases): a[0], p[0], and *p.

As illustrated in Figure 4-4, a pointer need not always point to the first element of an array. For example, suppose we set p to point to element 50 of list:*

```
p = &list[50];
```

Now, p[0] is an alias of list[50], p[1] is an alias of list[51], and so on. Likewise, p[-1] is an alias of list[49], p[-2] is an alias of list[48], and so on. Such negative subscripts are allowed in C but are meaningful only in situations like this, where p points to an element other than the first element of an array. Negative subscripts are *never* meaningful when subscripting an array name.

Pointers and Function Arguments

In Chapter 1 we saw how to pass the address of a variable to a function, thereby enabling the function to change the value of the variable. Nothing was said, however, of how the function actually used the address to achieve the desired end. Pointer variables and the

*The subscript operator has higher precedence than the address-of operator, so &list[50] represents the address of list[50].

Figure 4-4

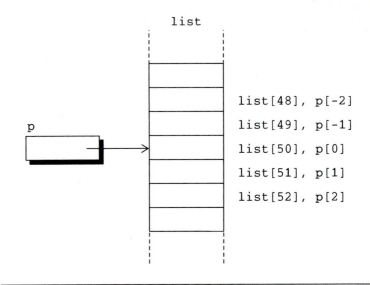

list

list[48], p[-2]

list[49], p[-1]

p   list[50], p[0]

list[51], p[1]

list[52], p[2]

indirection and subscripting operators provide us with the means to utilize addresses passed to functions.

For example, suppose we wish to write a function swap() that will swap the values of two int variables. After

```
int m = 10;
int n = 20;
swap(&m, &n);
```

the value of m will be 20 and that of n will be 10. Because swap() changes the values of m and n, their addresses (rather than their values) must be passed as arguments.

The formal arguments of swap() are declared like pointer variables so that they can receive address values. The body of the function uses the indirection operator to access the objects whose addresses were passed as arguments:

```
void swap(int *p, int *q)
{
    int temp;

    temp = *p;
    *p = *q;
    *q = temp;
}
```

When the function is called with &m and &n as actual arguments, the formal arguments are initialized as follows:

```
int *p = &m;
int *q = &n;
```

In the body of the function, *p and *q are aliases of m and n, respectively, and so give the function access to those variables.

When an array name is used as an argument, it is converted to the address of (the first element of) the array before being passed to the function. Thus arrays are always passed via their addresses; there is no way to pass the entire value of an array as a function argument.

For example, let's define zero() so that

```
zero(list, 50);
```

will assign 0 to the first 50 elements of list. The first argument is passed as an address of type pointer-to-int:

```
void zero(int *p, int count)
{
    int i;

    for (i = 0; i < count; i++)
        p[i] = 0;
}
```

Because only the address of an array is passed to a function, the function does not know the number of elements in the array. Unless this information can be deduced from the data in the array, we must tell the function how many elements to process.

Consider the following function, which returns the sum of a specified number of array elements:

```
long sum(const int *p, int count)
{
    int i;
    long total = 0;

    for (i = 0; i < count; i++)
        total += p[i];
    return total;
}
```

Because p is declared as a pointer to a constant object, we cannot use p[i] to assign to, increment, or decrement any of the elements of the array. A declaration of this form is a promise that the function will not change any of the data that it accesses via the pointer. Making such promises is the most frequent use of the `const` qualifier.

Functions often read their data from one or more arrays and store their results in another array. Pointers to arrays from which data is only read can be declared as pointers to constant objects. For example, the following function copies element values from the array pointed to by `source` to the array pointed to by `destin`:

```
void copy(int *destin, const int *source,
          int count)
{
    int i;

    for (i = 0; i < count; i++)
        destin[i] = source[i];
}
```

Of course, `destin` cannot be declared as a pointer to a constant object because it points to the array into which data is to be copied. If we were to inadvertently write

```
const int *destin
```

then we could not assign values to `destin[i]`, so

```
destin[i] = source[i];
```

would be invalid.

We can also use array notation for formal arguments corresponding to arrays. For example, `zero()` could have been declared by

```
void zero(int p[], int count);
```

The compiler automatically changes the array declaration

```
int p[]
```

to the pointer declaration

```
int *p
```

For one-dimensional arrays, C programmers usually just use the pointer notation to begin with.

Pointers to Functions

C allows both objects and functions to be designated by pointers. We declare p as a function pointer by writing a function declaration with `(*p)` in place of the function name:

```
void (*p)(void);
```

This declares p as a pointer to a function that takes no arguments and returns no value. We must enclose *p in parentheses because (void), which is a form of the function-call operator, has higher precedence than the indirection operator.

Function names behave much like array names: when a function name appears without being followed by a function-call operator, it is converted to the address of the function. If we wish, we can indicate this conversion explicitly by applying the address-of operator to the function name. Thus both

```
p = say_hello;
```

and

```
p = &say_hello;
```

set p to point to say_hello(). Note that say_hello() *must* have the function type declared for *p: the function must take no arguments and return no value.

The function-call operator is applied to the address of a function. In a function-call such as

```
say_hello();
```

the function name is converted to the address of the function before the function-call operator is applied. This means that we can apply the function-call operator to any expression that yields the address of a function. In particular, we can apply it to a variable that points to the function. If p has been set to point to say_hello(), we can call the function with

```
p();
```

The function-call operator is applied to the value of p, which is the address of the function.*

Multiway Selection with Function Pointers

An array of function pointers can sometimes eliminate the need for a switch statement. For example, suppose that selection contains

---

*Because *p is an lvalue that names the function pointed to by p, we could also call the function with

```
(*p)();
```

This call more closely resembles the function-pointer declaration than the simpler call just discussed. For obvious reasons, however, the simpler call is the one normally used. Remember, then, that the indirection operator is required when a function pointer is *declared*   ·t can be (and usually is) omitted when the function is *called*.

an integer from 1 to 4 representing a figure that the user wants printed. The four possible figures are printed by the following functions:

```
void print_box(void);
void print_block(void);
void print_triangle(void);
void print_diamond(void);
```

Instead of writing a switch statement to call the proper function, let's declare an array whose elements point to the four functions. To help keep the array declaration simple, we define fctn_ptr_t as a typedef name for our pointer-to-function type:

```
typedef void (*fctn_ptr_t)(void);
```

Remember that, except for the presence of typedef, a type definition has the same form as a declaration.

We now declare and initialize an array figure of function pointers:

```
fctn_ptr_t figure[4] = {print_box,
                        print_block,
                        print_triangle,
                        print_diamond};
```

Inside the braces, the function names represent the addresses of the four functions. We can call the selected function as follows:

```
fctn_ptr_t p;
p = figure[selection - 1];
p();
```

We set p to point to the selected function and call the function with p(), as before.

At the possible expense of readability, we could call the function with a single statement:

```
figure[selection - 1]();
```

The operators [] and () associate from left to right. Therefore, the subscript operator is applied to figure first, yielding a pointer to the selected function. The function-call operator is applied to this pointer, thereby calling the selected function.

It is crucial that the value of selection be in the range 1 to 4 so that the subscript is in the range 0 to 3. If the subscript is out of range, a garbage value will be used as the function pointer. The computer will try to execute code at an unknown location, and a crash will surely result.

More Complicated Declarations

Array, pointer, and function declarations can get complicated, particularly when the three kinds are mixed, as when declaring an array of pointers to functions. If we understand the principles behind such declarations, however, most can be deciphered without too much difficulty.

The declarations in question are constructed as follows. We start with an identifier, apply one or more subscript, indirection, and function-call operators, and state the type that results from those operations. To understand the declaration, we work backwards and determine what type the identifier must have in order for the indicated operations to yield the indicated type. For example,

```
int c[50];
```

states that applying the subscript operator to c yields an int result. This can be true only if c names an array with int elements. Note that the brackets represent the subscript operator even though they are also used for another purpose, to hold the number of elements in the array.

Likewise,

```
int *p;
```

states that applying the indirection operator to p yields an int result. This can be true only if p has type pointer-to-int.

And again,

```
int f(int, double);
```

says that if the function-call operator is applied to f (with an int and a double argument), the expression will yield an int value. Therefore, f must be a function that takes an int and a double argument and returns an int value. Note that the parentheses after the identifier represent the function-call operator, even though they may enclose argument types or formal-argument declarations.

In interpreting more complicated expressions, we must remember that the subscript and function-call operators have the same precedence and associate from left to right. Both have higher precedence than the indirection operator. We may need to use parentheses to override the precedences and produce the grouping we desire.

For example,

```
int *f(int);
```

declares a function that takes an int argument and returns a pointer-to-int value. Because () has higher precedence than *, the indirection operator is applied to the value returned by the function call. If the result of the indirection has type `int`, the returned value must have type pointer-to-`int`.

On the other hand,

```
int (*p)(int);
```

declares a pointer to a function that takes an `int` argument and returns an `int` value. Applying the function-call operator (with an `int` argument) to `*p` yields an `int` result. Therefore, `p` must point to a function with an `int` argument and `int` result.

For arrays,

```
int *a[5];
```

declares an array of pointers. Subscripting the array and then applying `*` yields an `int`; therefore, the array must have pointer-to-`int` elements. On the other hand,

```
int (*q)[5];
```

declares `q` to be a pointer to an array with five `int` elements (because subscripting `*q` yields an `int`). As with all pointers, we must use assignment or initialization to give `q` an appropriate address. If we declare

```
int a[5];
```

then

```
q = &a;
```

assigns `q` the address of `a`. Incidentally, this is one of the few cases where the address-of operator is applied to `a`. If we write

```
q = a;
```

the compiler will warn that `a` and `q` have different types. The type of `a` is pointer-to-`int`, whereas we might write the type of `q` as pointer-to-array-of-5-`int`s.

In the previous section we declared `figure` as an array of pointers to functions with no arguments and no return values. There we used a typedef name to help simplify the declaration. To illustrate the techniques in this section, we will declare the function without the aid of a typedef name.

To begin with, `figure` is an array of four elements, and subscripting it yields a pointer to a function. Therefore,

```
figure[4]
```

represents a pointer to a function. Applying `*` gives

```
*figure[4]
```

which yields an lvalue that designates a function with no arguments and no return value. Therefore, we declare `*figure[4]` as such a function:

```
void (*figure[4])(void) = {print_box,
                           print_block,
                           print_triangle,
                           print_diamond};
```

We know that we can omit the argument names in a function declaration that is not part of a function definition. When an argument name is omitted, the expression that remains represents the type of the argument. This same expression can be used to represent the corresponding type in a type cast.

For example, in the declaration

```
void copy(int *destin, const int *source,
          int count);
```

we can omit the argument names to get

```
void copy(int *, const int *, int);
```

Thus `int *` represents the type pointer-to-int, and `const int *` represents type pointer-to-constant-int. Just as the type-cast operator `(int)` converts its operand to type `int`, so `(int *)` converts its operand to type pointer-to-int and `(const int *)` converts its operand to type pointer-to-constant-int.

Here's another example. The following declares `f` as a pointer to a function with no arguments and no return value:

```
void (*f)(void);
```

Therefore,

```
void (*)(void)
```

represents the type of `f`. The type cast

```
(void (*)(void))
```

will, if possible, convert its operand to a pointer having the same type as `f`.

Additional Properties of Pointers

Pointers to `void`

We have seen that a pointer type must specify the type of the target object or function. Sometimes, however, we need to work with an address without making any commitment as to the type of the designated object. This can be accomplished by giving the address the type pointer-to-`void`, which does not specify the type of a target object. For example,

```
void *p;
```

declares `p` with type pointer-to-`void`. The value of `p` is an address, but no target object is defined. Any expression that would refer to the target of `p`, such as `*p` or `p[i]`, is invalid.

Pointer Conversions

C will convert a pointer from any object-pointer type to any other object-pointer type or from any function-pointer type to any other function-pointer type. Such conversions are often dangerous: converting an object pointer can cause the target object to be processed improperly; converting a function pointer can cause the target function to be called improperly. For this reason, the C compiler issues a warning message for any implicit pointer conversion. No warning is issued for explicit conversions, that is, those specified by type casts.

Conversions between pointer-to-`void` (or `void *`) and any other object-pointer type are considered safe and produce no warning. We use `void *` when the type of the target object is unknown or irrelevant. As soon as the type of the target object is known, we convert the pointer from `void *` to the appropriate type for the target object.

For example, assume that pointers `p`, `q`, and `r` are declared as follows:

```
long *p;
double *q;
void *r;
```

The implicit conversions in the following assignments produce warning messages:

```
p = q;    /* Warning */
q = p;    /* Warning */
```

These conversions can result in a `long` object's being mistaken for a `double` object, or vice versa, causing arithmetic calculations to be performed incorrectly. If the user requests the conversions with a type cast, however, the compiler will comply without complaint. The following produce no warnings:

```
p = (long *)q;
q = (double *)p;
```

Because conversion to and from `void *` is considered safe, none of the following produce warnings:

```
p = r;
q = r
r = p;
r = q;
```

An implicit conversion that removes a `const` or `volatile` qualifier will produce a warning, whereas one that imposes a qualifier will not. For example, suppose `p` and `q` are declared by

```
const int *p;
int *q;
```

After

```
q = p;   /* Warning */
```

`q` and `p` point to the same object. What's more, the value of the object can be changed via `q`, although this was not possible via `p`. The warning makes sure we understand that we have removed a previously imposed restriction on access to the target object. As usual, there is no warning if the conversion is done with a type cast:

```
q = (int *)p;
```

The reverse assignment,

```
p = q;
```

produces no warning, because access via `p` is more restrictive than the access already available via `q`.

A similar situation occurs when passing arguments to functions. If we declare

```
void fcn(int *r, const int *s);
```

then the actual argument passed to `s` can be a pointer to either constant or nonconstant objects. On the other hand, if we pass a pointer to constant objects to `r`, the compiler will complain because an access restriction is being removed.

Access restrictions can always be avoided, because it is so easy to change the types of pointers with type casts. But if a restriction was imposed for a good reason, avoiding it is likely to be unwise.

Integers can be converted to pointers, and vice versa. Most implementations provide some means of designating addresses by integers; these means vary, however, so conversions between integers and pointers are highly implementation dependent. For example,

```
int *p;
p = (int *)0x3f;
```

assign to p the address that corresponds, in some implementation-dependent fashion, to the integer 0x3f. Such integers can be used only to designate fixed addresses defined by the hardware or system software. The addresses of objects defined in a program are not known when the program is written and so cannot be designated by integer constants.

The Null Pointer

One integer that can be safely converted to any pointer type is integer 0, which is converted to the null pointer for any pointer type. The null pointer is a pointer value that is guaranteed *not* to point to a valid object. A null pointer is often used as a sentinel to signal the end of a sequence of valid pointers.

Depending on the implementation, the null pointer may best be represented by 0, 0L, or (void *)0. Therefore, a number of header files, including stdio.h and stdlib.h, define the macro NULL by one of these three expressions, whichever is most appropriate for the implementation at hand. If p has any pointer type, the statement

```
p = NULL;
```

is valid and produces no warning.

Reading and Printing Pointers

We can use the conversion specifier p to input pointers with scanf() and to output them with printf(). The pointers must have type void *. The printed representation of the pointers is entirely implementation dependent. For example, if we declare r and s by

```
void *r;
int *s;
```

then

```
scanf("%p", &r);
```

reads a value for r, and

```
printf("%p", (void *)s);
```

prints the value of s.

Statements such as these are used mainly to help debug programs that manipulate pointers. It is rare for an end user to need to know anything about the pointers that a program employs for its internal data organization.

MULTI-DIMENSIONAL ARRAYS

A multidimensional array is one that requires more than one subscript to specify an element. C provides multidimensional arrays, although they are used much less frequently than one-dimensional arrays. One reason for this is that often we can use pointers to create data structures with faster access and greater flexibility.

The declarations

```
int table[3][4];
double book[9][6][4];
```

declare `table` as a two-dimensional array with 3 rows and 4 columns. As the name suggests, we can think of the three-dimensional array `book` as a book with 9 pages, each containing a table with 6 rows and 4 columns. We refer to the element in row `i` and column `j` of `table` as `table[i][j]` rather than the more familiar `table[i, j]` (wrong!). Likewise, `book[i][j][k]` refers to the element on page `i` in row `j` and column `k`.

The order in which the elements are stored in memory is determined by letting the right-most subscript vary most rapidly and the left-most subscript least rapidly. For example, `table[0][0]` through `table[0][3]` are stored first, followed by `table[1][0]` through `table[1][3]` and finally `table[2][0]` through `table[2][3]`. Thus `table` is stored by rows, with row 0 first and row 2 last. Likewise, `book` is stored by pages, with each page being stored by rows.

We initialize a multidimensional array by listing the elements in the order in which they are stored in memory. Substructures such as rows and pages can be optionally enclosed in braces. For example, `table` could be declared and initialized using either

```
int table[3][4] = { {7, 9, 2, 5},
                     {8, 4, 6, 1},
                     {6, 5, 4, 2} };
```

or

```
int table[3][4] = { 7, 9, 2, 5,
                     8, 4, 6, 1,
                     6, 5, 4, 2 };
```

An advantage of enclosing the rows in braces is that fewer than four elements could be specified for some rows, in which case the remaining elements of the row would be set to 0.

Like one-dimensional arrays, multidimensional arrays are passed to functions via the address of the first element (that is, the one that is stored first in memory). When we declare a formal parameter for a multidimensional array, we can leave the first dimension unspecified but must specify all the remaining dimensions. For instance, consider the following function declaration:

```
void fctn(int p[][4], double q[][6][4]);
```

The actual argument corresponding to p is the address of the first element of a two-dimensional array. The array can have any number of rows, but it must have four columns. Likewise, the actual argument corresponding to q must point to the first element of a three-dimensional array. The array can have any number of pages, but each page must have 6 rows and 4 columns.

For example, the following function sums the elements in each row of a two-dimensional array and stores the result in the corresponding element of a one-dimensional array. The two-dimensional array can have any number of rows, but it must have eight columns:

```
void sum(long p[], int q[][8], int row_count)
{
   int i, j;
   long total;

   for (i = 0; i < row_count; i++) {
      total = 0;
      for (j = 0; j < 8; j++)
         total += q[i][j];
      p[i] = total;
   }
}
```

We could have used pointer notation for the one-dimensional array as well as for the first dimension of the two-dimensional array. Thus the function heading could have been written

```
void sum(long *p, int (*q)[8], int row_count)
```

MORE ABOUT IDENTIFIERS AND OBJECTS

To prepare for studying more complex programs, we need to look in greater detail at the properties of identifiers and objects.

Name Spaces

The identifiers in a C program are divided into categories called *name spaces*. In a given name space, each identifier has a single declaration and therefore a single use in the program. However, the same identifier can belong to several different name spaces. It will have a different declaration (and use) in each name space.

Certain name spaces can coexist peacefully, with no conflicts arising even if the same identifier is declared in more than one name space. When such coexistence is not possible, C favors one name space over its competitors. A declaration in the favored name space *masks* declarations of the same identifier in the other name spaces. A use of the identifier is associated with the declaration in the favored name space rather than with any of the masked declarations. For example, macro names form a name space. The preprocessor, which does not know about any other kinds of identifiers, will interpret an identifier as a macro name if at all possible. Therefore, a macro definition will mask a declaration of the same identifier in any other name space.

Any part of a source file that is not enclosed in a block is said to be at *file level*. There are two name spaces associated with each block and with the file level. One of these consists of *ordinary identifiers:* variable and formal-parameter names, function names, typedef names, and enumeration constants. The other consists of tags, such as the enumeration tags discussed earlier. These two name spaces coexist without conflict. For each occurrence of an identifier, the compiler can determine whether it is an ordinary identifier or a tag, and so can determine to which name space it belongs.

Identifiers representing formal arguments are handled differently for function definitions and function declarations. For a definition, the formal arguments are treated as if they were declared in the block that defines the function. The argument names, therefore, belong to the name space of ordinary identifiers for that block.

On the other hand, in a function declaration such as

```
double wages(int hours, double rate);
```

the argument identifiers `hours` and `rate` are optional placeholders that have no significance outside the declaration. Therefore, every function declaration has a separate name space for its argument identifiers. Like all other identifiers, these argument names can be masked by macro names. Beyond that, name spaces associated with function declarations cannot conflict with one another or with the name spaces associated with blocks or with file level. Note that the function name is *not* in the same name space as the argument identifiers. All function names are ordinary identifiers associated with file level.

Scope and Visibility of Identifiers

The *scope* of an identifier is the region of a program over which an identifier has a particular meaning—that is, the region over which the identifier is associated with a particular definition or declaration. For example, the scope of a macro name extends from the directive that defines the name to the end of the source file, unless the definition is explicitly canceled. We can cancel a macro definition with an `#undef` directive. Thus, if a source file contains the directive

```
#define PI   3.14159265
```

and later contains the directive

```
#undef PI
```

then the scope of `PI` will extend from the `#define` directive to the `#undef` directive.

The scope of an ordinary identifier or tag declared at file level extends from the declaration to the end of the source file. Such identifiers are said to have *file scope*. The scope of an identifier declared in a block extends from the declaration to the end of the block. Such identifiers can be said to have *block scope;* more commonly they are said to be *local* to the block.

An identifier is *visible* over that part of the program in which it can be used in statements and other constructions. An identifier is visible only within its scope. It may not be visible throughout its entire scope, however. Over part of the scope it may be masked by another identifier.

Because blocks can be nested one inside another, a block may be surrounded by other blocks and by file level. Such a block lies in the scope of any identifiers declared in outer blocks or at file level. For example, consider the nested blocks shown somewhat schematically as follows:

```
{float x, y; ... {int m, n; ...} ...}
```

The scopes of `x` and `y` extend to the end of the outer block, whereas the scopes of `m` and `n` extend only to the end of the inner block. Therefore, `x` and `y` are visible in both the inner and the outer blocks, whereas `m` and `n` are visible only in the inner block.

A conflict occurs when an identifier declared in an inner block is also declared in a surrounding block or at file level:

```
{float x; ... {int x; ... } ... }
```

The part of the inner block following `int x;` lies within the scopes of two conflicting declarations of `x`. The conflict is resolved by the rule that a declaration in a block masks any declarations of the same identifier in surrounding blocks or at file level. Thus the `float` variable `x` is visible in those parts of the outer block that are not included in the inner block. The `int` variable `x` is visible throughout the inner block.

Masking takes place separately for the two name spaces associated with a block. Thus, ordinary identifiers in a block can mask ordinary identifiers declared in surrounding blocks and at file level. Likewise, tags in a block can mask tags declared in surrounding blocks or at file level.

Storage Durations of Objects

The lifetime of an object—the time that it exists in memory—is determined by its *storage duration*.* There are two possible storage durations: static and automatic. Objects declared at file level have *static storage duration*. Such objects are created before program execution begins and remain in existence throughout the execution of the program. Unless we explicitly specify otherwise, objects declared in blocks (including formal parameters) have *automatic storage duration*. Such an object is created when the computer enters the block and is deleted when the computer leaves the block. If the block is executed more than once, the object is created anew each time the block is entered. Thus, an object with automatic storage duration cannot retain its value from one execution of the block to the next.

An object declared with the storage-class specifier `static` has static storage duration, even if it is declared within a block. For example, consider the following block:

```
{int m; static int n; ... }
```

The object designated by `m` has automatic storage duration. Because this object is created anew each time the block is entered, `m` cannot retain its value from one execution of the block to the next. On the other hand, the object designated by `n` is declared to have static storage duration. Because this object remains in existence throughout program execution, `n` can retain its value from one execution of the block to the next. For example, if the block is the body of a function, `n` will retain its value between successive function calls.

The storage-class specifier `auto` specifies automatic storage duration. Because automatic storage duration is the default for formal parameters and objects declared in blocks, which are the only objects that can have automatic storage duration, we never actually have to use `auto`.

The storage-class specifier `register` specifies that an object with automatic storage duration be stored, if possible, in a processor register. Access to objects stored in processor registers is normally much faster

---

Storage is a synonym for *memory*. Although we usually prefer the more popular term *memory*, *storage* is used when it occurs in standard C terminology.

than access to objects stored in main memory. The `register` specifier is portable, in the sense that it will be ignored if a particular implementation cannot store the object in a processor register. The *appropriate* use of `register` to speed up execution is highly implementation dependent, however. In some implementations, for example, inappropriate use of `register` can produce slower-executing code by interfering with the compiler's attempts to optimize register usage.

Because a `register` object might not be stored in main memory, we cannot compute its address either explicitly (with &) or implicitly (conversion of an array name to an address). For example, the declaration

```
register int i, j, k;
```

asks the compiler to store the values of `i`, `j`, and `k` in registers. Whether or not the compiler complies, the expressions `&i`, `&j`, and `&k` are invalid.

Storage Duration and Initialization

The storage duration of an object affects the way it can be initialized. The reason is that objects with static storage duration are created and initialized when the program is compiled, whereas those with automatic storage duration are created and initialized while the program is running.

If no initial value is specified for an object with static storage duration, then an integer or floating-point object is initialized to zero and a pointer object is initialized to `NULL`. On the other hand, no default initialization is performed for an object with automatic storage duration. If such an object is not explicitly initialized, it starts off containing garbage that may not even be a valid value of the object's type.

An object with static duration must be initialized with a *constant expression,* which is an expression that the compiler can evaluate without actually executing the program. A constant expression must be constructed from constant values; it may not use the values of variables or call functions, nor may it contain assignment, increment, or decrement operators. Note that addresses computed with & or represented by array or function names are constants and can be used in constant expressions.

An arithmetic or pointer object with automatic storage duration can be initialized with any expression that would be allowed in an expression statement. In particular, the initializing expression can use values of variables and values returned by functions. Initial values listed inside braces must be represented by constant expressions. Therefore, the elements of an array must be initialized with constant expressions, regardless of the storage duration of the array.

Linkage of Identifiers

Linkage is a mechanism whereby an identifier can be declared more than once, with each declaration causing the identifier to refer to the same object or function. Linkage can be internal or external. For *internal linkage*, all the declarations must be in the same source file. For *external linkage*, the declarations can be in different source files. If an identifier has *no linkage*, different declarations of the identifier must cause it to refer to different objects or functions.

For example, it is external linkage that allows us to refer to library functions by identifiers such as `scanf` and `printf`. The external linkage ensures that these identifiers refer to the same functions in our source files as they do in the source files from which the library was compiled. Also, it is linkage that connects a function declaration near the beginning of a source file with a corresponding function definition later in the file. In our programs so far this linkage has been external, which is the default linkage for functions. We could just as well have specified internal linkage, however, because the declaration and definition are in the same source file.

We can control the linkage with the storage-class specifiers `extern` and `static`. A default linkage applies when no storage-class specifier is used. Unfortunately, there are inconsistencies in how linkage is specified for functions and objects and at file and block level. At file level, for example, `static` specifies internal linkage but at block level it specifies no linkage.

Functions Declared at File Level

Let's begin with the most common case, functions declared or defined at file level. If the storage-class specifier is static, the function name has internal linkage. If there is no storage-class specifier, or if extern is used, the function name has what is sometimes called *previous linkage*. That is, if the function has already been declared at file level, the linkage will be the same as in the previous declaration. If there is no previous declaration, the function name has external linkage.

For example, if the first declaration of `wages()` is

```
double wages(int hours, double rate);
```

or

```
extern double wages(int hours, double rate);
```

the identifier `wages` has external linkage. If `wages()` has been declared previously, the linkage will be the same as for the previous declaration. If `wages()` is declared by

```
static double wages(int hours, double rate);
```

the function name has internal linkage. We often use `static` to restrict a declaration to one source file, thereby avoiding name conflicts if the declared name is used for other purposes in other source files.

Objects Declared at File Level

For objects declared at file level, external linkage is the default, and `static` specifies internal linkage. Thus, at file level,

```
int n;
```

declares n with external linkage, and

```
static int n;
```

declares n with internal linkage. Again, `static` is often used to prevent inadvertent name conflicts between source files.

Using `extern` causes an object to have previous linkage. Usually, an object identifier is declared only once in a source file, so that there is no previous declaration and `extern` produces external linkage.

Using `extern` has another important effect. Although we conventionally speak of variable and object *declarations*, these normally both *declare* an identifier (state its properties) and *define* the corresponding object (create it in memory). However, using `extern` produces a pure declaration that declares an identifier but does not define a corresponding object. Such an identifier can be used to refer to an object defined in another source file. For example,

```
extern int error_status;
```

declares `error_status` as an int object-identifier with external linkage, but does not create a corresponding object. The object must be defined elsewhere, usually in another source file, by a conventional declaration/definition such as

```
int error_status;
```

A pure declaration cannot specify an initial value. For example,

```
extern int error_status = 100;
```

is not a pure declaration, because the compiler must create an object to hold the initial value.

Functions Declared at Block Level

Function declarations (but not definitions) can occur inside a block. If there is a storage-class specifier, it must be `extern` (`static` is not allowed). Such declarations have previous linkage. Any previous file-level declaration used by previous linkage must be visible within the block. If no previous file-level declaration is visible within the block, previous linkage is the same as external linkage.

Objects Declared at Block Level

For object declarations inside a block, the absence of a storage-class specifier or the specifier static indicates no linkage. Thus the block-level declarations

```
int m;
static int n;
```

cannot be linked with any other declarations in the same or another source file.

As at file level, `extern` specifies previous linkage; if no initial value is specified then no object is defined. An object referred to by an identifier declared with `extern` has static duration (the same as if `static` were used). Identifiers that refer to objects with automatic duration must have no linkage.

A CASE STUDY

We conclude this chapter with a short case study, a program that plays craps with the user. We will confine our discussion of the code to a few major points. However, you are urged to work through the code in detail, because it is a good review of many of the C features that we have studied so far. Anyone who can read this code without too much difficulty is progressing quite satisfactorily in their study of C.

The program is shown in Listings 4-1 to 4-5. Like most real-world C programs, it consists of multiple source files, each of which contains a separate *module*—that is, a logically distinct part of the program. File `craps.c` (Listing 4-3) is a general-purpose game-playing module that could be used for any betting game. File `game.c` (Listing 4-4) contains all the code specific to craps, and `random.c` (Listing 4-5) provides the pseudorandom numbers required to simulate the rolling of dice. File `craps.c` defines `main()` which, as usual, is called directly by the system; `game.c` supplies functions for use by `craps.c`; and `random.c` supplies functions for use by `game.c`.

A header file serves as an interface to each source file that *exports* functions for use by other source files. The header file can contain

Listing 4-1

```
/* File game.h */
/* Interface to game module */

typedef enum {LOST, WON} outcome_t;

extern void init_game(void);
extern void play_round(outcome_t *outcome_p);
```

type and constant definitions as well as function declarations. File game.h (Listing 4-1) declares the two functions exported by game.c: init_game(), which initializes the game module, and play_round(), which plays one round of the game. This header file also defines the enumeration type outcome_t, which represents the outcome of a round of play, and the enumeration constants WON and LOST, which are used to test values of type outcome_t. Function play_round() takes an address argument and sets the corresponding variable to an outcome_t value representing the outcome of the round.

File random.h (Listing 4-2) declares the two functions exported by random.c: init_random(), which initializes the random-number module, and rand_1_to_n(), which returns a random number ranging from 1 to the function's argument n.

Each header file is included both in the source file that exports the functions and in any source file that uses them. In #include directives, the name of a programmer-defined header file is enclosed in quotation marks rather than in angle brackets:

```
#include "game.h"
#include "random.h"
```

The quotation marks tell the compiler to begin searching for the

Listing 4-2

```
/* File random.h */
/* Interface to random-number module */

extern void init_random(void);
extern int rand_1_to_n(int n);
```

header file in the programmer's working directory rather than in the directory reserved for implementation-defined header files.

Functions exported by a module are declared with `extern`, which could be omitted, however, because external linkage is the default for function declarations. Functions that are not to be exported are declared `static` to confine their use to a single source file. Likewise, in `game.c`, a file-level array is declared static to prevent it from being exported.

craps.c

File `craps.c` (Listing 4-3) includes `game.h` to *import*, or have access to, the functions exported by `game.c`. It also defines two functions for internal use: `get_stake()`, which reads and validates the user's stake, or bankroll, and `get_bet()`, which reads and validates each bet. The module calls `init_game()` to initialize the game module and `play_round()` to play a round and set `outcome` to WON or LOST.

Throughout `craps.c`, note the use of addresses as actual arguments and pointers as formal arguments. In `get_stake()` and `get_bet()`, note the use of pointer variables as actual arguments for `scanf()`. In our previous programs, address arguments for `scanf()` were always address constants formed with the address-of operator.

game.c

File `game.c` (Listing 4-4) includes both its own header file, `game.h`, and `random.h`, the header file for a module from which it imports functions. With the aid of a function imported from `random.h`, `roll_dice()` simulates the roll of a pair of dice and returns the number rolled, an `int` in the range 2 to 12.

The outcome of a round is returned by one of the functions `win()`, `lose()`, and `play_on()`. Functions `win()` and `lose()` always return WON and LOST, respectively; these functions are used when the outcome is determined on the first roll. Otherwise, `play_on()` is called to play the rest of the round and return WON or LOST as appropriate.

Function `play_on()` requires an `int` argument, the player's "point," which is the number that came up on the first roll. Because `win()`, `lose()`, and `play_on()` are to be accessed via the same pointer array, they all need to have the same function type. Therefore, `win()` and `lose()` also take an `int` argument but make no use of it, a fact that some compilers will note in a warning message.

The rules of craps for the first roll are implemented via an array of function pointers called `action_tab`. The subscript of

Listing 4-3

```c
/* File craps.c */
/* Main program module for craps program */

#include <stdio.h>
#include <stdlib.h>
#include "game.h"

static void get_stake(double *stake_p);
static void get_bet(double *bet_p, double stake);

main()
{
    outcome_t outcome;
    double stake;
    double bet;
    char another;

    init_game();
    get_stake(&stake);
    do {
        get_bet(&bet, stake);
        play_round(&outcome);
        if (outcome == WON) {
            stake += bet;
            printf("You win!\n");
        }
        else {
            stake -= bet;
            printf("You lose!\n");
        }
        printf("\nYou now have %.21f dollars\n", stake);
        if (stake > 0.0) {
            printf("Play another round (y/n)? ");
            scanf(" %c", &another);
        }
        else {
            printf("You're broke!\n");
            another = 'n';
        }
    } while ( (another == 'y') || (another == 'Y') );
    printf("\nLet's play again sometime!\n");
    return EXIT_SUCCESS;
}
```

```
/* Read and validate stake */

static void get_stake(double *stake_p)
{
    do {
        printf("How much do you have for betting? ");
        scanf("%lf", stake_p);
        if (*stake_p <= 0.0)
            printf("Invalid stake—please try again\n");
    } while (*stake_p <= 0.0);
}

/* Read and validate bet */

static void get_bet(double *bet_p, double stake)
{
    do {
        printf("\How much do you wish to bet? ");
        scanf("%lf", bet_p);
        if ( (*bet_p <= 0.0) || (*bet_p > stake) )
            printf("Invalid bet—please try again\n");
    } while( (*bet_p <= 0.0) || (*bet_p > stake) );
}
```

action_tab is the number rolled; each entry is the address of a corresponding function that calculates the outcome of the round. The first two entries are dummies, because neither a 0 nor a 1 can be rolled. The remaining entries conform to the rules of craps. If 7 or 11 is rolled, win() is called to report an immediate win. If 2, 3, or 12 is rolled, lose() is called to report an immediate loss. If any other possible value is rolled, play_on() is called to continue play.

Because action_tab incorporates the rules for the first roll and play_on() handles the remaining rolls, play_round() can be very simple. It begins by rolling the dice and initializing roll with the result:

```
int roll = roll_dice();
```

The value of roll is used in two ways: as a subscript for action_tab and as an argument to the function called via action_tab. In the following statement, action_tab[roll] points to the function to be called, and

A CASE STUDY

Listing 4-4

```
/* File game.c */
/* Source file for game module */

#include "game.h"
#include "random.h"

static int roll_dice();
static outcome_t win(int point);
static outcome_t lose(int point);
static outcome_t play_on(int point);

typedef outcome_t (*fct_ptr_t)(int);

static fct_ptr_t action_tab[13] =
    { lose, lose,                       /* dummies */
      lose, lose,                       /* rolled 2 or 3 */
      play_on, play_on, play_on,        /* rolled 4, 5, or 6 */
      win,                              /* rolled 7 */
      play_on, play_on, play_on,        /* rolled 8, 9, or 10 */
      win,                              /* rolled 11 */
      lose };                           /* rolled 12 */

/* Initialize game module */

extern void init_game(void)
{
    init_random();
}

/* Play one round */

extern void play_round(outcome_t *outcome_p)
{
    int roll = roll_dice();

    *outcome_p = action_tab[roll](roll);
}

/* Roll the dice; return number rolled */
```

```
static int roll_dice(void)
{
    int die_1 = rand_1_to_n(6);
    int die_2 = rand_1_to_n(6);

    printf("You rolled a %d and a %d\n", die_1, die_2);
    return die_1 + die_2;
}

/* Report win */

static outcome_t win(int point)
{
    return WON;
}

/* Report loss */

static outcome_t lose(int point)
{
    return LOST;
}

/* Play rest of game */

static outcome_t play_on(int point)
{
    int roll;

    do {
        roll = roll_dice();
        if (roll == 7) return LOST;
    } while (roll != point);
    return WON;
}
```

```
        action_tab[roll](roll)
```

calls that function with argument `roll`:

```
    *outcome_p = action_tab[roll](roll);
```

The result returned by the function is assigned to `*outcome_p`, the object whose address is supplied as an argument to `play_round()`.

If the player does not win or lose on the first roll, the remaining rolls are played by `play_on()`. To win, the player must roll until "making his point"—rolling the same value as on the first roll. If, while attempting this, 7 is rolled, the player immediately loses. Function `play_on()` uses a `do` statement to roll the dice until the player makes his point, after which the function returns with `WON`. An `if` statement returns with `LOST` if 7 is rolled.

Function `roll_dice()` simulates the rolling of two dice with the following statements:

```
int die_1 = rand_1_to_n(6);
int die_2 = rand_1_to_n(6);
```

When called with an argument of 6, `rand_1_to_n`, which is imported from `random.h`, returns a pseduorandom `int` in the range 1 to 6.

random.c

The C library provides, via `stdlib.h`, a random-number function `rand()` and a function `srand()` for initializing or seeding the random-number generator. However, the value returned by `rand()` is an `int` in the range 0 to RAND_MAX (often 32,767), which is not a very useful range for most purposes. (RAND_MAX is a macro defined in `stdlib.h`.) We therefore need `random.h` (Listing 4-5) to convert the output of `rand()` to a more useful range.

The function `srand()` initializes the random-number generator with an unsigned value that determines the sequence of numbers to be generated. For variety, we would like to use a different initial value each time the program is run. We can obtain such a value from `time()`, declared in `time.h`, which returns the *calendar time*—the number of seconds (or other time units) since a certain starting date and time. If `time()` is called with an address argument, it will also store the calendar time and the designated address. If we don't want to store a time, we call `time()` with NULL as its argument:

```
srand( (unsigned)time(NULL) );
```

The value returned by `time()`, usually of type `long`, may well be changed by converting it to `unsigned`. This doesn't matter, however, because the exact value is unimportant as long as we usually get a different value on each program run.

The job of `rand_1_to_n()` is to convert the output of `rand()` from the range 0 to RAND_MAX to the range 1 to n. This is most easily done by first converting the value returned by `rand()` into a floating-point number that ranges from 0.0 up to

Listing 4-5

```
/* File random.c */
/* Source file for random-number module */

#include <stdlib.h>
#include <time.h>
#include "random.h"

/* Seed random number generator with current time */

extern void init_random(void)
{
    srand( (unsigned)time(NULL) );
}

/* Return random integer in the range 1 to n */

extern int rand_1_to_n(int n)
{
    double f_rand;
    static double rand_count = (double)RAND_MAX + 1.0;

    f_rand = (double)rand() / rand_count;
    return (int)(n * f_rand) + 1;
}
```

(but not including) 1.0. We compute such a value by dividing the value of `rand()` by RAND_MAX + 1.0. Note that this addition must be done with floating-point arithmetic; often, RAND_MAX is the largest possible `int` value, so RAND_MAX + 1 would yield an invalid result.

In `rand_1_to_n()`, the static variable `rand_count` is initialized to RAND_MAX + 1.0:

```
static double rand_count = (double)RAND_MAX + 1.0;
```

Because `rand_count` is declared with static duration, it is initialized before program execution begins, and it retains its value from one call of the function to the next. Because no statements change the value of `rand_count`, it retains its initial value throughout the execution of the program.

The floating-point random number is computed by dividing the value of `rand()` by `rand_count`:

```
f_rand = (double)rand() / rand_count;
```

We can easily scale `f_rand` to the desired range. The value of

```
(int)(n * f_rand)
```

is an integer ranging from 0 to `n` – 1; adding 1 yields an integer in the desired range.

Compiling and Linking

To compile this program, we must compile each of the three source files to a corresponding object file, then link the object files to produce an executable file. The details of carrying out these steps vary considerably among implementations. For integrated development environments, however, the process is usually straightforward. We must first provide the IDE with a list of source files to be compiled; then, when we issue a "Make" or "Build" command, all compiling and linking is done automatically. These commands recompile only those source files that have been changed since the most recent previous compilation. A "Build all" or "Rebuild all" command will recompile all source files, regardless of when they were last changed.

EXERCISES

4-1. Write a function `sort()` to sort the elements of an `int` array into ascending order. You can use any sorting algorithm with which you are familiar. A simple (but inefficient) algorithm is the *bubble sort*, which makes repeated passes over the array. Each pass compares the values of adjacent elements and exchanges them if they are out of order. The passes are repeated until a pass finds no adjacent elements out of order and so does not have to make any exchanges.

4-2. A *shuffle* is the opposite of a sort, in that it attempts to destroy any order that exists in an array. Write a function `shuffle()` to shuffle the elements of an `int` array. To begin, select an element at random and exchange it with element 0; element 0 is now shuffled. Select one of the unshuffled elements at random and exchange it with element 1; elements 0 and 1 are now shuffled. Continue in the same way until all elements are shuffled. For the random selections, it will help to have a function `rand_m_to_n()` that returns a pseudorandom integer in the range `m` to `n`.

4-3. Write a program to read a series of letter grades terminated by a dollar sign, as in

A A F B C F D B A C C B D F $

The program should count and print the number of A's, B's, C's, and so on. *Hint:* Store the counts in an array count that is subscripted by `grade - 'A'`, where `grade` is the letter currently being counted. The array should have an unused element corresponding to the nonexistent grade E. Note that in both ASCII and EBCDIC, A through F have contiguous codes: `'B'` equals `'A' + 1`, `'C'` equals `'A' + 2`, and so on.

4-4. Following suggestions in this chapter, write a version of the program of Exercise 2-4 in which an array of function pointers is used to call the function corresponding to the user's selection. Be sure to validate the user's selection—check that it is in the proper range—before using it as an array subscript. One way to handle the `Quit` option is to define an additional function, `quit_program()`, and to let each function return a value indicating whether processing should continue. Function `quit_program()` will always indicate that processing should not continue, whereas the other functions will indicate that it should.

4-5. A *magic square* is a square array of integers such that every row, column, and diagonal has the same sum, as in

```
2  7  6
9  5  1
4  3  8
```

Write a program to check whether a square is magic by computing and comparing the sums of its rows, columns, and diagonals. The input data should consist of the *order* of the square—the number of rows or columns—followed by the elements in row-by-row order. The data for the example square would be:

```
3    2 7 6    9 5 1    4 3 8
```

The data should be stored in an array whose dimensions determine the order of the largest square that can be processed. The program should inform the user of this limit and reject any attempt to enter a square of larger order.

5
Pointers and Strings

*T*HIS CHAPTER continues the development of ideas introduced in Chapter 4. We begin with pointer arithmetic, which
provides an alternative to array subscripting. We then turn to a
detailed look at strings, which are stored as arrays and usually
accessed via pointers. Some of the library functions for string
processing will provide us with a variety of examples of pointer
manipulation.

POINTER ARITHMETIC

Although we can always use subscripting to refer to array elements
via a pointer, there are alternative techniques that are sometimes more
efficient. These techniques make use of *pointer arithmetic*—arithmetic
involving integers and pointers. For any operation of pointer arithmetic, pointer operands and pointer results must all point to elements of the same array. Pointer arithmetic is not defined for pointers that do not point to array elements or that point to elements of
different arrays.

We can add an integer to a pointer with the following effect: if
p points to element 0 of an array, then p + 1 points to element 1,
p + 2 points to element 2, and so on. Thus *p is an alias for p[0],
*(p + 1) is an alias for p[1], *(p + 2) is an alias for p[2],
and so on.

If p points to an array element other than the first, then subtracting an integer from p is also useful. For example, if p points to
a[10], then p - 1 points to a[9], p - 2 points to a[8], and
so on.

Figure 5-1
The lvalues `*p`, `*(p + 1)`,
`*(p + 2)`, *and so on, refer to*
successive array elements starting
with the element pointed to by `p`.
Likewise, `*(p - 1)`, `*(p - 2)`,
and so on, refer to successive array
elements preceding the element
pointed to by `p`. *The expressions*
`*(p + i)` *and* `p[i]` *refer to*
the same array element.

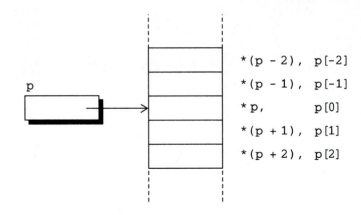

Figure 5-1 illustrates the general case, where `p` points to some element within an array. The lvalues `*p`, `*(p + 1)`, `*(p + 2)`, and so on, refer to successive array elements starting with the element pointed to by `p`. Likewise, `*(p - 1)`, `*(p - 2)`, and so on, refer to successive array elements preceding the element pointed to by `p`. The expressions `*(p + i)` and `p[i]` refer to the same array element.

When carrying out pointer arithmetic, C takes into account the sizes of the array elements. Thus expressions such as `*(p + 1)` and `*(p - 1)` will work as expected regardless of how many bytes are occupied by each array element.

With subscripting, we leave the pointer pointing to the first element of the array and use the subscript operator to designate the element that we actually wish to access. An alternative is to use pointer arithmetic to move the pointer through the array so that it always points to the element we wish to access, eliminating the need for subscripts. For example, if `a` is an `int` array, then after

```
int *p = a;
```

`p` points to element 0 of `a`, and we can use `*p` to refer to `a[0]`. If we execute

```
p = p + 1;
```

`p` will point to element 1 of `a`, and we can use `*p` to refer to `a[1]`. If we again execute

```
p = p + 1;
```

p will refer to element 2 of a, and we can use *p to refer to a[2]. Proceeding in that way, we can step through all the elements of a, at each step using *p to refer to the element currently pointed to by p.

The compound assignment operators += and -= also can be used with pointers. For example,

```
p += 5;
```

is equivalent to

```
p = p + 5;
```

Both statements move the value of p forward in the array by five elements. Likewise,

```
p -= 7;
```

is equivalent to

```
p = p - 7;
```

Both statements move the value of p backwards in the array by seven elements.

The increment and decrement operators work with pointers just as they do with numbers. The expression p++ moves the value of p forward in the array by one element; the value of p++ is the old value of p, the value before the increment operator was applied. Likewise, ++p also moves the value of p forward in the array by one element, but the value of ++p is the new value of p. The decrement operator, --, works similarly, except that it moves backward instead of forward.

The expression

```
*p++
```

occurs frequently and can confuse the unwary. Postfix ++ has higher precedence than prefix *, yielding the grouping

```
*(p++)
```

Thus the increment operator is applied to the pointer p, *not* to *p, the target data object. The subexpression p++ increments p so that it points to the next element of the array. The value of p++, however, is the value of the pointer *before* it was incremented. Applying the indirection operator, *, yields the element that p pointed to before it was incremented. Thus *p++ increments p and, at the same time, names the element that p pointed to before it was incremented.

On the other hand, prefix ++ and prefix * have the same precedence and associate from right to left. Therefore *++p, which
groups as *(++p), increments the value of p and, at the same time,
names the element that p points to after it is incremented. For example, if we execute

```
*p++ = *q++;
```

then (1) the value of *q will be assigned to *p, and (2) p and q will
each be incremented to point to the next array element. Executing
this statement repeatedly will step p and q through their respective
arrays, at each step assigning the value of *q to *p. Thus our array-
copying function can be defined as follows:

```
void copy(int *p, const int *q, int count)
{
    int i;

    for (i = 0; i < count; i++)
        *p++ = *q++;
}
```

Likewise, we can define the summation function by

```
int sum(const int *p, int n)
{
    int i;
    int total = 0;

    for (i = 0; i < n; i++)
        total += *p++;
    return total;
}
```

In

```
total += *p++;
```

*p++ returns the value of *p and increments p so that it points to
the next element of the array.

In most cases it is more efficient to apply the increment operator
than to apply the subscript operator. Therefore, the versions of copy()
and sum() that use pointer arithmetic are at least marginally more
efficient than those that use subscripting.

We can also subtract pointers that point to elements of the same
array; the result is an integer equal to the difference of the corre-

sponding array subscripts. For example, if `p` points to `a[10]` and `q` points to `a[15]`, then `q` - `p` has the value 5, the result of subtracting 10 from 15. The value of `q` - `p` is the number of array elements from `*p` up to but not including `*q`. If we include `*q`, then the count must be increased by one. Thus the number of array elements from `*p` through `*q`, including both `*p` and `*q`, is `q` - `p` + `1`.

Pointers can be compared with the equality and relational operators. The expression `p` == `q` yields 1 (*true*) if `p` and `q` point to the same object and 0 (*false*) if they point to different objects. Likewise, `p` != `q` yields 1 if `p` and `q` point to different objects and 0 if they point to the same object.

We are already familiar with the null pointer, which does not point to any object, and which is represented by the macro `NULL`. We use `p` == `NULL` and `p` != `NULL` to test whether the value of `p` is the null pointer. Such tests are common, because the null pointer is frequently used to mark the end of a series of pointers or (as with `time()`) to indicate the absence of a valid pointer.

Relational operators such as `<` and `>=` can be used to compare pointers that point to elements of the same array. The result is the same as if the corresponding array subscripts were compared. Thus if `p` points to `a[5]` and `q` points to `a[6]`, then `p` < `q` and `p` <= `q` both yield *true*, because 5 is less than 6. For the same reason, `p` > `q` and `p` >= `q` both yield *false*.

STRINGS

Strings are stored in memory as arrays of `char` values. To indicate where a string ends, the final character of the string is followed by the *null character*, whose code is zero.[*] All string-processing functions assume that every string is terminated by a null character; they will yield incorrect results and possibly crash the program if a terminating null character is missing.

We can represent the null character by the escape sequence `\0`, which designates the character with octal code zero. We can demonstrate that the null character terminates a string by executing

```
printf("abcd\0efgh");
```

The computer prints

```
abcd
```

[*]Be sure not to confuse the null character with the null pointer.

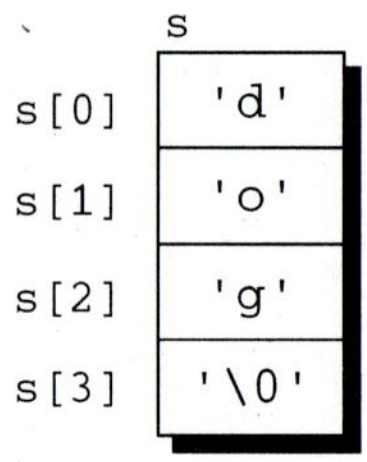

Figure 5-2

The string `"dog"` *is stored in a
four-element array. The first three
elements hold the characters* `d`, `o`,
and `g`. *The final element holds the
null character, designated* `\0`,
which signals the end of the string.

because the first null character encountered is taken to indicate the
end of the string.

We can declare an array `s` to hold strings of up to three characters as follows:

```
char s[4];
```

The number of array elements must be one more than the number
of characters, to provide room for the terminating null character.
The following declaration initializes `s` with the string `"dog"`:

```
char s[4] = "dog";
```

Figure 5-2 illustrates the array `s`, whose elements have the same values as if we had written

```
char s[4] = {'d', 'o', 'g', '\0'};
```

Note the terminating null character, which does not appear in the
usual quotation-mark notation.

As usual for initialized arrays, we can leave it to the compiler to
determine the number of array elements:

```
char s[] = "dog";
```

Again, `s` is given four elements—three for `'d'`, `'o'`, and `'g'` and one
for the terminating null character. Because the null character, and not
the size of the array, indicates where a string ends, the array can have
more elements than needed for the string. If we declare `s` by

```
char s[10] = "dog";
```

then, as shown in Figure 5-3, `s` has 10 elements, but only the first
four are used for the string. String-processing functions will ignore
the six unused elements, because the null character following `'g'`
indicates where the string ends.

Figure 5-3

The string `"dog"` *occupies only the first four characters of the 10-character array* `s`. *The null character* `\0` *signals the end of the string, and the remaining array elements are unused.*

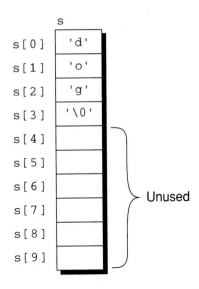

We have seen that when an array name such as `s` is used in an expression, it yields a pointer to the first element of the array. Likewise, when a string literal such as `"dog"` is used in an expression, it yields a pointer to the first character of the string. Specifically, whenever we use a string literal, the compiler creates a character array to hold the characters of the string; when the string literal is used in an expression, it yields a pointer to the first element of the corresponding array.

We can pass a string argument to a function or operator using either a string literal or the name of a character array. If `s` has been declared and initialized as in any of the preceding examples, then

```
printf(s);
```

and

```
printf("dog");
```

both cause the computer to print `dog`. In each case, a pointer to the beginning of the string is passed to the operator. The pointer has type `char *` or pointer-to-`char`.

Array names and string literals can also be used to initialize and assign values to pointers. Thus

```
char *p = s;
```

initializes p to point to the first character of s, and

```
char *p = "dog";
```

initializes p to point to the first character of "dog". Because strings are passed to functions as pointers, the statement

```
printf(p);
```

also causes the computer to print "dog".

In explanations, it is common to refer to strings and other arrays by the pointers to their first elements. Thus when we mention "string p" and "array q," we are referring to the string and array whose first elements are designated by the values of p and q, respectively.

FUNCTIONS FOR STRING PROCESSING

The standard library provides a number of string-processing functions, which are declared in the header file string.h. Because these functions are in the standard library, we do not have to define them ourselves. However, looking at some of their definitions will not only familiarize us with the string functions but will also provide some good examples of programming with pointers, arrays, and strings.

The library function

```
char *strcpy(char *p, const char *q);
```

copies string q (that is, the string pointed to by q) into array p (that is, the array pointed to by p); the const in the declaration assures us that the function will not change the string q. The function returns a pointer to the newly created copy.

The array p *must* have enough elements to hold all the characters of string q. The function has no way of determining whether the target array is large enough. If it is not, some characters will be stored in memory locations intended for other purposes, and the program will probably crash.

For example, if we declare s by

```
char *s[10];
```

then the statement

```
strcpy(s, "canine");
```

copies the string "canine" into the first seven (not six!) elements of s. All that is passed to strcpy() are two pointers: one to the first element of s and one to the first character of "canine".

There are a number of ways to write the definition of `strcpy()`. The following is a straightforward approach using subscripting:

```c
char *strcpy(char *p, const char *q)
{
    int i;

    for (i = 0; q[i] != '\0'; i++)
        p[i] = q[i];
    p[i] = q[i];    /* copy null character */
    return p;
}
```

The `for` statement has the form we are familiar with, *except* for the control expression, which determines whether repetitions will continue. We are used to something like

```c
i < COUNT
```

that allows repetitions to continue as long as the value of `i` is less than the number of elements to be processed. But we do not know how many characters are in the string to be copied; all we know is that the string is terminated by a null character. Therefore, we use the control expression

```c
q[i] != '\0'
```

to copy characters until the null character is encountered. The `for` statement does *not* copy the null character (why?); therefore, a separate assignment statement is needed for that purpose.

Because subscripting does not change the values of `p` and `q`, `p` still points to the array into which string `q` was copied. Therefore, `p` points to the copy of string `q` that the function created, and

```c
return p;
```

returns a pointer to this copy.

We can make this code more compact at the expense of making it somewhat harder to read. First, recall that a control expression is considered *true* if it yields any nonzero value and *false* if it yields zero. The value of `q[i]` is zero for the null character and nonzero otherwise. Therefore, the control expression `q[i] != '\0'` can be replaced by just `q[i]`:

```c
for (i = 0; q[i]; i++)
    p[i] = q[i];
p[i] = q[i];    /* copy null character */
```

We can go even further in this direction. The assignment

```
p[i] = q[i]
```

is itself an expression whose value is the character being copied; that value will be zero when the null character is copied and nonzero otherwise. Thus strcpy() can be coded

```
char *strcpy(char *p, const char *q)
{
    int i;

    for (i = 0; p[i] = q[i]; i++)
        ;
    return p;
}
```

In this version, the control expression both copies a character and determines whether the copying should continue. All the work of the for statement is done in the expressions within the parentheses; therefore the controlled statement is the null statement, which is indicated by an isolated semicolon. This version of the for statement also copies the null character (why?), so no additional assignment statement is required for that purpose.

Despite the preceding discussion, and similar ones later in the chapter, you should not feel compelled to write code in the most compact form possible. Highly compact code can be tricky to write and difficult to read. Studying such code, however, can help you appreciate the possibilities of C expressions and statements.

The code for strcpy() can also be written using pointer arithmetic. Because the values of the pointers will be changed, we will have to save the initial value of p so that it can be returned as the value of the function:

```
char *strcpy(char *p, const char *q)
{
    char *temp = p;

    while (*q)
        *p++ = *q++;
    *p = *q;
    return temp;
}
```

The value of *q will be zero only if q points to the null character, so we can use *q as the control expression. Recall that *p++ =

`*q++` assigns the value of `*q` to `*p` and increments both pointers. Again, the control statement does not copy the null character (why?), so an additional assignment statement is needed.

We can make this code more compact by giving another job to `*p++ = *q++`, which is already doing double duty (assignment and pointer incrementation). As with any other assignment expression, the value of `*p++ = *q++` is the value assigned, which is zero for the null character and nonzero otherwise. Therefore, `*p++ = *q++` can also serve as the control expression:

```
char *strcpy(char *p, const char *q)
{
    char *temp = p;

    while (*p++ = *q++)
        ;
    return temp;
}
```

In this version, the `while` statement also copies the null character (why?), so no additional statement is needed for that purpose.

Your compiler may give a warning when it compiles this version of `strcpy()`. Because people frequently write = when they mean ==, many compilers issue a warning if they find an assignment operator where an equality or relational operator is more likely. In this case, however, we are using the assignment operator intentionally, so the warning should be ignored.

The function

```
size_t strlen(const char *p);
```

returns the number of characters in the string pointed to by p; this count does *not* include the null character. We recall that `size_t` is the typedef name for the integer type used for the sizes of memory areas. To find the length, we must first find where the string ends, which we do by searching for the null character:

```
size_t strlen(const char *p)
{
    size_t i;

    for (i = 0; p[i]; i++)
        ;
    return i;
}
```

The `for` statement sets `i` to the subscript of the null character (why?). The subscript of an array element is equal to the number of array elements that precede the element designated by the subscript; for example, `p[0]` is preceded by zero elements, `p[1]` is preceded by one element, `p[2]` is preceded by two elements, and so on. Thus the subscript of the null character is the result we are seeking: the number of string characters that precede (and therefore do not include) the null character.

This function can also be coded with pointer arithmetic:

```
size_t strlen(const char *p)
{
    const char *p_first = p;

    while (*p)
        p++;
    return p - p_first;
}
```

The `while` statement sets `p` to point to the terminating null character. Because `p - p_first` is the number of characters from `*p_first` (the first character of the string) up to but not including `*p` (the null character), this difference is the result we are seeking. Note that `p_first` must have type `const char *`, because the compiler will complain if we attempt to remove the constant-data restriction from the value of `p`.

If we write the `while` statement as

```
while (*p++)
    ;
```

will the function still return the correct result? If not, can we change the `return` statement so that the returned length will be correct?

The function

```
int strcmp(const char *p, const char *q);
```

compares strings for lexicographical order—a generalized alphabetical order in which the order of the characters is the same as the numerical order of their codes. In ASCII, for example, Z follows A in lexicographical order because the value of `'A'` is 65 and the value of `'Z'` is 90. Some of the ordering is less obvious; for example, a follows Z in ASCII because the value of `'a'` is 97. And 9 precedes A because the value of `'9'` is 57.

The function `strcmp()` returns zero if the two strings are equal, a negative integer if the first string precedes the second, and a positive integer if the second string precedes the first. If one string equals the initial part of the other, as in `"program"` and `"programmer"`, the shorter string precedes the longer.

One way to code the function is as follows:

```
int strcmp(const char *p, const char *q)
{
    while (*p == *q) {
        if (*p == '\0') return 0;
        p++;
        q++;
    }
    return *p - *q;
}
```

The `while` statement scans the two strings, comparing corresponding characters, as long as the corresponding characters are equal. The `if` statement determines if the value of `*p` is the null character; if it is, then so is the value of `*q`, because the control expression has verified that the values of `*p` and `*q` are equal. When the condition `*p == '\0'` is true, then, the ends of both strings have been reached and all the corresponding characters in the strings have been found to be equal. In this case the `return` statement exits from the `while` statement and from the function, returning the value 0 to indicate that the strings are equal.

If the `while` statement terminates normally, then two corresponding characters have been found to be unequal. The order of the codes for these two characters determines the order of the strings. Therefore, the difference of the codes for the two unequal characters is returned:

```
return *p - *q;
```

Verify for yourself that this function also yields the correct result when one string equals the initial part of the other.

INPUT AND OUTPUT OF CHARACTERS AND STRINGS

We already know how to write characters and strings with `printf()` and how to read single characters with `scanf()`. In this section we will look at several format specifications that allow us to read either sequences of characters* or strings with `scanf()`. Also, we will look at other input and output functions that, by spe-

---

*A sequence of characters is stored without a terminating null character and therefore is not a string.

cializing in characters and strings, are able to read and write them more efficiently than `printf()` and `scanf()`.

Reading Characters and Strings with `scanf()`

For each conversion specification that reads a sequence of characters or a string, the corresponding argument must point to the first element of a `char` array large enough to hold all the characters and, for a string, the terminating null character as well.

We know that when the conversion specifier `c` is used without a field width, a single character is read and stored. If a field width is used, `scanf()` reads and stores the number of characters specified by the field width. Thus `%10c` reads and stores a sequence of 10 characters, `%30c` reads and stores a sequence of 30 characters, and so on. No terminating null character is supplied, so the stored characters do not constitute a string. As usual for `c`, no whitespace is skipped before reading the characters.

The conversion specification `%s` reads a sequence of non-whitespace characters. Specifically, it skips any initial whitespace, then reads characters until whitespace is again encountered. For example, suppose that the format string is `"%s%s%s%s"` and the input line is

```
Now is the time
```

The first `%s` will read `Now`, the second will read `is`, the third will read `the`, and so on. Characters read with `%s` are stored as a string, so they are followed by a terminating null character.

A field width specifies the maximum number of characters to be read. Thus `%10s` stops reading after 10 characters even if the next character is not whitespace. Limiting the number of characters that can be read ensures that they cannot overflow the array in which they are to be stored. For example, in

```
char s[26];
scanf("%25s", s);
```

the array `s` cannot overflow because at most 25 characters can be read. Note that, because of the terminating null character, `s` must have 26 elements to accommodate a 25-character string.

A *scanset specifier* is a conversion specifier that defines a set of characters called the *scanset*. The scanset specifier reads characters until it encounters a character that is not in the scanset. No whitespace is skipped before reading, and the characters read are stored as a string.

A scanset specifier is delimited by the square brackets [and]. The characters in the scanset can be simply listed between the square brackets. For example, the scanset specifier

```
[0,1,2,3,4,5,6,7,8,9]
```

defines a scanset containing the digits 0 through 9. The conversion specification

```
%[0,1,2,3,4,5,6,7,8,9]
```

reads characters until a nondigit character is encountered. For example, if the input is

```
13459XA257B
```

the characters 3459 will be read and stored as a string.

Many implementations let us use a hyphen to specify a range of characters. In such an implementation, the conversion specification

```
%[0-9,A-Z,a-z]
```

will read the largest possible string consisting of only digits, uppercase letters, and lowercase letters.

If the opening left bracket is followed by ^, the listed characters are those that are *not* to be included in the scanset. For example, [^A-Z,a-z] defines a scanset consisting of all characters *except* the uppercase and lowercase letters. The statement

```
scanf("%[^A-Z,a-z]", s);
```

reads characters into array s until it encounters an upper- or lowercase letter.

Because of the roles that] and – play in the notation, they must be placed in special positions if they are to be included among the listed characters. To list] we must place it immediately after [or [^; to list – we must place it either (1) immediately after [or [^, or (2) immediately before the closing]. For example, the scanset defined by

```
[],a-z,-]
```

includes both] and –; the scanset defined by

```
[^],a-z,-]
```

excludes both] and –.

As usual, a field width specifies the maximum number of characters to be read. For example, %25[^0-9] reads characters until a digit is encountered or until 25 characters have been read. As with the s conversion specifier, it is important to use a field width to guard against overflowing the array in which the string is to be stored.

Input and Output for Arbitrary Streams

As we know, `scanf()` reads from the standard input stream `stdin`, and `printf()` writes to the standard output stream `stdout`. These functions have counterparts `fscanf()` and `fprintf()` that read from or write to the stream specified by the first argument of the function. Thus

```
scanf("%80s", line);
```

is equivalent to

```
fscanf(stdin, "%80s", line);
```

and

```
printf("%s", line);
```

is equivalent to

```
fprintf(stdout, "%s", line);
```

Unfortunately, some functions for arbitrary streams are not equivalent to their counterparts for the standard streams. This is why we are taking up both kinds of functions now, even though we will not learn how to declare and open our own streams until Chapter 7. For now, the only streams we will use are `stdin`, `stdout`, and the standard error-message stream `stderr`. Messages written to `stderr` appear on the console even if `stdout` has been redirected.

Using `stdin` and `stdout`

It may seem that programs using only the standard streams are very limited, but this is not true if the operating system supports file redirection and *pipes*. We already know that file redirection allows us to specify which files or devices a program will use for input and output. For example, the command line

```
prog < input.txt > output.txt
```

runs the program `prog` with `stdin` connected to the file `input.txt` and `stdout` connected to the file `output.txt`.

A pipe, which is represented by the symbol |, connects the output of one program to the input of another. For example, as a result of

```
prog1 < input.txt | prog2 | prog3 > output.txt
```

prog1 reads from input.txt and passes its output to prog2; prog2 gets its input from prog1 and sends its output to prog3; prog3 gets its input from prog2 and writes its output to output.txt. A program intended for use with pipes is sometimes called a *filter* because, like a filter for light or for a gas or a fluid, it performs a specified operation on the data that flows through it.

With the aid of redirection and pipes, programs that access only stdin and stdout (and perhaps stderr) can do much useful processing. The main limitation is that each program can have only one input file and one output file. If more sources of input or destinations for output are needed, streams other than stdin and stdout will have to be used.

Functions for Character Input and Output

The character input/output functions for stdin and stdio are getchar() and putchar(), which are declared by

```
int getchar(void);
int putchar(int c);
```

Function getchar() reads a character from the standard input stream and returns the corresponding character code as the value of the function; putchar() writes to the standard output stream the character whose code is supplied as a function argument. Note that in both cases the character code is represented by an int value. This can be converted to or from type char as needed. For example, the value returned by getchar() can be assigned to a char variable, and putchar() can take a char variable as its argument.

On input, if an error occurs because the end of the file has been reached, getchar() returns a special sentinel value represented by the macro EOF. EOF has a negative value, −1 in most implementations. If an output operation is successful, putchar() returns the character that was written; if an error occurred, EOF is returned.

Consider the code for copying the input file to the output file unchanged. If ch is an int variable, we could write

```
ch = getchar();
while (ch != EOF) {
   putchar(ch);
   ch = getchar();
}
```

The first statement initializes `ch` to the first input character (or to EOF). The `while` statements checks if the value of `ch` is EOF. If it is not, the current value of `ch` is written, a new value is read, and so on.

Most C programmers would probably write this code in the following more cryptic form, which avoids repeating the assignment statement:

```
while ( (ch = getchar()) != EOF )
    putchar(ch);
```

The expression

```
(ch = getchar())
```

assigns the value returned by `getchar()` to `ch` and returns that value as the value of the expression. This value is compared with EOF to see whether to continue writing the value of `ch` to the output file.

The corresponding functions for arbitrary files are `fgetc()`, `getc()`, and `fputc()` and `putc()`, which are declared as follows:

```
int fgetc(FILE *stream);
int getc(FILE *stream);
int fputc(int c, FILE *stream);
int putc(int c, FILE *stream);
```

A stream is declared as a pointer to an object of type `FILE`. Except for the presence of the stream argument, `fgetc()` and `getc()` are equivalent to `getchar()`, and `fputc()` and `putc()` are equivalent to `putchar()`. Thus,

```
ch = getc(stdin);
```

reads a character from `stdin` and assigns its code to `ch`, and

```
putc(ch, stdout);
```

writes the character with code `ch` to `stdout`.

What's the difference between `getc()` and `putc()` on the one hand and `fgetc()` and `fputc()` on the other? For the sake of speedy execution, some functions are also implemented as *function macros*—macros that take arguments like a function. (Function macros are discussed in more detail later in this chapter.) Because macro calls are processed before function calls are compiled, the macro will normally be used in place of the function. The programmer can force the function to be used by enclosing the function name in parentheses, as in

```
(putchar)(ch);
```

The parentheses invalidate the macro call but not the function call. For `getc()` and `putc()`, however, a simpler course is possible:

`getc()` and `putc()` have macro definitions, but `fgetc()` and `fputc()` do not. Therefore, we call `getc()` or `putc()` if we want the macro (we usually do—it's faster) and `fgetc()` or `fputc()` if we want the true function.

The functions `getchar()` and `putchar()` also have macro definitions.

Finally, when input is read character by character, it is often necessary to read one character too many. For example, if a number is being read digit by digit, the only way to detect the end of the number is to read the first nondigit character that follows it. Often we need to push this extra character back into the input stream so that later it can be reread and processed properly by another part of the program. In C, pushback is accomplished with `ungetc()`, which is declared as follows:

```
int ungetc(int c, FILE *stream);
```

Character `c` is pushed back into `stream`. If `ungetc()` is successful, it returns the character it pushed back; if unsuccessful, it returns EOF. The character pushed back need not be the same as the one just read. However, at least one character must have been read from a stream before `ungetc()` is called. There can be at most one pushed-back character; that character must be reread before `ungetc()` can be called again.

Error Returns for `printf()` and `scanf()`

Functions in the `printf()` and `scanf()` families also return integer values that can be used to diagnose errors. Functions `printf()` and `fprintf()` return the number of characters written, if all went well, and a negative value if an error occurred. Functions `scanf()` and `fscanf()` return the number of values that were assigned to variables, or EOF if no values were assigned. A return of EOF or of a smaller count than expected indicates that reading was terminated prematurely, either because an error occurred or because the end of the input file was reached.

`ctype.h` and Uppercasing Letters

Listing 5-1 shows a short filter program, `upper.c`, that yields a copy of the input file in which all lowercase letters have been

	FUNCTION NAME	FUNCTION RETURNS NONZERO VALUE FOR:
Table 5-1	`isalnum()`	Letter or digit
Functions for	`isalpha()`	Letter
Testing Characters	`iscntrl()`	Control character
	`isdigit()`	Digit
	`isgraph()`	Printing character except space
	`islower()`	Lowercase letter
	`isprint()`	Printing character (includes space)
	`ispunct()`	Printing character other than space, letter, or digit
	`isspace()`	Whitespace character
	`isupper()`	Uppercase letter
	`isxdigit()`	Hexadecimal digit

changed to uppercase. On a system that provides file redirection, and uses the notation discussed earlier, the command line

```
upper < text.in > text.out
```

makes `text.out` a copy of `text.in` in which all letters have been uppercased.

To change lowercase letters to uppercase, the program uses a function declared in `ctype.h`, which provides a number of functions for testing characters and two for converting between uppercase and lowercase. Each function takes an `int` argument and returns an `int` result. All the functions have macro implementations for speed of execution.

Table 5-1 lists the functions for testing characters; each function returns a nonzero value if its argument is as described in the right-hand column, and returns 0 otherwise. The two conversion functions are given in Table 5-2. They can be applied to any character. If the argument is not a letter of the appropriate case, it is returned unchanged.

The program `upper.c` uses the functions we have studied in a straightforward way. It uses `getchar()` to read each character from the input file, `toupper()` to change a lowercase character to uppercase, and `putchar()` to write a character to the output file.

	FUNCTION NAME	ACTION
Table 5-2	`tolower()`	Converts uppercase letter to lowercase
Conversion Functions	`toupper()`	Converts lowercase letter to uppercase

Listing 5-1

```
/* File upper.c */
/* Change lowercase letters to uppercase */

#include <ctype.h>
#include <stdlib.h>
#include <stdio.h>

int main(void)
{
    int ch;

    while ( (ch = getchar()) != EOF ) {
        ch = toupper(ch);
        putchar(ch);
    }
    return EXIT_SUCCESS;
}
```

Processing continues while the value returned by `getchar()` is not EOF.

Functions for String Input and Output

We use `gets()` or `fgets()` to read a line of text and store it as a string, and `puts()` or `fputs()` to print a string as a line of text. Unfortunately, the functions for the standard input and output streams are not precisely equivalent to those for arbitrary streams.

The functions for the standard streams are declared as follows:

```
char *gets(char *s);
int *puts(const char *s);
```

The argument of `gets()` points to the first element of the array in which string characters are to be stored. The function reads and stores characters until it encounters a newline. The newline is discarded, and the stored string is terminated with a null character. If a string is successfully read, `gets()` returns the value of its argument, which now points to the first character of the string that was read. If an error or end-of-file condition occurred, `gets()` returns the null pointer. If an error occurred, the contents of the array are indeterminate.

For example,

```
char s[255];
gets(s);
```

reads a line of text and stores it in array `s`. The following code reads and processes strings until end-of-file or an error is encountered:

```
while (get(s) != NULL) {
    /* Process contents of s */
}
```

The argument for `puts()` points to the first character of the string to be written. The function outputs the characters of the string and then outputs a newline to terminate the line. If the string is written successfully, `puts()` returns a nonnegative value (which may be zero); if an error occurred, `puts()` returns EOF. For example, in

```
char s[255];
gets(s);
puts(s);
```

`puts()` prints the line of text that was read by `gets()`.

Unfortunately, `gets()` has a serious problem: it provides no means for limiting the number of characters read. We cannot prevent the input from overflowing the array into which it is being read, which will likely crash the program. Thus `gets()` should not be used in any program where a crash could have serious consequences, such as losing the user's data. In particular, `gets()` should never be used where system security is at stake. By deliberately overflowing an array, an intruder can place hostile code in memory areas that would otherwise be inaccessible. This was precisely one of the techniques that the infamous Internet worm used to invade thousands of computers.

The functions for arbitrary streams differ from `gets()` and `puts()` in two ways: (1) the array-overflow problem with `gets()` is corrected, and (2) newlines are handled differently. We declare `fgets()` and `fputs()` as follows:

```
char *fgets(char *s, int n, FILE *stream);
int *fputs(const char *s, FILE *stream);
```

The second argument, `n`, of `fgets()` specifies the size of the array in which the string is being stored. The function will read and store at most `n - 1` characters, thereby ensuring that the input characters and the terminating null character will all fit into array s. For example, in

```
char s[255];
fgets(s, sizeof s, stdin);
```

we can be absolutely sure that the input will not overflow the array. No such assurance can be given for gets().

We have seen that gets() discards the newline at the end of an input line, and puts() supplies a newline after printing a string. In contrast, fgets() stores the newline as the last string character (immediately preceding the terminating null character), and fputs() does not supply an extra newline. The upshot is that strings read with fgets() will end with a newline, whereas those read with gets() will not. In the former case we may need to eliminate the newline, which usually serves no useful purpose for strings stored in memory.

Trimming Whitespace

The program in Listing 5-2 removes whitespace from the end of a line, leaving only the newline that is needed to terminate the line. Because the job done by this program is line-oriented—only white-space *at the end of a line* is to be eliminated—the program reads its input and writes its output one line at a time.

Each input line is stored temporarily in the 255-character array buf. For reading lines, we use fgets() rather than gets(), to eliminate the possibility of overflowing buf. To trim the line, we start with the last string character (other than the null character) and scan backward toward the beginning of the line. The scan stops when a non-whitespace character is found or (if the entire line is whitespace) the scan runs past the beginning of the line:

```
last = strlen(buf) - 1;
for (i = last; i >= 0; i—)
    if (!isspace(buf[i])) break;
```

Remember that ! is the logical NOT operator. When a non-white-space character is found, the break statement exits the for statement with i equal to the subscript of the right-most non-whitespace character. If no such character is found (the entire string is white-space), the for statement terminates with i equal to −1.

The statement

```
buf[i+1] = '\0';
```

stores a null character immediately after the last non-whitespace character, terminating the string at that point. If the entire string is

Listing 5-2

```
/* File trim.c */
/* Remove trailing whitespace from strings */

#include <ctype.h>
#include <stdio.h>
#include <stdlib.h>
#include <string.h>

int main(void)
{
    char buf[255];
    int last, i;

    while ( fgets(buf, sizeof buf, stdin) != NULL ) {
        last = strlen(buf) - 1;
        for (i = last; i >= 0; i--)
            if (!isspace(buf[i])) break;
        buf[i+1] = '\0';
        puts(buf);
    }
    return EXIT_SUCCESS;
}
```

whitespace, the null character is stored in `buf[0]` to yield the null string, the string with no characters.

Because newlines are whitespace, our trimming code has removed the newline that `fgets()` stores at the end of each string. To write a string, therefore, we use `puts()`, which outputs a newline after writing a string. If you use `fputs()` instead of `puts()`, as the author did on the first try, you will find that all the text in your file has been run together into one long line.

DYNAMIC MEMORY MANAGEMENT

In our work so far, memory has been allocated and deallocated in a rigid manner over which the programmer has little control. Memory for static objects is allocated before program execution begins and deallocated only after program execution terminates. Memory for the automatic objects declared in a block is allocated when the block is entered and deallocated when the block is exited.

Often we need more flexible ways of managing memory. For example, we may want to allocate memory only as it is needed. That way, a program will fail for want of memory only if the data that it actually stores on a particular run exceeds memory capacity. When we are through with a block of memory, we may wish to recycle it—deallocate it so that it can later be reallocated for another purpose. File `stdlib.h` declares several library functions that support such dynamic memory management.

The simplest memory allocation function is `malloc()`, which is declared as follows:

```
void *malloc(size_t size);
```

The argument specifies the number of bytes to be allocated. If successful, `malloc()` returns a pointer to the first byte of the block; if unsuccessful (due to insufficient memory), `malloc()` returns the null pointer. The returned pointer has type `void *`; we can convert this, via assignment or type cast, to the pointer type appropriate for the object to be stored in the allocated memory.

As an example, let's see how we would allocate memory for a `double` object (although in practice we would probably not use dynamic memory allocation for such a small object):

```
double *p;
p = malloc(sizeof(double));
```

If the allocation was successful, `p` points to a newly allocated `double` object. We can refer to this object via `*p`, as usual:

```
*p = 3.1416;
printf("%f", *p);
```

Note the use of `sizeof` to determine the number of bytes to be allocated. Note also that the assignment implicitly converts the pointer-to-`void` value returned by `malloc()` to the pointer-to-`double` value that must be assigned to `p`. If we wish, we can indicate this conversion explicitly with a type cast:

```
p = (double *)malloc(sizeof(double));
```

We can determine if an allocation was not successful by testing whether `malloc()` returned the null pointer:

```
p = malloc(sizeof(double));
if (p == NULL) {
   fprintf(stderr, "Out of memory\n");
   exit(EXIT_FAILURE);
}
```

The body of the if statement is executed if `malloc()` returns the null pointer. We use `fprintf()` to write a message to the standard error-message stream. The function `exit()`, declared in `stdlib.h`, terminates program execution with the function argument as the return code.

We could have embedded the assignment within the test expression for the if statement:

```
if ( (p = malloc(sizeof(double))) == NULL ) {
    /* ... */
}
```

However, because this version does not actually save any memory space—it does not avoid repeating any code—the longer, clearer version is recommended.

It is not uncommon to read a string into a temporary buffer area, then copy it for permanent storage to a block of memory allocated with `malloc()`. The number of bytes in a string is one more than the value returned by `strlen()`, because `strlen()` does not count the terminating null character:

```
char buffer[255];
char *p;

fgets(buffer, sizeof buffer, stdin);
p = malloc(stdlen(buffer) + 1);
if (p == NULL) {
    /* Handle out-of-memory error */
}
strcpy(p, buffer);
```

This code uses `strlen()` to determine the length of the string stored in `buffer`, and `strcpy()` to copy the string from `buffer` to the array pointed to by p.

Although we can allocate memory for an array with `malloc()` (as we did in the preceding example), this task is often simplified by the array-allocation function `calloc()`:

```
void *calloc(size_t nelem, size_t size);
```

The first argument is the number of elements in the array; the second is the number of bytes in one element. For example, we can allocate an array of 500 `double` elements as follows:

```
double *p;
p = calloc(500, sizeof(double));
```

Note that p has type `double  *` because it is to point to the first element of the array. We can use `p[0]` through `p[499]` to refer to the elements of the newly allocated array.

Like `malloc()`, `calloc()` returns the null pointer if the allocation is not successful. We thus check for this error in the same way as for `malloc()`:

```
p = calloc(500, sizeof(double));
if (p == NULL) {
   /* Handle out-of-memory error */
}
```

The function `realloc()` declared by

```
void *realloc(void *ptr, size_t size);
```

changes the size of an allocated block. We can use `realloc()` to expand the size of a memory block to accommodate more data or to contract the size to free unused memory. For example,

```
p = realloc(p, 1000 * sizeof(double));
```

changes the size of the block pointed to by p to 1000 `double` elements. Any data stored in the old block is preserved if it fits into the new block. The new value of p—the value returned by `realloc()`—may differ from the old value because `realloc()` may have to move the data to a new address to find room for a block of the required size. If `realloc()` fails, it returns the null pointer as usual.

The function `free()` declared by

```
void free(void *ptr);
```

deallocates the block of memory pointed to by its argument. For example,

```
free(p);
```

frees the memory block pointed to by p. We can call `free()` only for memory blocks allocated with `malloc()`, `calloc()`, or `realloc()`.

Sorting Strings

We illustrate memory management with a program for sorting strings (Listing 5-3). The input file is read line by line and each line is stored as a string. Memory is allocated for each string after it is read. The strings are referred to via an array of pointers; memory for the pointer array is allocated as needed. Once the input file has been

Listing 5-3

```
/* File sort.c */
/* Sort lines into ascending lexicographical order */

#include <ctype.h>
#include <stdio.h>
#include <stdlib.h>
#include <string.h>

void read_data(char ***array_pp, unsigned *count_p);
void write_data(const char **array_p, unsigned count);
int compare(const void *p, const void *q);

int main(void)
{
    char **array_p;
    unsigned count;

    read_data(&array_p, &count);
    qsort(array_p, count, sizeof(char *), compare);
    write_data(array_p, count);
    return EXIT_SUCCESS;
}

/*  Read strings; allocate memory for strings and
    pointer array; return (via address arguments)
    pointer to array and count of strings read */

void read_data(char ***array_pp, unsigned *count_p)
{
    char buffer[255];
    char **array_p;
    char *str_p;
    unsigned count = 0;
    unsigned max_count = 4;
    unsigned str_len;
    size_t new_size;

    array_p = calloc(max_count, sizeof(char *));
    if (array_p == NULL) {
        fputs("Insufficient Memory\n", stderr);
        exit(EXIT_FAILURE);
    }
```

```c
    while ( fgets(buffer, sizeof buffer, stdin) != NULL ) {
        if (count == max_count) {
            max_count *= 2;
            new_size = max_count * sizeof(char *);
            array_p = realloc(array_p, new_size);
            if (array_p == NULL) {
                fputs("Insufficient Memory\n", stderr);
                exit(EXIT_FAILURE);
            }
        }
        str_len = strlen(buffer);
        str_p = malloc(str_len + 1);
        if (str_p == NULL ) {
            fputs("Insufficient Memory\n", stderr);
            exit(EXIT_FAILURE);
        }
        strcpy(str_p, buffer);
        array_p[count++] = str_p;
    }
    *array_pp = array_p;
    *count_p = count;
}

/* Write sorted strings to output file */

void write_data(const char **array_p, unsigned count)
{
    unsigned i;

    for (i = 0; i < count; i++)
        fputs(array_p[i], stdout);
}

/* Compare two strings, ignoring case.  Arguments p and q
   point to the array elements that, in turn, point to
   the first character of each string */

int compare(const void *p, const void *q)
{
    char *p1 = *(char **)p;
    char *q1 = *(char **)q;

    while ( toupper(*p1) == toupper(*q1) ) {
        if (*p1 == '\0') return 0;
        p1++;
        q1++;
    }
    return toupper(*p1) - toupper(*q1);
}
```

Figure 5-4

The data structure used by the string-sorting program (Listing 5-3). Pointer variable `array_p` *points to the first element of an array, each element of which points to the first character of a string. Because* `array_p` *points to an array element that points to a* `char` *value,* `array_p` *is declared with type* `char **`.

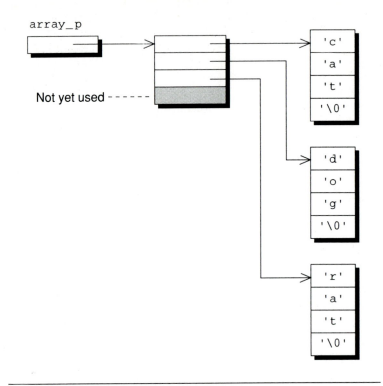

read, the pointer array is sorted so that the strings are in ascending lexicographical order, and the strings are written in sorted order to the output file.

Figure 5-4 shows the data structure used by the program. As usual, each string is stored as a `char` array and is referred to by a pointer to its first element; such pointers have type pointer-to-`char` or, in C notation, `char *`. These pointers are stored in an array, which is itself referred to by a pointer to its first element. Because the first element of the pointer array has type pointer-to-`char`, the pointer to this first element has type pointer-to-pointer-to-`char`, or `char **`. The pointer to the pointer array is stored in a pointer variable `array_p` declared by

```
char **array_p;
```

Still another level of indirection arises in defining the function `read_data()`, which reads the input file and creates the data structure just described. We want to pass `read_data()` the addresses of variables `array_p` and `count`:

```
read_data(&array_p, &count);
```

After reading the input, `read_data()` will set `array_p` to point to the pointer array and set `count` to the number of strings read. We declare `read_data()` as follows:

```
void read_data(char ***array_pp,
               unsigned *count_p);
```

Each formal argument points to a variable to which the function is to assign a value. Because `count_p` points to an `unsigned` variable, it has type `unsigned  *`. Likewise, because `array_pp` points to a `char  **` variable, it has type `char  ***`.

These declarations with multiple indirection operators are quite typical of C. Readers should make sure they understand them thoroughly before preceding.

As just mentioned, `read_data()` reads the input and creates the data structure. During input, `array_p` points to the pointer array, and `count` holds the number of elements in the pointer array. The value of `max_count` is the maximum number of elements that can be currently stored in the pointer array; if need be, however, we can increase `max_count` and allocate a correspondingly larger array with `realloc()`. For debugging, we give `max_count` the initial value of 4, which would be on the small side for a production program, but which ensures that even small test files will require that additional memory be allocated for the pointer array.

The pointer array is initially allocated with `calloc()`, with the number of elements determined by the initial value of `max_count`:

```
array_p = calloc(max_count, sizeof(char *));
```

After each allocation, the program checks to see if the null pointer was returned. Although we will hereafter omit such checks from our discussion, they are essential parts of the program.

Input lines are read with `fgets()` and stored in the `char` array `buffer`. For permanent storage of the string, a memory area of the appropriate size is allocated with `malloc()`, and the string is copied to this area. A pointer to the string in its new location is stored in the pointer array, and `count` is incremented.

Before storing a new string, however, `read_data()` must see if there is room for it in the pointer array. If not, the size of `max_count` must be increased (we double the size), and a larger pointer array must be allocated with `realloc()`:

```
if (count == max_count) {
   max_count *= 2;
   new_size = max_count * sizeof(char *);
   array_p = realloc(array_p, new_size);
   /* ... */
}
```

Having ensured that there is room in the pointer array,
read_data() next allocates memory for the current input line:

```
str_len = strlen(buffer);
str_p = malloc(str_len + 1);
```

The string is then copied from buffer to the newly allocated area:

```
strcpy(str_p, buffer);
```

A pointer to this string is stored in the pointer array, and the value
of count is incremented:

```
array_p[count++] = str_p;
```

Just before returning, read_data() assigns values to the variables
pointed to by its formal parameters:

```
*array_pp = array_p;
*count_p = count;
```

We now have to sort the elements of the pointer array in such a
way that the corresponding strings are in ascending order. The standard C library provides a function, qsort(), which sorts an array
using the efficient quicksort algorithm. The comparison function,
which determines the order of two array elements, is supplied by the
user. Because of this, qsort() does not have to know anything
other than the size and number of the elements to be sorted. In our
case, only the comparison function—which we write—needs to
know that each element is a pointer to a string, and that the strings
are to be compared for lexicographical order.

The qsort() function is declared in stdlib.h as follows:

```
void qsort(void *base, size_t nelem, size_t size,
           int (*cmp)(const void *p, const void *q));
```

Argument base points to the first element of the array whose elements are to be sorted; because qsort() knows nothing about the
type of these elements, base has type void *. Argument nelem
is the number of elements in the array, and size is the size in bytes
of each element.

The final argument, cmp, points to the comparison function. The arguments to this function point to the array elements to be compared. Again because qsort() does not know the type of the array elements, these arguments have type const void *. Like strcmp(), the comparison function returns a negative integer if element *p precedes element *q, zero if the two elements are equal, and a positive integer if element *q precedes element *p.

The quicksort function is called as follows:

```
qsort(array_p, count, sizeof(char *), compare);
```

Because any object-pointer type can be converted to void *, array_p will be converted from char ** to void * without a warning message. The number of elements in the pointer array is given by count, and sizeof(char *) yields the size of an array element. The last argument, compare, yields the address of our comparison function.

Our comparison function is similar to strcmp(), discussed earlier, except that the arguments point to elements of the pointer array rather than to strings. Because each argument is passed with type void *, we must first convert it to type char **, the type of a pointer to an array element. We can do this with a type cast (char **):

```
(char **)p
(char **)q
```

These expressions point to array elements whose values are the string pointers that we need. To get the string pointers, then, we apply the indirection operator to each of the preceding expressions:

```
*(char **)p
*(char **)q
```

The resulting expressions are used to initialize the char * pointers p1 and q1, each of which initially points to the first character of a string:

```
char *p1 = *(char **)p;
char *q1 = *(char **)q;
```

As before, make sure you understand every detail of how these pointers are used. For example, you should be able to draw a diagram similar to Figure 5-4 showing (in a typical case) what is pointed to by p, q, *p1, and *q1.

The rest of compare() is similar to strcmp(), using pointers p1 and q1 to scan the strings being compared. One difference is that `compare()` changes lowercase letters to uppercase before comparing them, thereby making the comparisons case independent. Thus, instead of comparing `*p1` and `*q1`, `compare()` compares `toupper(*p1)` and `toupper(*q1)`.

After sorting, the function `write_data()` is called to write the sorted strings to the output file. The strings are written with `fputs()`. Note that the newline stored at the end of each string by `fgets()` is still there and will be written to the output file by `fputs()`.

FUNCTION MACROS

When a function is called, a certain amount of time is required to pass arguments to the function, transfer control to it, allocate memory for its variables, return its value, and transfer control back to the code following the function call. This overhead can be eliminated by replacing a function call by *inline code*—an expression that accomplishes the same purpose without calling the function. Function macros provide a simple means of replacing certain function calls by inline code.

Function macros are defined like other macros except that one or more formal arguments are listed in parentheses after the macro name. The formal arguments are used in the expression that defines the macro. For example, the function macro defined by

```
#define sumsqr(x, y)   x*x + y*y
```

has two formal arguments, `x` and `y`. A macro call specifies what text will be substituted for each formal argument when the call is expanded. For example, if we write

```
u = sumsqr(a, 2.75);
```

then `a` will be substituted for `x`, `2.75` will be substituted for `y`, and the statement will expand to

```
u = a*a + 2.75*2.75;
```

Because text is substituted without any regard for the structure of expressions, the previous definition of `sumsqr()` is a poor one that will often yield unexpected results. For example, when

```
sumsqr(a + b, c)
```

is expanded, `x` is replaced by `a + b`, giving

```
a + b*a + b + c*c
```

instead of the expected

```
(a + b)*(a + b) + c*c
```

Likewise,

```
2.0*sumsqr(a, b)
```

expands to

```
2.0*a*a + b*b
```

instead of the expected

```
2.0*(a*a + b*b)
```

We can avoid these problems by writing the definition with parentheses around each formal argument as well as around the entire defining expression. Thus sumsqr() should have been defined by

```
#define sumsqr(x, y)  ((x)*(x) + (y)*(y))
```

Now, sumsqr(a + b, c) expands to

```
((a + b)*(a + b) + (c)*(c))
```

and 2.0*sumsqr(a, b) expands to

```
2.0*((a)*(a) + (b)*(b))
```

The expanded expressions yield the expected results even though they contain a few more parentheses than we would normally write.

The preprocessor recognizes a call to a function macro only if the name of the macro is followed by a left parenthesis. This provides the way, mentioned earlier, of using parentheses around a function name to call the function rather than calling a macro with the same name. The call

```
(sumsqr)(a, b);
```

is not a valid macro call because the macro name is not followed by a left parenthesis. It is, however, a valid call to a function sumsqr() because the function-call operator can be preceded by any expression that yields the address of the function.

In fact, whenever the function name is used to represent the address of the function, it refers to the true function rather than to the macro (as it must, because a macro has no address). Thus

```
p = sumsqr;
```

sets p to the address of the function `sumsqr()`, and

```
p(a, b);
```

calls the function—not the macro.

EXERCISES

5-1. The library function

```
char *strchr(const char *s, int c);
```

searches for the first occurrence of character c in string s. For the purpose of this search, the terminating null character is considered to be part of string s. If the search is successful, the function returns a pointer to the character that was found; otherwise, the function returns the null pointer. Write two or more different definitions for `strchr()`.

5-2. The library function

```
char *strpbrk(const char *s1, const char *s2);
```

is similar to `strchr()` except that it searches for the first occurrence in string s1 of *any* character of string s2. For example,

```
strpbrk("now is the time", "aeiou")
```

returns a pointer to o, the first vowel in `"now is the time"`. For the purpose of this search, the terminating null character of each string is considered to be part of the string. If, however, the character found by the search is the terminating null character, the null pointer is returned (rather than the address of the terminating null character). Write two or more different definitions for `strpbrk()`.

5-3. To *concatenate* two strings is to join the end of one to the beginning of the other; for example, the concatenation of `"never"` and `"more"` is `"nevermore"`. The library function

```
char *strcat(char *s1, const char *s2);
```

concatenates string s2 to string s1; specifically, it copies string s2 into array s1, with the first character of the copy replacing the null character that previously terminated string s1. The function returns the value of s1, which now points to the concatenation of the two strings. Write two or more definitions for `strcat()`.

5-4. One string is a *substring* of another string if it matches a sequence of adjacent characters in the other string; the terminating null characters of the strings are *not* included in the matching. Thus `"never"` is a substring of `"nevermore"` and `"cat"` is a substring of `"concatenate"`. The library function

```
char *strstr(const char *s1, const char *s2);
```

searches for the first occurrence of string `s2` as a substring of string `s1`. If the search is successful, the function returns a pointer to the first character of the matching sequence; if the search is unsuccessful, the function returns the null pointer. Thus the call

```
strstr("concatenate", "ate")
```

returns a pointer to the first `a` (not the second) of `"concatenate"`, and the call

```
strstr("concatenate", "eat")
```

returns the null pointer. Write two or more different definitions of `strstr()`.

5-5. Write a program that inputs a file of English text and outputs a list of the words in the text, with each word on a separate line. Each word should appear on the word list only once regardless of how many times it occurs in the text. On the other hand, the words on the list can be in any convenient order. If we need the words in alphabetical order, we can pipe the output of this program to a sorting program such as the one presented earlier (Listing 5-3). To avoid duplicating words, the word list must be kept in memory while the input file is being read. Use the same techniques for string storage and memory management that were used in the sorting program.

6

Structures, Unions, Bitfields, and Bitwise Operators

STRUCTURES, WHICH ARE known as *records* in most other languages, define objects that can store more than one data item. The data items, called the *members* of the structure, can have different types. In contrast, all the elements of an array must have the same type. Unions are similar to structures except that the members represent alternatives: the value of only one member at a time can be stored in a union object. Unions in C serve the same purpose as record variants in Pascal.

We will also look in more detail at bitfields, which are declared in much the same way as structure members. And while on the subject of bits, we will look at the bitwise logical operators and the shift operators, which provide additional means of accessing and manipulating individual bits.

STRUCTURES

We declare a structure by the keyword `struct` followed by an optional tag and a brace-enclosed list of member declarations. For example,

```
struct item {
    unsigned long item_num;
    unsigned quantity;
    double price;
};
```

declares a structure with tag `item` and with three members: `item_num`, `quantity`, and `price`. Figure 6-1 illustrates two objects having this structure.

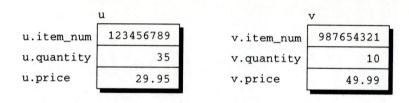

Figure 6-1

Two structure objects, both of which have the same structure. The structure has three members, named item_num, quantity, *and* price.

As was the case with enumerations, there are three ways to use a structure for declaring variables. First, the variables can be declared in the structure declaration. For example, the following declares s and t as variables with the specified structure:

```
struct item {
    unsigned long item_num;
    unsigned quantity;
    double price;
} s, t;
```

Second, if a tag is defined, we can use the keyword struct followed by the tag to declare variables:

```
struct item u, v;
```

Variables u and v have the same structure as s and t. Tags are most useful for declaring *self-referential structures*, in which member declarations can refer to the structure being defined.

The final method, which we will use most often, is to define a typedef name for a structure type. For example,

```
typedef struct {
    unsigned long item_num;
    unsigned quantity;
    double price;
} item_t;
```

define item_t as the type whose values have the specified structure. We can use item_t in declarations just like any other type name. Thus variables u and v could have been declared by

```
item_t u, v;
```

Note that in such a declaration, a tag name is preceded by struct but a typedef name is not.

A structure is initialized much like an array, with a brace-enclosed list giving the values of the structure members. For example, the following declarations and initializations yield the objects illustrated in Figure 6-1:

```
item_t u = { 123456789, 35, 29.95 };
item_t v = { 987654321, 10, 49.99 };
```

We access the members of a structure with the *member-access operator* . (dot or period), which yields an lvalue that refers to a particular member of an object. For example, `u.item_num`, `u.quantity`, and `u.price` are lvalues referring to the three members of u. If u has the value shown in Figure 6-1, the value of `u.item_num` is 123456789, that of `u.quantity` is 35, and that of `u.price` is 29.95. Likewise, the statements

```
v.item_num = 123123123;
v.quantity = 5;
v.price = 19.99;
```

assign the indicated values to the members of v.

The member-access operator is on the highest priority level—the same as for the subscript and function-call operators—and associates from left to right. Its left operand is always a structure or union; its right operand is a member name.

In stark contrast to arrays, we are free to manipulate the entire value of a structure object, not just the values of individual members. Structure values can be assigned to variables and can be passed to and returned by functions. For example,

```
u = v;
```

assigns the value of v to u. This structure assignment is equivalent to the following three member assignments:

```
u.item_num = v.item_num;
u.quantity = v.quantity;
u.price = v.price;
```

Likewise, the function

```
item_t change_price(item_t itm, double delta_p);
```

takes a structure value as its first argument and returns such a value as its result. We might define `change_price()` by

```
item_t change_price(item_t itm, double delta_p)
{
    itm.price += delta_p;
    return itm;
}
```

Argument `delta_p` gives the amount by which the price is to be changed. As usual, changing the value of a formal argument has no effect on the actual argument. If we wish to change the value of the actual argument, we must assign it the value returned by the function, as in

```
u = change_price(u, 5.00);
```

Tags and member names can be masked by macro names but cannot conflict with other identifiers. All tags—enumeration tags, structure tags, and union tags—form a separate name space. Thus tags can conflict with one another (including different kinds of tags, such as enumeration and structure tags), but no conflict between tags and ordinary identifiers is possible. Tags obey the same scope rules as ordinary identifiers. If a tag is declared at file level, its scope extends to the end of the source file; if it is declared in a block, its scope extends to the end of the block.

There is a separate name space for the member names of each structure or union. Except when a member name is used with the member access operator, its scope extends only to the end of the structure or union in which it is declared. Member names cannot conflict with other identifiers, nor can member names declared in different structures or unions conflict with one another.

The member-access operator provides special access to the member names of a structure or union, enabling us to use a member name to select the corresponding member. A member name used in this way cannot be confused with any other kind of identifier because only a member name can follow a member-access operator.

Example: A Complex-Number Module

It is not unusual to augment the arithmetic types of a language via modules, or "packages," that provide new arithmetic types along with functions for manipulating their values. Examples include complex numbers (used in science and engineering), binary-coded decimal (BCD) numbers (used in business), and rational numbers with arbitrarily large numerators and denominators (used in mathematics).

Our first use of structures will be for a complex-number module. As in previous examples, such a module consists of a header file, which is included by the program that uses the module, and a source file, which defines the functions declared in the header file. Listing 6-1 shows the header file `complex.h`, and Listing 6-2 shows the source file `complex.c`.

Listing 6-1

```
/* File complex.h */
/* Interface to complex-number module */

typedef struct {
    double re;
    double im;
} complex;

complex cmplx_cons(double, double);
complex cmplx_conj(complex);
complex cmplx_add(complex, complex);
complex cmplx_sub(complex, complex);
complex cmplx_mul(complex, complex);
complex cmplx_div(complex, complex);
```

A complex number consists of two floating-point numbers, which are called the real and the imaginary parts of the complex number. We thus define type `complex` by a structure whose members are the required real and imaginary parts:

```
typedef struct {
    double re;
    double im;
} complex;
```

This definition is placed in the header file so that type `complex` can be used in the source file for the module as well as in any program that uses the module.

The function `cmplx_cons()` constructs a complex number from given real and imaginary parts:

```
complex cmplx_cons(double x, double y)
{
    complex z;

    z.re = x;
    z.im = y;
    return z;
}
```

The function declares z as a complex variable, assigns the desired

Listing 6-2

```
/* File complex.c */
/* Source file for complex-number module */

#include "complex.h"

/* Construct a complex value from
   its real and imaginary parts */

complex cmplx_cons(double x, double y)
{
   complex z;

   z.re = x;
   z.im = y;
   return z;
}

/* Compute complex conjugate */

complex cmplx_conj(complex u)
{
   u.im = -u.im;
   return u;
}

/* Add two complex numbers */

complex cmplx_add(complex u, complex v)
{
   complex z;

   z.re = u.re + v.re;
   z.im = u.im + v.im;
   return z;
}

/* Subtract two complex numbers */

complex cmplx_sub(complex u, complex v)
{
   complex z;
```

```
    z.re = u.re - v.re;
    z.im = u.im - v.im;
    return z;
}

/* Multiply two complex numbers */

complex cmplx_mul(complex u, complex v)
{
    complex z;

    z.re = u.re * v.re - u.im * v.im;
    z.im = u.im * v.re + u.re * v.im;
    return z;
}

/* Divide two complex numbers */

complex cmplx_div(complex u, complex v)
{
    complex z;
    double denom = v.re * v.re + v.im * v.im;

    z.re = (u.re * v.re + u.im * v.im) / denom;
    z.im = (u.im * v.re - u.re * v.im) / denom;
    return z;
}
```

values to its real and imaginary parts, and returns the value of z as the value of the function.

The function `cmplx_conj()` returns the complex conjugate of its argument, which is computed by changing the sign of the imaginary part:

```
complex cmplx_conj(complex u)
{
    u.im = -u.im;
    return u;
}
```

Because the argument is passed by value, changing the value of the formal argument does not effect the actual argument. The modified argument value, however, is returned as the value of the function.

Functions `cmplx_add()`, `cmplx_sub()`, `cmplx_mul()`, and `cmplx_div()` carry out the corresponding arithmetic operations on complex values. We add two complex numbers by adding the corresponding real and imaginary parts:

```
complex cmplx_add(complex u, complex v)
{
    complex z;

    z.re = u.re + v.re;
    z.im = u.im + v.im;
    return z;
}
```

Again we declare a complex variable z, assign the required values to its real and imaginary parts, and return the value of z as the value of the function.

The definition of `cmplx_sub()` is similar to that of `cmplx_add()`, except that the real and imaginary parts are subtracted rather than added. The definitions of `cmplx_mul()` and `cmplx_div()` are also similar, although more complicated expressions are needed to calculate the real and imaginary parts of the result.

A program using this module might contain code such as

```
complex a, b, c, d;
a = cmplx_cons(3.0, 5.0);
b = cmplx_cons(2.0, 6.0);
c = cmplx_add(a, b);
d = cmplx_sub(a, b);
printf("c = (%.1f, %.1f)\n", c.re, c.im);
printf("d = (%.1f, %.1f)\n", d.re, d.im);
```

The sum of a and b is stored in c, and the difference of the two is stored in d. We print a complex number by printing its real and imaginary parts, enclosed in parentheses for ease of reading. (A more elaborate complex-number module would include functions for reading and printing complex numbers.) The example code produces the following printout:

```
c = (5.0, 11.0)
d = (1.0, -1.0)
```

STRUCTURES, ARRAYS, AND POINTERS

We frequently use arrays whose elements have structure types. For example,

```
complex z[50];
```

declares an array of 50 complex numbers. When accessing an element, the subscript and member-access operators are applied in left-to-right order. For example, in

```
z[10].re
```

the subscript operator first selects element 10 of the array, after which the member-access operator selects the real part (member `re`) of element 10.

We can also declare an array directly in a structure declaration. For example,

```
struct {
    unsigned long item_num;
    unsigned quantity;
    double price;
} table[100];
```

declares `table` as an array of 100 elements, each of which has the specified structure.

A member of a structure can also be an array. For example, in

```
struct {
    unsigned count;
    double data[100];
} d;
```

member `data` is an array of 100 `double` elements. To access element 25, we would write

```
d.data[25]
```

The member-access operator selects the desired member of `d`, and the subscript operator selects the desired array element.

The alignment considerations discussed in Chapter 3 may force a structure object to contain unused bytes. For example, suppose that a `long` value occupies four bytes and must be aligned on a four-byte boundary—that is, its address must be a multiple of 4. Consider the following structure, illustrated in Figure 6-2:

Figure 6-2

Alignment of structure members.
The shading designates three
unused bytes that must be inserted
after member c so that member n
will be properly aligned—so its
address will be a multiple of 4.

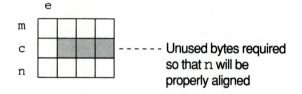

Unused bytes required
so that n will be
properly aligned

```
struct {
    long m;
    char c;
    long n;
} e;
```

Assume that m is properly aligned. Then c, which takes up only one byte, must be followed by three unused bytes so that n will be properly aligned—so its address will be a multiple of 4.

Unused bytes are reflected in the value returned by the `sizeof` operator, so `sizeof` e yields 12 rather than 9, as we might expect at first glance.

Now consider the following, illustrated in Figure 6-3:

```
struct {
    long m;
    long n;
    char c;
} f[50];
```

In this case, no unused bytes are needed between structure members. However, because the structure objects are the elements of an array, c must still be followed by three unused bytes so that member m in the following array element will be properly aligned.

C assumes that any structure can be used to declare array elements. Therefore, the C compiler inserts in any structure all the unused bytes needed to ensure that the members in *an array of* structure objects will be properly aligned. This policy ensures that `sizeof` will return the same value for an object of a given type regardless of whether the object is or is not an array element. It also ensures that we can always calculate the size of an array by multiplying the size of one element (computed with `sizeof`) by the number of elements in the array.

Figure 6-3

Alignment of structure members in an array of structures. In this array of structure objects, the last member of each element must be followed by three unused bytes so that the first member of the following element will be properly aligned. C assumes that any structure can be used for array elements and so always includes any unused bytes needed to align the next array element.

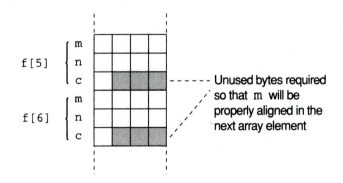

Structures and Pointers

Objects with structure types are frequently designated by pointers. For example,

```
complex *p;
```

declares p as a pointer to an object of type complex. Likewise,

```
struct {
    unsigned long item_num;
    unsigned quantity;
    double price;
} *q;
```

declares q as a pointer to a specified structure.

We *could* refer to the members of the object pointed to by p as

```
(*p).re
(*p).im
```

The parentheses are needed because the indirection operator has lower precedence than the member-access operator. However, because structure members are so frequently accessed via pointers, C provides a special member-access operator, ->, for use with pointers. The expressions

```
p->re
p->im
```

are equivalent to the preceding ones and refer to members `re` and `im` of the object pointed to by `p`.

Likewise, we can refer to the members of an object pointed by `q` as

```
q->item_num
q->quantity
q->price
```

The `->` operator has the same precedence and associativity as the dot operator. The two operators differ only in the significance of their left operands. The left operand of the dot operator is an lvalue that names a structure object. The left operand of `->` is a pointer to a structure object.

EXAMPLE: INFORMATION RETRIEVAL

Listings 6-3, 6-4, and 6-5 show an in-memory information retrieval program that stores inventory and price-list data as an array of structure objects. The array is allocated dynamically and reallocated as needed to increase its size. Listing 6-3 shows the header file `store.h`, which provides an interface to the module that stores the data. The corresponding source file, `store1.c`, is shown in Listing 6-4. Later in this chapter, we will look at an alternate storage module, `store2.c` (Listing 6-6), which uses the same interface (header file `store.h`) but stores the data in a completely different manner. Listing 6-5 shows the main program, which inserts, finds, and deletes data items as requested by the user. This program can be used with either of the two alternate storage modules. Because most of our attention will be focused on the storage modules, a detailed examination of Listing 6-5 will be left to the reader.

Header File `store.h`

In Listing 6-3, the storage module provides four functions: `init()`, `insert()`, `locate()`, and `delete()`. Function `init()` initializes the storage module if necessary. Only `store1.c` requires initialization. (In `store2.c`, `init()` is a dummy function provided only for compatibility with `store1.c`.)

Each stored data item has the same three components that we used in previous examples: an item number, a quantity, and a price. The item number is the *key* that will be used to identify a particular data item. Function `insert()` takes these three components as arguments and, if possible, stores the resulting data item. The arguments of `locate()` are an item number and *the addresses of* vari-

Listing 6-3

```
/* File store.h */
/* Interface to data storage module */

typedef enum { SUCCESS, NOT_FOUND,
               ALREADY_THERE, OUT_OF_MEMORY } result_t;

extern result_t init(void);

extern result_t insert(unsigned long item_num,
                       unsigned quantity,
                       double price);

extern result_t locate(unsigned long item_num,
                       unsigned *quantity_p,
                       double *price_p);

extern result_t delete(unsigned long item_num);
```

ables in which a quantity and a price can be stored. If an item with the given item number is found, those variables are set to the corresponding quantity and price. Function `delete()` takes an item number as its only argument; the function searches for the item and deletes it if it is found.

Each function returns a value of the enumerated type `result_t`, which is defined in `store.h`. All functions return SUCCESS if no error occurred. Function `init()` returns OUT_OF_MEMORY if it cannot allocate the memory initially required by the storage module. Function `insert()` returns ALREADY_THERE if an item with the given item number is already stored, and OUT_OF_MEMORY if there is insufficient memory for a new item. Functions `locate()` and `delete()` both return NOT_FOUND if an item with the given item number is not stored. If an error occurs, `insert()` and `delete()` do not change the stored data, and `locate()` (which never changes the stored data) does not change the quantity and price variables whose addresses it has been passed.

Module `store1.h`

In Listing 6-4, data items are stored as values of type `item_t`, which is the structured type we have already used in a number of

Listing 6-4

```
/* File store1.c */
/* Store data as array */

#include <stdlib.h>
#include <string.h>
#include "store.h"

typedef struct {
    unsigned long item_num;
    unsigned quantity;
    double price;
} item_t;

static int compare(const void *k, const void *e);

static item_t *table;
static size_t count = 0;
static size_t max_count = 4;

/* Allocate memory for table */

extern result_t init(void)
{
    table = calloc(max_count, sizeof(item_t));
    if (table == NULL)
        return OUT_OF_MEMORY;
    else
        return SUCCESS;
}

extern result_t insert(unsigned long item_num,
                       unsigned quantity,
                       double price)
{
    size_t i, m_count;
    item_t *p;

    i = 0;
    while ( (i < count) && (table[i].item_num < item_num) )
        i++;
    if ( (i < count) && (table[i].item_num == item_num) )
        return ALREADY_THERE;
```

```
    if (count == max_count) {
        m_count = max_count * 2;
        p = realloc(table, m_count * sizeof(item_t));
        if (p == NULL)
            return OUT_OF_MEMORY;
        else {
            table = p;
            max_count = m_count;
        }
    }

    if (i < count)
        memmove( &table[i+1], &table[i],
                 (count-i)*sizeof(item_t) );
    count++;

    table[i].item_num = item_num;
    table[i].quantity = quantity;
    table[i].price = price;
    return SUCCESS;
}

/* Return quantity and price for given item_num */

extern result_t locate(unsigned long item_num,
                       unsigned *quantity_p,
                       double *price_p)
{
    item_t *p;

    p = bsearch(&item_num, table, count,
                sizeof(item_t), compare);
    if (p == NULL)
        return NOT_FOUND;
    else {
        *quantity_p = p->quantity;
        *price_p = p->price;
        return SUCCESS;
    }
}
```

(continued)

```
/* Delete item with given item_num */

extern result_t delete(unsigned long item_num)
{
    item_t *p, *q;

    p = bsearch(&item_num, table, count,
                sizeof(item_t), compare);
    if (p == NULL) return NOT_FOUND;

    count--;
    q = &table[count];
    if (p != q)
        memmove( p, p+1, (char *)q - (char *)p );
    return SUCCESS;
}

/* Compare key with array element */

static int compare(const void *k, const void *e)
{
    unsigned long k1 = *(unsigned long *)k;
    unsigned long k2 = ((item_t *)e)->item_num;

    if (k1 < k2)
        return -1;
    else if (k1 == k2)
        return 0;
    else
        return 1;
}
```

---

examples. The module declares three global variables, which are accessible throughout the module but not outside of it:

```
static item_t *table;
static size_t count = 0;
static size_t max_count = 4;
```

Variable `table` points to the first element of the array of `item_t` objects used to store the data. Variable `count` gives the number of items currently stored in the array, and `max_count` gives the maximum number that can be stored without increasing the size of the array.

Function `init()`

Function `init()` allocates the initial array with the number of elements given by the initial value of `max_count`:

```
table = calloc(max_count, sizeof(item_t));
```

If `calloc()` returns `NULL`, `init()` returns `OUT_OF_MEMORY`, in which case the storage module cannot be used.

Function `insert()`

Function `insert()` searches the array for an item with a given number and, if no such item is found, inserts an item with the given item number, quantity, and price. If an item with the given item number is already present, `insert()` reports an error.

We wish to insert each new item in the proper position so that the stored items will be in ascending order according to their key values. This will allow `locate()` and `delete()` to use a library binary-search function, `bsearch()`, to search for items. We cannot use `bsearch()` for `insert()`, however, because `bsearch()` provides no information as to where a nonexistent item should be inserted. Therefore, `insert()` uses a simple sequential search to find either the item with a given key or the proper place to insert such an item.

The sequential search starts at the beginning of the table and continues until the end of the table is reached or until it finds an item whose key is greater than or equal to the given item number:

```
while ( (i < count) && (table[i].item_num < item_num) )
    i++;
```

Note that there can be no confusion between the member name `item_num` and the formal parameter with the same name: the one that follows the member-access operator (and only that one) is the member name.

The test expression in the `while` statement makes use of the short-circuit property of `&&`: the right operand is not evaluated if the left operand yields *false*. Such an evaluation could in fact be invalid. If `i` equals `count` and if `count` equals `max_count`, then `table[i]` is outside the bounds of the array. (The array has `max_count` elements, so valid subscripts range from 0 to `max_count - 1`.) In a system with memory protection, attempting to refer to an invalid array element can cause a run-time error.

When the search terminates, the key of `table[i]` is greater than or equal to the given item number. If the two are equal, then an item with the given number is already in the table. We regard this as an error, so the function should return with the error code `ALREADY_THERE`:

```
if ( (i < count) && (table[i].item_num == item_num) )
   return ALREADY_THERE;
```

The next step is to increase the size of the array, if necessary, to accommodate a new element. The code for doing this should now be reasonably familiar:

```
if (count == max_count) {
   m_count = max_count * 2;
   p = realloc(table, m_count * sizeof(item_t));
   if (p == NULL)
      return OUT_OF_MEMORY;
   else {
      table = p;
      max_count = m_count;
   }
}
```

Note that the values of `p` and `m_count` are *not* assigned to `table` and `max_count` until it is known that the reallocation was successful. If it was not, the existing array is preserved (`realloc()` does not deallocate the existing memory unless the requested new allocation can be made).

Having ensured that enough memory is available, we are now ready to store a new item in `table[i]`, where `i` still has the value set by the search. If `i` equals `count`, `table[i]` is then currently unused, and we are free to store the new item in it. If `i` is less than `count`, however, the items now stored in `table[i]` through `table[count-1]` must be moved forward by one array element, thereby freeing `table[i]` to hold the new item. Figure 6-4 illustrates this move.

We choose a function from `string.h` to perform the move. This header file provides two kinds of functions: those whose names begin with `str` apply to strings (which are terminated by null characters); those whose names begin with `mem` apply to arbitrary arrays of bytes (no null-character termination). There are two functions for moving a block of n bytes:

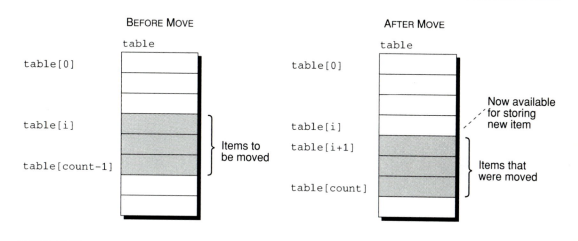

Figure 6-4
To make room for a new item in `table[i]`, *the items stored in* `table[i]`
through `table[count-1]` *must be moved forward by one array element.*

```
void *memcpy(void *p1, const void *p2, size_t n);
void *memmove(void *p1, const void *p2, size_t n);
```

For each function, `p2` points to the first byte of the block to be
moved, `p1` gives the desired new address of the first byte. The difference between the two is that `memmove()` allows the new and
old positions of block to overlap, ensuring that, in the overlap
region, the existing value of each byte will be moved before a new
value is stored. Because the new and old positions of our array elements will overlap, we need `memmove()` rather than `memcpy()`.

We need to move the items in array elements `table[i]`
through `table[count-1]` to elements `table[i+1]` through
`table[count]`. The number of items to be moved is `count-i`;
the number of *bytes* to be moved is `(count-i)*sizeof(item_t)`.
The following code performs the move (if necessary) and increments
`count` to reflect the new table element:

```
if (i < count)
    memmove( &table[i+1], &table[i],
             (count-i)*sizeof(item_t) );
count++;
```

All that remains to be done is to assign the components of the new
item to the members of `table[i]`.

```
table[i].item_num = item_num;
table[i].quantity = quantity;
table[i].price = price;
```

Again, there can be no confusion between the member names and the names of the formal parameters.

The Library Function bsearch()

In the interest of getting acquainted with more library functions, we will, as mentioned, use the binary-search function bsearch() in locate() and delete(). This function is declared in stdlib.h as follows:

```
void *bsearch( const void *key, const void *base,
               size_t nelem, size_t size,
               int (*cmp)(const void *k,
                          const void *e));
```

Argument key points to a key value, and base points to the first element of the array to be searched. Argument nelem gives the number of elements in the array, and size is the number of bytes in each element. The final argument, cmp, points to a function that compares the key pointed to by k with that of the array element pointed to by e. The function returns a pointer to the array element that was found, or the null pointer if the search was unsuccessful.

If the comparison function (which we must supply) is compare, we can call bsearch() as follows:

```
p = bsearch(&item_num, table, count,
            sizeof(item_t), compare);
```

The item_t array pointed to by table is searched for an element with key item_num. If the search is successful, p is set to point to the element found; if it is unsuccessful, p is set to NULL.

Function compare()

The function compare() must return an int that is negative if the given key precedes that of the array element, zero if they are equal, and positive if the given key follows that of the array element. If the keys were int values, we could just subtract them and return the result. However, attempting to convert such a difference from long to int could change the all-important sign. Therefore, we compare the two keys with two nested if-else statements, which return the appropriate int result.

First, however, we have to dereference the pointers and select the id_num member of the array element. Because the arguments are void * pointers, each must be converted to the correct type before dereferencing or member selection can take place:

```
unsigned long k1 = *(unsigned long *)k;
unsigned long k2 = ((item_t *)e)->item_num;
```

The key pointer k is converted to type unsigned long * and dereferenced with the indirection operator; the element pointer e is converted to type item_t *, and the member item_num is selected. We can now compare the two keys and return the appropriate int result:

```
if (k1 < k2)
    return -1;
else if (k1 == k2)
    return 0;
else
    return 1;
```

Function locate()

We can now easily understand the function locate(). The function bsearch() is called as before. If p was set to the null pointer, a NOT_FOUND error is reported. Otherwise, the values of p->quantity and p->price are assigned to the variables pointed to by arguments quantity_p and price_p:

```
if (p == NULL)
    return NOT_FOUND;
else {
    *quantity_p = p->quantity;
    *price_p = p->price;
    return SUCCESS;
}
```

Function delete()

Like locate(), delete() starts out by calling bsearch() and setting p to the result returned. If p is set to the null pointer, the item to be deleted was not found, and the function returns the error code NOT_FOUND.

If the item to be deleted is present, we decrement count to reflect the deletion of one element and set q to point to the last element that contains a valid item:

```
count—;
q = &table[count];
```

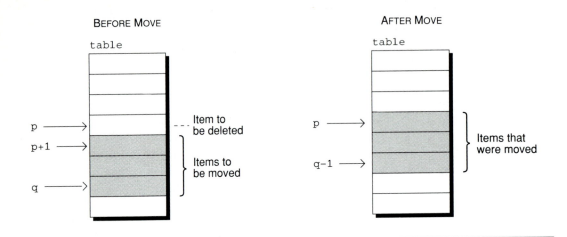

BEFORE MOVE

table

p →

p+1 →

q →

Item to be deleted

Items to be moved

AFTER MOVE

table

p →

q-1 →

Items that were moved

Figure 6-5
To eliminate the hole left by deleting the item in `*p`*, the items following* `*p` *must be moved up by one element. Specifically, items in elements* `* (p+1)` *through* `*q` *must be moved to elements* `*p` *through* `* (q-1)`.

If p (which points to the item to be deleted) equals q (which points to the last item), we are through. Just decrementing `count` is enough to drop the last item off the end of the table.

If p is not equal to q, however, the items following `*p` must be moved up by one element to eliminate the hole left by the deleted item. Specifically, items in elements `* (p+1)` through `*q` must be moved to elements `*p` through `* (q-1)`. (Remember that, in pointer arithmetic, adding or subtracting 1 moves an element pointer forward or backward by one element.) Figure 6-5 illustrates this move.

The number of items to be moved is `q-p`. For `memmove()`, however, we need to know the number of *bytes* to move, which we can compute by converting p and q to byte pointers before subtracting them:

```
(char *)p - (char *)q
```

The following `if` statement determines if a move is necessary and, if so, carries it out:

```
if (p != q)
    memmove( p, p+1, (char *)q - (char *)p );
```

Module `info.c`

As mentioned, we will leave a detailed analysis of `info.c` (Listing 6-5) to the reader, for it is similar to other command-driven programs we have studied earlier. If the call to `init()` fails, the pro-

Listing 6-5

```
/* File info.c */
/* Program to maintain inventory in memory */

#include <stdio.h>
#include <stdlib.h>
#include "store.h"

void do_insert(void);
void do_find(void);
void do_delete(void);

typedef enum {FALSE, TRUE} Boolean;

int main(void)
{
   char selection;
   Boolean running = TRUE;

   if (init() == OUT_OF_MEMORY) {
      printf("Insufficient memory to run\n");
      exit(EXIT_FAILURE);
   }
   do {
      printf("\nSelect Insert, Find, Delete, or Quit\n");
      printf("Enter letter for selection: ");
      scanf(" %c", &selection);
      switch (selection) {
      case 'i':
      case 'I':
         do_insert();
         break;
      case 'f':
      case 'F':
         do_find();
         break;
      case 'd':
      case 'D':
         do_delete();
         break;
```

(continued)

```
            case 'q':
            case 'Q':
                running = FALSE;
                break;
            default:
                printf("Invalid selection\n");
                printf("Please try again\n");
                break;
        }
    } while (running);
    return EXIT_SUCCESS;
}

/* Insert item */

void do_insert(void)
{
    unsigned long item_num;
    unsigned quantity;
    double price;
    result_t r;

    printf("Item number? ");
    scanf("%lu", &item_num);
    printf("Quantity? ");
    scanf("%u", &quantity);
    printf("Price? ");
    scanf("%lf", &price);
    r = insert(item_num, quantity, price);
    if (r == ALREADY_THERE)
        printf("This item number already present\n");
    if (r == OUT_OF_MEMORY)
        printf("Insufficient Memory for item\n");
}

/* Look up item with given item number */

void do_find(void)
{
    unsigned long item_num;
    unsigned quantity;
    double price;
    result_t r;
```

```
        printf("Item number? ");
        scanf("%lu", &item_num);
        r = locate(item_num, &quantity, &price);
        if (r == NOT_FOUND)
            printf("Item not found\n");
        else {
            printf("Quantity: %u\n", quantity);
            printf("Price: %.2f\n", price);
        }
    }

    /* Delete item with given item number */

    void do_delete()
    {
        unsigned long item_num;
        result_t r;

        printf("Item number? ");
        scanf("%lu", &item_num);
        r = delete(item_num);
        if (r == NOT_FOUND)
            printf("Item not found\n");
    }
```

gram terminates, because no data array can be created. Failures of other `store1.c` functions do not terminate the program, however, because the user can carry out other commands even if one fails. Indeed, these other commands can remedy the failure by, for instance, deleting old items to make room for new ones.

From a practical point of view, the greatest failing of this program is that it makes no provision for saving the data to disk and reloading it the next time the program is run. Ways to remedy this deficiency are discussed in Chapter 7.

SELF-REFERENTIAL STRUCTURES AND LINKED LISTS

Structure members can be pointers, and such pointers are often used to link structure objects into more complex data structures. A particular interesting (and common) case is when a structure object contains pointers to objects of the same structure type. The corresponding structure declaration is self-referential, because one or more of the member declarations must refer to the structure declaration of which they are a part.

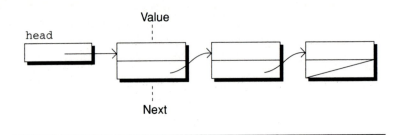

For example, consider the *linked list* illustrated in Figure 6-6. Each object on the list contains a floating-point value and a pointer to the following object. The last object on the list contains the null pointer, which is indicated in diagrams by a diagonal line through a pointer variable. A pointer variable head points to the first object on the list.

We can describe a list object, or cell, by the following structure:

```
struct cell {
    double value;
    struct cell *next;
};
```

A cell has two members: value, which contains a floating-point number, and next, which points to the next object on the linked list.

One problem with self-referential declarations is how to refer to the entity being declared. In C, tags come to the rescue. By specifying cell as a tag for our structure, we can use

```
struct cell *next;
```

to declare a pointer to another object with same structure. Not all self-referential declarations are valid. For example, suppose we omit the asterisk in the declaration of next:

```
struct cell {
    double value;
    struct cell next;
};
```

This declaration is invalid because it is physically impossible for a cell to contain another cell as one of its members. Nothing, however, prevents a cell from containing *a pointer to* another cell.

As usual, we can define a typedef name for the cell structure type:

```
typedef struct cell {
    double value;
    struct cell *next;
} cell_t;
```

Note that we still use the tag, and not the typedef name, for self-reference. The compiler does not encounter the typedef name (and hence does not define it) until after processing the structure declaration. We use the typedef name as usual to declare pointers to cells:

```
cell_t *head, *p;
```

The -> operator is particularly convenient for working with linked lists. If p points to a particular cell, then p->value is the value member of that cell, and p->next is the pointer to the next cell (if any). The statement

```
p = p->next;
```

sets p to point to the next cell on the list (or to null if there is no next cell). The statement

```
for (p = head; p != NULL; p = p->next)
    printf("%f\n", p->value);
```

prints all the values on the list. This is also a good example of the power of the C for statement, which is not limited to stepping an integer variable through a series of values.

If head points to the first cell on a linked list, then pointers to successive cells on the list (which we assume all exist) are the values of the following expressions:

```
head                       /* first cell */
head->next                 /* second cell */
head->next->next           /* third cell */
head->next->next->next     /* fourth cell */
/* and so on */
```

(Remember that -> associates from left to right.)

EXAMPLE: INFORMATION RETRIEVAL REVISITED

As promised, we will now look at a different version of the storage module for our information program. Listing 6-6 shows the new version, store2.c, which stores data as a *binary tree* rather than as an array. Both store1.c and store2.c use the same header file, store.h, and either can be used with the information retrieval program info.c.

Listing 6-6

```
/* File store2.c */
/* Store data as binary tree */

#include <stdlib.h>
#include "store.h"

typedef struct item {
    unsigned long item_num;
    unsigned quantity;
    double price;
    struct item *left_branch;
    struct item *right_branch;
} item_t;

static item_t *root = NULL;

static item_t **search(unsigned long key);

/* Dummy initialization function present only
   for compatibility with array version */

extern result_t init(void) { return SUCCESS; }

/* Insert new item */

extern result_t insert(unsigned long item_num,
                       unsigned quantity,
                       double price)
{
    item_t **p, *q;

    p = search(item_num);
    if (*p != NULL) return ALREADY_THERE;
    q = malloc(sizeof(item_t));
    if (q == NULL) return OUT_OF_MEMORY;
    q->item_num = item_num;
    q->quantity = quantity;
    q->price = price;
    q->left_branch = q->right_branch = NULL;
    *p = q;
    return SUCCESS;
}
```

```c
/* Return quantity and price for given item_num */

extern result_t locate(unsigned long item_num,
                       unsigned *quantity_p,
                       double *price_p)
{
    item_t *q;

    q = *search(item_num);
    if (q == NULL) return NOT_FOUND;
    *quantity_p = q->quantity;
    *price_p = q->price;
    return SUCCESS;
}

/* Delete item with given item_num */

extern result_t delete(unsigned long item_num)
{
    item_t **p, **q, *r, *s;

    p = search(item_num);
    r = *p;
    if (r == NULL) return NOT_FOUND;

    if (r->left_branch == NULL)
        *p = r->right_branch;
    else if (r->right_branch == NULL)
        *p = r->left_branch;
    else {
        q = &r->right_branch;
        while ( (*q)->left_branch != NULL )
            q = &(*q)->left_branch;
        s = *q;
        *q = s->right_branch;
        *p = s;
        s->left_branch = r->left_branch;
        s->right_branch = r->right_branch;
    }
    free(r);
    return SUCCESS;
}
```

(continued)

```
/* Search for item with given key */

static item_t **search(unsigned long key)
{
    item_t **p = &root;

    while ( (*p != NULL) && ((*p)->item_num != key) )
        if (key < (*p)->item_num)
            p = &(*p)->left_branch;
        else
            p = &(*p)->right_branch;
    return p;
}
```

Binary Trees

We begin with a brief introduction to (or review of) binary trees, which can be diagrammed as in Figure 6-7. Each of the circles is a *node* and corresponds to a stored data item; the number in a circle is the key (that is, the item number) of the corresponding data item. The lines connecting the nodes are *branches*.

A node can be connected by descending branches to at most two other nodes; they are its *children* and it is their *parent*. The child reached by following the *left branch* down from a node is its *left child*; the one reached by following the *right branch* is its *right child*. When a node has only one child, it is still classified as a left child or a right child, and the branch leading to it is classified as a left or a right branch.

The top-most node, which has no parent, is the *root* of the tree. The bottom-most nodes, which have no children, are *leaves*. A tree that is part of a larger tree is a *subtree*. There is a subtree suspended from each branch leading downward from a node. A subtree suspended from a left branch is the *left subtree* of the parent node; a subtree suspended from a right branch is the *right subtree* of the parent node. The *descendants* of a node consist of all the nodes in its left and right subtrees. They include its children, its grandchildren, its great grandchildren, and so on.

The following simple principle governs the organization of a binary tree: For each node, all descendants whose keys precede that of the node go in its left subtree, and all descendants whose keys follow that of the node go in its right subtree. If we are at a given node, then, and are looking for descendants with smaller keys, we follow

Figure 6-7

A binary tree. The data items are stored in the nodes, which are represented here by circles. The number in each node is the key of the corresponding data item. The nodes are connected by branches. The topmost node is the root of the binary tree; the bottom-most nodes are its leaves.

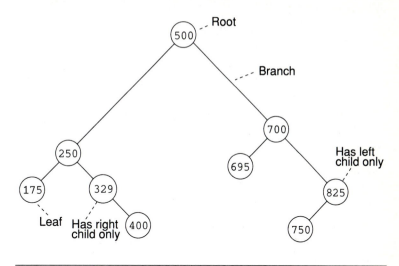

the left branch and search the left subtree. If, on the other hand, we are looking for descendants with larger keys, we follow the right branch and search the right subtree.

This organization leads to a simple algorithm for finding a node with a given key. Start at the root and compare the key you are searching for with the key of the node. If the two are equal, you have found the desired node and the search is over. Otherwise, if the search key is less than the key of the node, follow the left branch; if the search key is greater than the key of the node, follow the right branch. Repeat this process for every node encountered, until you find the desired node or until you try to follow a nonexistent branch. If the latter occurs, then the key you are searching for is not present. (For practice, use this algorithm to locate several nodes in the tree of Figure 6-7.)

The same algorithm is used to find where to insert a new node. First, search for the key of a new node; if a node with that key is found, the user is informed and no insertion is carried out. If a nonexistent branch is encountered, it is replaced by a branch leading to the new node. We know that any future search will find the new node, because the search we just conducted found the nonexistent branch that has now been replaced by a branch to the new node. (For practice, use this algorithm to insert several new nodes in the tree of Figure 6-7, then convince yourself that these nodes will be found by subsequent searches.)

Module `store2.c`   In Listing 6-6, a node is represented by a value of the structure type `item_t`, which is defined as follows:

```
typedef struct item {
    unsigned long item_num;
    unsigned quantity;
    double price;
    struct item *left_branch;
    struct item *right_branch;
} item_t;
```

The left and right branches are represented by members `left_branch`, which points to the node's left child, and `right_branch`, which points to the node's right child. If a branch does not exist, the corresponding member holds the null pointer.

The root node is pointed to by the global variable `root`, which is declared and initialized as follows:

```
static item_t *root = NULL;
```

Figure 6-8 shows a small binary tree and illustrates how it is represented using objects of type `item_t`. Remember that a diagonal line through a pointer variable indicates that it holds the null pointer.

We now need to think about how to keep track of our position in the tree as we move from node to node. The obvious solution would be to maintain a pointer to the current node, the one we are currently examining. The problem with this is that we sometimes need access to the variable or member that points to the current node. Let's call this variable or member the *parent variable* of a node.[*] We will keep track of our position in the tree by maintaining a pointer to the parent variable of the current node.

As illustrated in Figure 6-9, the parent variable is always one of the following: (a) the variable `root`, if the current node is the root; (b) the member `left_branch` in the parent of the current node; or (c) the member `right_branch` in the parent of the current node. If p points to the parent variable, then `*p` *is* the parent variable and therefore its value points to the current node. We can refer to members of the current node by expressions such as `(*p)->item_num` and `(*p)->quantity`. The parentheses are required because the `->` has higher precedence than the `*`.

A basic operation in searching or manipulating a binary tree is moving from the current node to its left or right child. As before,

---

[*]*Parent variable* is not standard terminology.

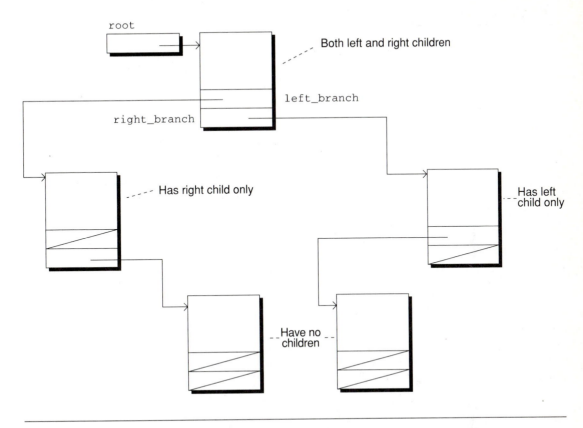

Figure 6-8
A small binary tree represented using objects of type `item_t`. *In each node, member* `left_branch` *points to the left child of the node and member* `right_branch` *points to the right child. If a particular child is not present, the corresponding member contains the null pointer.*

suppose `p` points to the parent variable of the current node so that `*p` points to the current node. The parent variable of the left child of the current node is the member `(*p)->left_branch`; the parent variable of the right child is `(*p)->right_branch`. To move from the current node to one of its children, `p` must be set to *the address of* one of these new parent variables. Therefore one (and only one) of the following statements must be executed:

```
p = &(*p)->left_branch;
p = &(*p)->right_branch;
```

The address-of operator, `&`, has lower precedence than `->`. It therefore applies to the entire expression that follows it, and not just to `(*p)`.

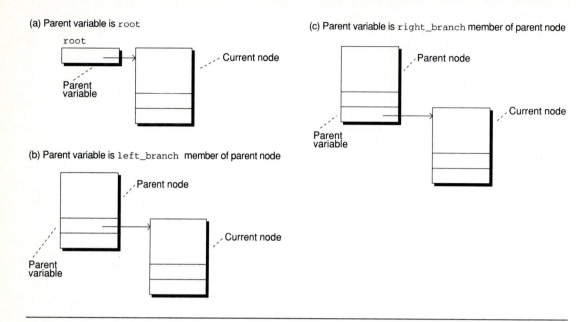

(a) Parent variable is `root`

root

Parent variable

Current node

(b) Parent variable is `left_branch` member of parent node

Parent node

Current node

Parent variable

(c) Parent variable is `right_branch` member of parent node

Parent node

Parent variable

Current node

Figure 6-9

As illustrated here, the parent variable *is always one of the following: (a) the variable* root, *if the current node is the root; (b) the member* left_branch *in the parent of the current node; or (c) the member* right_branch *in the parent of the current node.*

Function `search()`

The function `search()` (in Listing 6-6) finds the node having a given key or, failing that, finds where such a node can be inserted. The function is called with the search key as its argument; it returns a pointer to a parent variable that can be used to access the node that was found or, if none was, to insert a node with the given key.

As explained, we will work through the tree with `p` always pointing to the parent variable of the node currently being examined. We begin by declaring `p` and initializing it to the address of `root`, the parent variable for the root node:

```
item_t **p = &root;
```

Variable `p` has type `item_t **`, because it points to an object (the parent variable) that in turn points to an object of type `item_t` (the current node).

The search, which implements the algorithm given earlier, is carried out by a `while` statement and an `if` statement:

```
while ( (*p != NULL) && ((*p)->item_num != key) )
    if (key < (*p)->item_num)
        p = &(*p)->left_branch;
    else
        p = &(*p)->right_branch;
```

The search continues until it encounters a nonexistent branch or until it encounters a node with the desired key. It therefore continues while (1) the parent variable, `*p`, is not null (which would signify a missing branch) and (2) the item number of the current node, `(*p)->item_num`, is not equal to the given key. Note that the short-circuit property of `&&` is crucial to the validity of the test expression. If `*p` is null, then `(*p)->item_num` is invalid, because `*p` doesn't point to any object, let alone one of type `item_t`.

If the search is to continue, then, as per the algorithm, we compare the search key with `(*p)->item_num`, the key of the current node. If the search key precedes that of the current node, we follow the left branch, which we do (as explained earlier) by setting `p` to the address of `(*p)->left_branch`. If the search key follows that of the current node, we follow the right branch, which we do by setting `p` to the address of `(*p)->right_branch`.

When the search terminates, we have two possibilities. If it terminated because `(*p)->item_num` equals `key`, then `*p` points to the desired node. If it terminated because `*p` equals the null pointer, then no node with the desired key is present, but we can insert such a node by setting `*p` to point to it. The final value of `p` is returned as the value of the function and (depending on the value of `*p`) can be used for either accessing the node that was found or inserting a new node.

Function `insert()`

As before, the function `insert()` inserts a new node with a given item number, quantity, and price. It begins by searching for a node with the given item number, and returning if such a node is found:

```
p = search(item_num);
if (*p != NULL) return ALREADY_THERE;
```

Next we allocate a new node

```
q = malloc(sizeof(item_t));
if (q == NULL) return OUT_OF_MEMORY;
```

and assign values to its members:

```
q->item_num = item_num;
q->quantity = quantity;
q->price = price;
q->left_branch = q->right_branch = NULL;
```

Note the last line: the new node does not yet have any children. Finally, we set `*p`, the parent variable found by `search()`, to point to the new node:

```
*p = q;
```

If the search were repeated, `search()` would return the same value of p. However, then `*p` would not be null but would point to the newly inserted node.

Function `locate()`

Like `insert()`, `locate()` begins by searching for a node with a given item number. However, `locate()` does not need the parent variable but just its value, which (if the search was successful) points to the node that was found. Therefore, `locate()` applies * to the value returned by `search()`, getting a pointer to the desired node or (if the search failed) the null pointer:

```
q = *search(item_num);
if (q == NULL) return NOT_FOUND;
```

If the search was successful, the quantity and price in the node that was found are assigned to the variables pointed to by `quantity_p` and `price_p`:

```
*quantity_p = q->quantity;
*price_p = q->price;
```

Function `delete()`

All that remains to be discussed is the `delete()` function. Unfortunately, deleting a node from a binary tree is tricky: if we don't watch out, our tree will break up into three parts that cannot be reassembled without having a part left over.

If a node has at most one child, it can be deleted without difficulty. The branch coming down from the parent of the deleted node is connected to the child (if any) of the deleted node. The deleted node is thus bypassed and never will be missed. If the node to be deleted has two children, however, we have a problem. The branch coming down from the parent of the deleted node can be connected to one child, but the other child and its descendants have been disconnected from the rest of the tree.

The solution, which is discussed more fully in computer science texts, is to find another node that (1) can be deleted from its current position and (2) can be substituted for the deleted node without upsetting the order of the keys. Such a node is the *successor* to the deleted node, in the sense that is it is the node having the next largest key value. Because it has the next largest key value, it can be substituted for the node to be deleted without upsetting the order of the keys. And in its current position it has no left child and so can be easily deleted. (If it had a left child, the key of the left child would lie between the key of the deleted node and that of the successor node, contrary to the definition of the latter.)

We find the successor node by taking the right branch from the node to be deleted, then taking only left branches until we encounter a node with no left branch.

Turning to the code, we first search for the node to be deleted and return if it is not found:

```
p = search(item_num);
r = *p;
if (r == NULL) return NOT_FOUND;
```

After these statements, `r` points to the node to be deleted, and `p` points to its parent variable.

The rest of the deletion is handled by a three-way `if` statement. The `if` and `else-if` parts handle the two special cases that allow easy deletion. If the node to be deleted has no left child, we connect its parent to its right child:

```
*p = r->right_branch;
```

If the node to be deleted has no right child, we connect its parent to its left child:

```
*p = r->left_branch;
```

If neither of these special cases holds, then the node to be deleted has two children and must be replaced by its successor. Using `q` as a pointer to parent variables, we search for the successor by first taking a right branch, then taking left branches until we hit one that is null:

```
q = &r->right_branch;
while ( (*q)->left_branch != NULL )
    q = &(*q)->left_branch;
s = *q;
```

After these statements, s points to the successor node, and q points to its parent variable.

Because the successor node has no left child, we can delete it from its current position by connecting its parent to its right child:

```
*q = s->right_branch;
```

We next substitute the successor node for the node to be deleted. The parent of the node to be deleted is connected to the successor node:

```
*p = s;
```

and the successor node is connected to the children of the node to be deleted:

```
s->left_branch = r->left_branch;
s->right_branch = r->right_branch;
```

Finally, we call `free()` to reclaim the memory occupied by the deleted node (which is still pointed to by r):

```
free(r);
```

UNIONS

A *union* is declared in much the same way as a structure. However, the members of a union represent *alternatives*—that is, they describe data values that, at different times, can occupy the union object. The union object must be large enough to accommodate the largest value that will be stored in it. As with structures, unused bytes may be inserted to ensure that the elements of an array of union objects will be properly aligned. For example,

```
union {
    long l_val;
    double d_val;
    char *cp_val;
} u;
```

declare u as a variable capable of holding a `long` value *or* a `double` value *or* a character-pointer value. If a long value occupies four bytes, a double value eight bytes, and a character-pointer value two bytes, the size of u must be eight bytes. A `long` value will occupy only the first four bytes of u, a `double` value will occupy all eight bytes, and a character-pointer value will occupy the first two bytes.

A union object can be initialized only with a value for its *first* member. Therefore, if u is to be initialized, it must be initialized with a `long` value (or a value that can be converted to `long`):

```
union {
    long l_val;
    double d_val;
    char *cp_val;
} u = { 100L };
```

We use member names and the member-access operator to tell the compiler what type of value we are storing in or retrieving from a union. For example, if we write

```
u.d_val = 3.14;
```

the double value 3.14 is stored in u without change. On the other hand, if we write

```
u.l_val = 3.14;
```

then 3.14 will be converted to type long, and the long integer 3 will be stored in u.

Likewise, each of the following additions is done with a different kind of arithmetic, because in each the union supplies a value of a different type:

```
u.l_val + 5
u.d_val + 5
u.cp_val + 5
```

The first addition is done with long integer arithmetic, the second with double floating-point arithmetic, and the third with character-pointer arithmetic.

When retrieving a value from a union object, we must use the same member name that was used when the value was stored. For example, if we assign a value to u with

```
u.d_val = 1.5;
```

then we can only use u.d_val to refer to the value of u. The expressions u.l_val and u.cp_val will yield garbage, because they will misinterpret part of the code for a double value as representing a long value or a character-pointer.

Given a union object, we need to determine the type of data stored in it so we can retrieve the data via the proper member name (and so we will know what to do with the data once we have retrieved it). A common solution is to make the union a member of a structure, and to use another member of the structure to specify the type of data in the union. For example, consider the following declarations:

```
typedef enum { LONG_INT, DOUBLE_FLT,
               CHAR_PTR } u_tag_t;
struct {
   u_tag_t u_tag;
   union {
      long l_val;
      double d_val;
      char *cp_val;
   } u_part;
} s;
```

Structure s has two members, u_tag and u_part, with the value of u_tag specifying the type of data stored in u_part. (The member that specifies the type of data is often called a *tag*; this has nothing to do with the enumeration, structure, and union tags that are part of the C language.) When we assign a value to u_part, we also set u_tag to reflect the type of the stored data:

```
s.u_part.d_val = 3.14;
s.u_tag = DOUBLE_FLT;
```

When the program needs the value of s.u_part, it can examine the value of s.u_tag and determine that the desired value has type double and must be retrieved via s.u_part.d_val.

As a slightly more realistic example, recall the linked-list cells discussed earlier:

```
typedef struct cell {
   double value;
   struct cell *next;
} cell_t;
```

Here the value stored in a cell is restricted to type double. But a list-processing language such as LISP might allow a list cell to contain an integer, a floating-point number, a pointer to a string, or a pointer to (the first cell of) another list. By making value a union, we can easily allow a list cell to accommodate all these types:

```
typedef enum { LIST, STRING,
               LONG_INT, DOUBLE_FLT } value_tag_t;
typedef struct cell {
   value_tag_t value_tag;
   union {
      struct cell *list_v;
      char *string_v:
```

```
        long long_v;
        double double_v;
    } value;
    struct cell *next;
} cell_t;
```

Note that we now have two members that refer to the structure being declared via the structure tag cell. Member list_v refers to another list via a pointer to its first cell.

Suppose we use a pointer p to scan through the cells of a linked list, as discussed earlier. For each new cell, the program would first examine p->value_tag to determine the type of data stored in the cell. That determined, the data can be accessed via the proper member names and processed as needed.

BITFIELDS

Bitfields were introduced in Chapter 3 as representing parts of larger memory locations. Further discussion was postponed until now because bitfields can be declared only as members of structures or unions. When possible, successive bitfield members are packed into a single memory location. Both the size of location used for packing bitfields and the order in which the bitfields are stored are implementation dependent. If you need to match an existing hardware- or software-defined data format, you must investigate how your implementation packs bitfields.

A bitfield can be either signed, unsigned, or plain (not specified as either signed or unsigned). Like type char, a plain bitfield can be either signed or unsigned, depending on the implementation. The following declares three bitfields that could fit into a 16-bit location; the number after each colon gives the size of each bitfield:

```
struct {
    signed   s : 7;
    unsigned u : 6;
    int      p : 3;
} fields;
```

Signed bitfield s occupies seven bits and stores a signed integer; unsigned bitfield u occupies six bits and stores an unsigned integer; plain bitfield p occupies three bits and may store a signed or an unsigned integer (depending on the implementation).

For a more realistic example, suppose we are writing a program to simulate a microprocessor design. A microprocessor normally has a *status register* that contains a number of one-bit flags representing the status of the microprocessor; typical flags would be `carry` (whether or not the most recent arithmetic operation produced a carry), `overflow` (whether or not the most recent arithmetic operation produced an overflow), `sign` (the sign of the most recently computed arithmetic result), and so on. Using bitfields, we can declare a structure for the status register as follows:

```
struct {
     unsigned carry              : 1;
     unsigned auxiliary_carry    : 1;
     unsigned overflow           : 1;
     unsigned sign               : 1;
     unsigned zero               : 1;
     unsigned interrupts_enabled : 1;
} status;
```

It frequently happens that certain bits in a hardware-defined register are unused; we can represent a group of unused bits by a bitfield with no name or type:

```
struct {
     unsigned carry              : 1;
     unsigned auxiliary_carry    : 1;
     unsigned overflow           : 1;
                                 : 3;
     unsigned sign               : 1;
                                 : 5;
     unsigned zero               : 1;
     unsigned interrupts_enabled : 1;
} status;
```

There are three unused bits between the `overflow` and `sign` fields and five unused bits between the `sign` and `zero` fields.

Because a bitfield occupies only part of a memory location, it has no address (addresses refer only to whole locations). Therefore, we cannot get the address of a bitfield with the address-of operator, `&`.

OPERATORS FOR BIT MANIPULATION

Bitfields are one way of accessing groups of bits within an integer value. C also provides bitwise logical operators and shift operators, which are a time-honored means of achieving the same end. An advantage of the operators is that they can be applied to values of any integer type. In contrast, the type of value into which bitfields are packed is determined by the implementation.

Bitwise Logical Operators

The bitwise logical operators & (AND), | (inclusive OR), ^ (exclusive OR), and ~ (NOT) carry out logical operations on the individual bits making up an integer value. Be careful not to confuse the bitwise operators with the logical operators &&, ||, and !. The logical operators treat an entire integer as representing a single logical value, with 0 representing *false* and any nonzero value representing *true*. The bitwise operators act on the individual bits that make up an integer value, with each 0 bit representing *false* and each 1 bit representing *true*.

As shown in Table A2-1 in Appendix 2, the unary NOT operator, ~, has the same precedence as most other prefix unary operators and, like them, associates from right to left. The remaining bitwise operators are all binary and associate from left to right. Their precedences are greater than those of the logical operators and less than those of the relational and equality operators. The & operator has greater precedence than ^, which in turn has greater precedence than |. For example, in

```
a|b^c&~d
```

~ has the highest precedence, followed in order of decreasing precedence by &, ^, and |. Therefore, the expression is grouped as follows:

```
a|(b^(c&(~d)))
```

The bitwise operators act separately on each bit position in the operands and result. Thus the bit in a given position in the result depends only on the bits in the corresponding positions in the operands. The bitwise AND operator, &, produces a 1 bit in the result only if the corresponding bits in the operands are both 1:

```
    11010110
&   10010101
    10010100
```

The bitwise *inclusive* OR operator | produces a 1 bit in the result if either *or both* of the corresponding bits in the operands are 1:

```
  11010110
| 10010101
  11010111
```

The bitwise *exclusive* OR operator ^ produces a 1 bit in the result if either, *but not both*, of the corresponding bits in the operands is 1:

```
  11010110
^ 10010101
  01000011
```

The bitwise NOT operator ~ produces a 1 bit in the result if the corresponding bit in the operand was 0, and vice versa:

```
~ 11010110
  00101001
```

Like the arithmetic operators, the binary bitwise operators, &, |, and ^, can be combined with the assignment operator to give &=, |=, and ^=, which assign the result of the operation to the left operand. For example, if n is an integer variable, the statement

```
n &= 0x7fff;
```

"ands" the contents of n with the bit pattern represented by 0x7fff and stores the result back into n.

Shift Operators

The shift operators are >> (right shift) and << (left shift). These operators associate from left to right; their precedence is greater than that of the relational operators and less than that of the + and - operators.

The left shift operator shifts the bits of its first operand to the left by the number of places specified in the second operand:

```
     1111111111111111
<<                  3
     1111111111111000
```

Zeros are shifted into the right end. Any bits shifted out of the left end are lost.

The right shift operator shifts the bits of its first operand to the right by the number of places specified in the second operand:

```
     1111111111111111
>>                  5
     0000011111111111
```

6 STRUCTURES, UNIONS, BITFIELDS

It is implementation dependent whether 0s or 1s will be shifted into the left end. There are two possibilities: If a *logical* right shift is implemented, 0s are shifted in, as just illustrated. If an *arithmetic* right shift is implemented, copies of the sign bit (the original left-most bit) are shifted in.

Like the binary arithmetic and bitwise operators, the shift operators also can be combined with the assignment operator to give >>= and <<=, each of which modifies the first operand by shifting its bits the number of places specified in the second operand. Thus, if n is an integer variable, then

```
n <<= 7;
```

shifts each bit of object n seven places to the left, and

```
n >>= 4;
```

shifts each bit of object n four places to the right.

EXERCISES

6-1. Write your own version of the binary-search routine `bsearch()`. (The binary search algorithm can be found in any computer science text.) As with `qsort()`, `bsearch()` regards the data array as an array of bytes, with each of the `nelem` data items represented by a block of `size` bytes. Only the user-supplied function `*cmp` knows how to compare two data items.

6-2. Write a version of the storage module that stores items in a linked list. As with the binary tree, keep track of the current position in the list via a pointer to the variable or member that, in turn, points to the current cell.

6-3. Write a storage module that uses a *doubly linked list*: every list cell has two pointers, one to its predecessor and one to its successor. The predecessor pointer of the first node and the successor pointer of the last node are null. The "parent variable" idea is neither useful nor necessary for doubly linked lists; keep track of the current position in the list via a pointer to the current cell. It is convenient for the first cell of the list to be a dummy cell that is never deleted. This will avoid the special cases of inserting a cell into an empty list and deleting the last cell on a list.

6-4. Write a storage module that uses a doubly linked version of the binary tree: in addition to pointers to its children, each node also contains a pointer to its parent. As with doubly linked lists, use a pointer to the current node to keep track of position. To avoid special cases, it is convenient to provide a dummy root, which cannot be deleted and whose only child is the actual root.

6-5. For the binary-tree storage module (Listing 6-6), write a function that lists all the stored data in a three-column printout. The data items should be printed with their keys in ascending order. To do this, we must *traverse* the tree—visit every node—in such a way that the nodes are visited in increasing-key order. This is most easily done with a *recursive* function—one that calls itself. For each node, the traversal function should (1) call itself to traverse the left subtree of the node, (2) print the data for the node, and (3) call itself to traverse the right subtree of the node. Each recursive call should be made only if the corresponding subtree actually exists. C supports recursion, but in some cases you may have to specify a larger size for the *stack*—the area from which memory for function calls is allocated.

7 Streams and Files

S O FAR WE HAVE learned to read text from the standard input stream and write it to the standard output stream. In this chapter we extend our capabilities to reading text or binary data from any valid source and writing it to any valid destination. We will conclude our study of C with two additional topics: functions with varying numbers of arguments (`printf()` and `scanf()` are examples) and conditional preprocessor directives (often found in header files).

PROCESSING STREAMS AND FILES

The C language itself does not make any provisions for input and output. All input/output facilities are provided by library functions declared in `stdio.h`. Fortunately, a number of these functions have been standardized, so that the C programmer can assume that the standard input and output functions are available in any implementation (many other nonstandard functions may also be available). We begin our discussion by looking at files and streams as envisioned by the designers of the input/output library.

Files

A *file* is any source from which data can be read or any destination to which it can be sent. Although we usually think of files as sets of data stored on disk, the term can also refer to devices such as the keyboard, the display, a printer, or a communications port.

A file contains a sequence of bytes, which can represent either text or arbitrary binary data. C recognizes that a *text file* is divided into lines, and functions such as `scanf()` can recognize text representing numbers and strings. On the other hand, C views a *binary file* as nothing more than a sequence of bytes; C does not recognize any larger structures, such as records. For a binary file, all C will do is read or write a specified number of bytes; it is up to the programmer to know how the bytes are organized and to see that they are read and written in an appropriate manner.

In a text file, the end of each line is marked in some system-dependent way. In writing to a text file, each `\n` is translated into the system-dependent end-of-line marking; the reverse translation is performed when text is read from the file. For this reason, the characters read from or written to a text file may not coincide exactly with the characters stored in the file. In contrast, bytes are not changed when they are read from or written to a binary file. The bytes in the file conincide exactly with those that will be read or that have been written.

All files provide *sequential access*, in which bytes are read or written in the order in which they are stored in the file, or in which they are produced or consumed by a device. Some files, such as disk files, also offer *direct access* or *random access*, which allows the user to specify the byte position at which reading or writing will take place. Once a position is specified, a number of bytes are usually read or written sequentially before another position is specified.

Files are designated by *external names* that are known to the operating system (for devices) or listed in disk directories (for disk files). File-naming conventions vary from system to system, but the names can always be represented as strings. External names are too cumbersome to use every time we want to carry out an operation on a file. Thus programs designate files by simpler data items such as pointers or integers. All programming languages face the problem of associating the external names of files with the data items that designate the files in a program.

Streams

A file is represented in a C program by a *stream*, which abstracts the concept of a stream of bytes. Input, output, and related operations can be carried out in a uniform manner on streams, even though the physical nature of the corresponding files may vary considerably. A file is *opened* when it is connected to a stream and *closed* when that connection is broken.

Specifically, when a file is opened, C creates an object of type `FILE` to hold the information needed to access the file and to keep track of its status. There can only be one such object for each open file. We must not make copies of a `FILE` object (such as by assignment or by argument passing) because file operations carried out on one copy would not update other copies to reflect the altered state of the file. Therefore, the unique `FILE` object for each open file is referred to via a pointer, of which we can make as many copies as we need. It is these pointers that represent streams in C.

`FILE` is a macro that expands to a structure; `FILE` objects have the corresponding structure type. We declare streams as pointers to `FILE` objects:

```
FILE *inStream, *outStream, *ioStream;
```

We never actually declare `FILE` objects, but only pointers to them. Creation of `FILE` objects is reserved for the system.

A stream has certain properties, which are reflected by information stored in the `FILE` object. For example, a *text stream* is assumed to be connected to a file containing text, and a *binary stream* to a file containing binary data. Input and output operations on a text stream perform the \n translation described earlier; operations on a binary stream perform no such translation.

The operating-system calls that transfer data to and from a file are relatively expensive in terms of time. Transferring a block of bytes on each call is thus much faster than transferring the data byte by byte. We can accomplish such block transfers with the aid of a memory area called a *buffer*. Bytes written to the stream are stored in the buffer until enough have been accumulated to write to the file. Each block of bytes read from the file is stored in the buffer, allowing the data to be read from the stream byte by byte. The main drawback of buffering is that, by delaying transfers of input and output data, it can make the system less responsive to an interactive user.

A stream can be unbuffered, line buffered, or fully buffered. An *unbuffered* stream transfers each byte as soon as possible. A *fully buffered* stream transfers bytes in fixed-size blocks. *Line buffering*, which transfers one line of characters at a time, is a compromise between the efficiency of fully buffered streams and the responsiveness of unbuffered ones. Responsiveness is further improved by another feature: characters awaiting output will be transferred if input is requested from an unbuffered steam or from another line-buffered stream. This ensures that a prompt will always be printed before the program begins waiting for the user's response.

We can force buffered output to be transferred to a file by calling the function `fflush()`:

```
int fflush(FILE *stream);
```

The function causes the buffer for `stream` to be *flushed*: any output that has not yet been transferred to the file is transferred when the function is called. If the argument of `fflush()` is the null pointer, this flushing action is performed on all streams that permit output (input-only streams are not affected). The function returns 0 if successful and `EOF` if an error occurs while writing to a file.

For a file that allows positioning requests, a stream maintains a *file position indicator* giving the current position. The file position indicator can designate any byte in the file, or it can designate the end-of-file position, which is one position beyond the last byte. Functions are available for determining and changing the current position. An input or output operation transfers bytes sequentially, beginning at the current position.

Every stream has an end-of-file indicator and an error indicator. The *end-of-file indicator* is set if a read operation cannot be completed because the end of the file has been reached. The *error indicator* is set if an operation fails for any reason other than attempting to read beyond the end of the file.

We are already familiar with the predefined streams `stdin`, `stdout`, and `stderr`, which are created automatically at program startup. To ensure that error messages are delivered in a timely manner, `stderr` cannot be fully buffered—it must be unbuffered or line buffered. Stream `stdin` or `stdout` can be fully buffered only if it is *not* connected to an interactive device—that is, if the stream has been redirected to a disk file.

Streams vs. Handles

Because files are represented by streams, the standard I/O functions are sometimes called the *stream I/O* functions. Many implementations also provide another set of I/O functions in which files are represented by *handles*[*]—`int` file numbers generated by the operating system when each file is opened. A file is characterized entirely by its handle—the C program does not maintain any additional information, such as a `FILE` object, nor does it provide any buffering beyond that provided by the operating system. For this reason, the handle functions are sometimes referred to as the *unbuffered I/O* functions.

[*]Handles are known more formally as *file descriptors*.

Because some features of the unbuffered I/O functions are implementation dependent, only the stream I/O functions were standardized. For the sake of conforming to the ANSI standard, then, the stream functions are preferred over the unbuffered functions. On the other hand, implementations often provide a large number of nonstandard I/O functions, and these nonstandard functions often require handles as arguments rather than as streams. If you need the file operations provided by these nonstandard functions, you will have to provide them with the handles they require.

Fortunately, such implementations generally provide a nonstandard function that yields the handle of a file represented by a stream. Thus we can use the standard stream I/O functions as much as possible, then convert a stream to the corresponding handle when it is necessary to invoke a nonstandard function.

Generally, this book covers only stream I/O. In a later example, however, we will see how to use a handle and a nonstandard function to determine the size of a disk file, something that cannot be done with any standard function.

Opening and Closing Files

The function `fopen()` creates a stream with specified properties, connects it to a specified file, and returns a `FILE *` pointer representing the stream. This pointer is normally assigned to a `FILE *` variable, which is used thereafter to refer to the stream. If the attempt to open a file fails, `fopen()` returns the null pointer.

The function `fopen()` is declared in `stdio.h` as follows:

```
FILE *fopen(const char *filename, const char *mode);
```

Both arguments represent strings: `filename` is the external name of the file, and `mode` specifies some properties of the stream and some details of how the file will be opened.

The `mode` string contains one or more characters, each with its own significance. Generally, `r` specifies reading from an existing file, `w` specifies writing to a newly created file (or to an existing file whose previous contents have been discarded), and `a` specifies appending to the end of a new or existing file. A `b` specifies a binary file; its absence specifies a text file. A + indicates that the file is opened for both reading and writing. Table 7-1 lists all standard `mode` strings; additional implementation-dependent characters can follow the standard characters shown in the table.

Table 7-1

Standard mode *Strings*

mode STRING	FUNCTION
`"r"`	Open an existing text file for reading
`"w"`	Create a new text file (or discard the current contents of an existing one) for writing
`"a"`	Open an existing text file or create a new one for writing at the end of the file. The file position indicator is set to the end-of-file position before each write
`"rb"`	Open an existing binary file for reading
`"wb"`	Create a new binary file (or discard the current contents of an existing one) for writing
`"ab"`	Open an existing binary file or create a new one for writing at the end of the file. The file position indicator is set to the end-of-file position before each write
`"r+"`	Open an existing text file for reading and writing
`"w+"`	Create a new text file (or discard the current contents of an existing one) for reading and writing
`"a+"`	Open an existing text file or create a new one for reading and for writing at the end of the file. The file position indicator is set to the end-of-file position before each write
`"r+b"` or `"rb+"`	Open an existing binary file for reading and writing
`"w+b"` or `"wb+"`	Create a new binary file (or discard the current contents of an existing file) for reading and writing
`"a+b"` or `"ab+"`	Open an existing binary file or create a new one for reading and for writing at the end of the file. The file position indicator is set to the end-of-file position before each write

For example, if `inStream` has been declared as a `FILE *` pointer, then the statement

```
inStream = fopen("input.txt", "r");
```

tries to open for reading the existing text file with external name `input.txt`. If the file is opened successfully, `inStream` is set to point to the corresponding `FILE` object. If the attempt to open `input.txt` fails (as, for example, if no such file exists), `inStream` is set to the null pointer. To be safe, therefore, we should always follow a call to `open()` by code such as the following:

```
if (inStream == NULL) {
   fprintf(stderr, "Cannot open input file\n");
   exit(EXIT_FAILURE);
}
```

If we had written

```
inStream = fopen("input.bin", "rb");
```

then `input.bin` would have been opened for reading as a binary file.

If `outStream` is likewise a `FILE *` pointer, then

```
outStream = fopen("output.txt". "w");
```

opens a text file, `output.txt`, for writing only. If no such file currently exists, `open()` creates a new file named `output.txt`. If a file named `output.txt` is already present, it is opened but its current contents are discarded. In either case, the program is given an empty file to write to.

To open an output file without discarding existing data, we use `a` (append) mode:

```
outStream = fopen("output.txt", "a");
```

If `output.txt` does not exist, it is created, as before. If it does exist, it is opened with the file position indicator at the end-of-file position, just past the existing data. Writing is allowed only at the end of the file, so whatever new data is written is appended to the existing data.

Modes such as `r+b` and `w+b` open a file for both reading and writing. However, a function call that reads from the file cannot be followed immediately by a call that writes to the file, or vice versa. Before switching between reading and writing, you must call one of the positioning functions `fseek()`, `fsetpos()`, or `rewind()`. (These functions are discussed in the upcoming section on direct access.)

We can change the file to which a stream is connected with `freopen()`:

```
FILE *freopen(const char *filename,
              const char *mode,
              FILE *stream);
```

The function closes the file currently attached to `stream` and opens file `filename` with mode `mode`. If the operation is successful, `freopen()` returns the value of `stream`; otherwise, it returns the null pointer.

The most common use for freopen() is to connect the standard streams to other files. We cannot generally assign new pointer values to stdin, stdout, and stderr, which are macros whose expansions are implementation dependent. On the other hand, the statement

```
inStream = freopen("input.bin", "rb", stdin);
```

connects stdin to the binary file input.bin, which can now be referred to as stdin. All we need the value of inStream for is to determine if the function call was successful.

We close a stream (and the file attached to it) with fclose():

```
int fclose(FILE *stream);
```

The function returns 0 if successful and EOF if not. After a call such as

```
fclose(outStream);
```

the value of outStream is no longer valid and must not be used thereafter for any purpose.

All open files are closed automatically if a program terminates normally or via a call to exit(). They may not be closed, however, in the event of a hardware or software malfunction. A file that has been written to should be closed as soon as possible; if a crash occurs while the file is open, some or all of the data written to it may be lost.

Using Program Parameters

Obviously, a program must somehow obtain the external names of the files it is to open. A simple way is to prompt the user to enter the needed file names. A more complicated approach (from the program's point of view) is to display file names from a disk directory and have the user select the ones desired.

Still another popular approach is to pass the file names as *program parameters*. These are often called *command-line parameters*, because they are traditionally typed on the command line that executes a program. However, some operating systems with visual (mouse and menu) interfaces provide means for passing program parameters even though those systems do not have command lines. For example, the command line

```
trim text.in text.out
```

might call the program `trim` with `text.in` as its input file and `text.out` as its output file. The program would be passed three parameters by the operating system. Parameter 0 is always the name of the program, which in this case is `trim`. Parameter 1 would be the first data-file name, `text.in`, and parameter 2 would be the second data-file name, `text.out`

Program parameters are passed via arguments to `main()`. If a program is to receive program parameters, `main()` must declare two arguments, as follows:

```
int main(int argc, char** argv)
```

The value of `argc` is the number of program parameters. Remember that the name of the program is always passed as the first parameter and so is included in the count, which would be 3 for this example.

As shown in Figure 7-1, `argv` points to an array whose elements, in turn, point to parameter strings. Because `argv` points to the first element of an array, and that element points to the first character of a string, the type of `argv` is pointer-to-(pointer-to-char), or `char **`.

The first array element, `argv[0]`, points to a string containing the name of the program. If for any reason the program name cannot be supplied, `argv[0]` points to a null string. Elements `argv[1]` through `argv[argc - 1]` point to the strings for the remaining program parameters. Element `argv[argc]` contains the null pointer, which signals the end of the parameter array.

Listing 7-1 shows a version of the program `trim.c` (Listing 5-2) that reads from and writes to files named by program parameters. Because command lines are often garbled by hurried typing, we must be careful to check for errors caused by bad parameters. The program checks that the number of parameters is correct, and checks for errors after opening each file.

A couple of other minor changes to Listing 5-2 are necessary. In Listing 5-2, we wrote output strings with `puts()`, which supplied a newline at the end of each string. (The original newline read by `fgets()` was eliminated as whitespace.) Now, however, in order to write to a given stream, we must use `fputs()`, which does *not* supply a newline. We thus must store both a newline and a null character after the right-most non-whitespace character:

```
buf[i+1] = '\n';
buf[i+2] = '\0';
```

Figure 7-1

The elements of `argv` *point to successive command-line parameters. Element* `argv[0]` *points to the program name, and elements* `argv[1]` *through* `argv[argc - 1]` *point to the remaining parameters. Element* `argv[argc]` *contains a null pointer.*

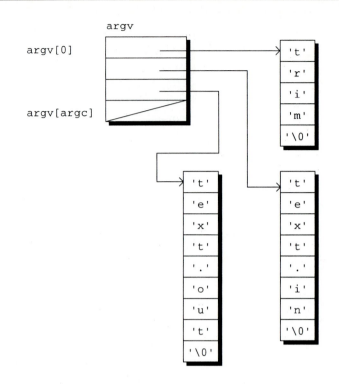

Command line: `trim text.in text.out`

To ensure that there is room in the `buf` for two additional characters, `sizeof buf - 1` is passed as the array size to `fgets()`. Were this not done, we could overflow `buf` if `fgets()` stopped reading because `buf` was full, and if the last character read was not whitespace. In that case there would be room in `buf` for only one character beyond the right-most whitespace character.

Reading and Writing Binary Data

Binary files allow values to be stored in their internal binary formats without having to be converted to character form on output and converted back into binary form on input. Binary values generally take up less space and can be stored and retrieved faster than the equivalent text values. The main drawback of binary files is that they cannot be written on one computer and read on another if the com-

Listing 7-1

```
/* File trim.c */
/* Remove trailing whitespace from strings */

#include <ctype.h>
#include <stdio.h>
#include <stdlib.h>
#include <string.h>

int main(int argc, char** argv)
{
   FILE *inStr, *outStr;
   char buf[255];
   int last, i;

   if (argc != 3) {
      fprintf(stderr, "Wrong number of parameters\n");
      exit(EXIT_FAILURE);
   }
   inStr = fopen(argv[1], "r");
   if (inStr == NULL) {
      fprintf(stderr, "Cannot open %s\n", argv[1]);
      exit(EXIT_FAILURE);
   }
   outStr = fopen(argv[2], "w");
   if (outStr == NULL) {
      fprintf(stderr, "Cannot open %s\n", argv[2]);
      exit(EXIT_FAILURE);
   }
   while ( fgets(buf, sizeof buf - 1, inStr) != NULL ) {
      last = strlen(buf) - 1;
      for (i = last; i >= 0; i--)
         if (!isspace(buf[i])) break;
      buf[i+1] = '\n';
      buf[i+2] = '\0';
      fputs(buf, outStr);
   }
   return EXIT_SUCCESS;
}
```

puters use different internal data formats. The big endian/little endian distinction, mentioned in Chapter 3, may intervene even when data formats would otherwise be compatible.

Because C does not recognize any internal structure in a binary file, it is up to the programmer to determine how many bytes to read or to write. If only one byte need be read or written, `fgetc()` or `fputc()` can be used. When more than one byte needs to be transferred, we usually use `fread()` or `fwrite()`:

```
size_t fread(void *ptr, size_t size,
            size_t nelem, FILE *stream);
size_t fwrite(void *ptr, size_t size,
            size_t nelem, FILE *stream);
```

The memory area from which bytes are to be read or into which they are to be written is treated as an array. The array begins at address `ptr` and has `nelem` elements, each containing `size` bytes. On input, `fread()` transfers `size * nelem` bytes from `stream` to the memory area designated by `ptr`. On output, `fwrite()` transfers the same number of bytes from the memory area to the stream.

Each function returns the number of complete elements that were successfully read or written. If `fread()` returns a value less than `nelem`, either the end of the file was encountered or a read error occurred. If `fwrite()` returns a value less than `nelem`, a write error occurred.

These functions can be used with either text or binary files, but their most common use is reading and writing binary data. For example, suppose we need to read or write one or more values of type `item_t`:

```
typedef struct {
    unsigned long item_num;
    unsigned quantity;
    double price;
} item_t;
```

Specifically, we want to read or write the array `items`, declared by

```
#define COUNT   150
item_t items[COUNT]:
```

The array name `items` yields a pointer to the first element, `sizeof(item_t)` yields the size of an element, and `COUNT` yields the number of elements. The statement

```
num_read = fread(items, sizeof(item_t), COUNT, inStream);
```

reads items from `inStream` into `items` and sets `num_read` to the number of items successfully read. Likewise,

```
num_written = fwrite(items, sizeof(item_t), COUNT, outStream);
```

writes items from `items` to `outStream`; `num_written` is set to the number of items successfully written.

If only one item is to be read or written, we can treat it as an array of one element. For example, suppose `item` is declared by

```
item_t item;
```

We can read a value of `item` with

```
fread(&item, sizeof item, 1, inStream);
```

and write a value with

```
fwrite(&item, sizeof item, 1, outStream);
```

Note that & is used with `item` but not with `items`. An array name is automatically converted to an address, but the address of a non-array variable must be computed with &.

Load and Save-As Commands for `store1.c` and `info.c`

As mentioned in Chapter 6, a fatal flaw of our information retrieval program (Listings 6-4 and 6-5) is that it cannot load data from or save data to disk files. Such capabilities are crucial for a practical program, because disk files are the only form of long-term storage available on many computers. We will now see how these capabilities can be added to the main program and to the array version of the storage module.

The revised version of `store1.c` provides two additional functions, `load()` and `save()` (Listing 7-2), each of which takes a binary stream as its argument:

```
result_t load(FILE *stream);
result_t save(FILE *stream);
```

Function `load()` reads a new data table from the given stream, and `save()` writes the current data table to the given stream. These declarations must be added to the header file `store.h`. Also, the enumeration type `result_t`, declared in `store.h`, must be

Listing 7-2

```
/* Additional functions for store1.c */

/* These functions give store1.h the ability to load or save
   a data table using a given stream.  Declarations for
   load() and save() must be placed in store.h, and the
   definition of result_t (in store.h) must be extended to
   define the additional constant IO_ERROR */

extern result_t load(FILE *stream)
{
    item_t *p;
    long file_size;
    size_t m_count;

    file_size = filelength(fileno(stream));
    if (file_size == -1L) return IO_ERROR;
    m_count = (size_t)file_size / sizeof(item_t);

    if (m_count > max_count) {
        p = realloc(table, (size_t)file_size);
        if (p == NULL)
            return OUT_OF_MEMORY;
        else {
            table = p;
            max_count = m_count;
        }
    }
    count = fread(table, sizeof(item_t), m_count, stream);
    if (count < m_count) return IO_ERROR;
    return SUCCESS;
}

extern result_t save(FILE *stream)
{
    size_t number;

    number = fwrite(table, sizeof(item_t), count, stream);
    if (number < count) return IO_ERROR;
    return SUCCESS;
}
```

extended to define the additional constant `IO_ERROR`, which the new functions will use to report read or write errors.

We begin with `save()`, which is the simpler of the two. This function uses a single call to `fwrite()` to write the entire data array:

```
number = fwrite(table, sizeof(item_t), count, stream);
```

Here `table` points to the first element (and hence the first byte) of the data array, the expression `sizeof(item_t)` yields the size of an element, `count` is the number of elements to be written, and `stream` is the stream to which the data is to be written. The value assigned to `number` is the number of elements actually written; if `number` is less than `count`, a write error occurred:

```
if (number < count) return IO_ERROR;
```

We can read the data array most efficiently if we know its size in advance. We can then allocate a large enough array to hold the data, and read the entire array with a single call to `fread()`. Unfortunately, there is no standard function that will give the size of a disk file. To illustrate using a nonstandard function, particularly one that requires a handle, we will use `filelength()`, which is provided by many implementations of C for MS-DOS. We will also need the nonstandard function `fileno()`, which returns the handle for the file attached to a given stream. The two functions are declared as follows:

```
long filelength(int handle);
int fileno(FILE *stream);
```

The declaration of `filelength()` is in io.h, a nonstandard header file that contains declarations for a number of nonstandard I/O functions. The declaration for `fileno()` is in `stdio.h`.

We compute the size of the file by applying `filelength()` to the handle returned by `fileno()`:

```
file_size = filelength(fileno(stream));
```

In case of error, `filelength()` returns the value −1:

```
if (file_size == -1L) return IO_ERROR;
```

If no error occurred, we compute the number of elements, `m_count`, in the file by dividing the file size by the size of one element:

```
m_count = (size_t)file_size / sizeof(item_t);
```

The type cast converts the file size from type `long` (which is returned by `filelength()`) to type `size_t` (which is used by the standard I/O functions for object sizes).

If the number of elements to be read is greater than the current size of the data array, the array must be reallocated:

```
if (m_count > max_count) {
    p = realloc(table, (size_t)file_size);
    if (p == NULL)
        return OUT_OF_MEMORY;
    else {
        table = p;
        max_count = m_count;
    }
}
```

With these preliminaries out of the way, we call `fread()` to read `m_count` elements:

```
count = fread(table, sizeof(item_t), m_count, stream);
```

The number of elements actually read is assigned to `count`. If `count` is less than `m_count`, the number of elements we have determined to be in the file, then an error must have occurred:

```
if (count < m_count) return IO_ERROR;
```

Listing 7-3 shows the functions `do_load()`, `do_save_as()`, and `do_save()` that must be added to `info.c` to support loading and saving files. Declarations for these functions must be placed near the beginning of `info.c`, along with the declarations for the other `do_` functions. The prompt and the switch statement must be extended to call these functions in response to corresponding commands. The usual command letters are L for `do_load()`, S for `do_save()`, and A for `do_save_as()`.

Also declared at file level is the array that holds the current file name:

```
char fileName[256] = "";
```

Declaring `fileName` as a global variable allows the file name set by `do_load()` or `do_save_as()` to be used as a default for `do_save()`.

There is a macro, **FILENAME_MAX**, that gives the array size needed for a file name. However, we want to read the file name with `scanf()`, and a macro is not suitable for specifying a `%s` field

Listing 7-3

```
/*  Additional functions for info.c */

/* These functions provide info.c with the ability to load
   its data from or save its data to a specified disk file.
   Declarations for do_load(), do_save_as(), and do_save()
   must be placed near the beginnning of info.c, along with
   the following declaration: */

char fileName[256] = "";

/* We declare fileName at file level so the value set by
   do_load() or do_save_as() can be used as a default for
   do_save().  The prompt and the switch statement must be
   updated to call these functions in reponse to specified
   commands. */

void do_load(void)
{
    FILE *inStr;
    result_t r;

    printf("File to load: ");
    scanf("%255s", fileName);

    inStr = fopen(fileName, "rb");
    if (inStr == NULL) {
       printf("Cannot open file\n");
       fileName[0] = '\0';
       return;
    }
    r = load(inStr);
    fclose(inStr);
    if (r == SUCCESS) return;
    fileName[0] = '\0';
    if (r == OUT_OF_MEMORY)
       printf("Insufficient memory to load file\n");
    if (r == IO_ERROR)
       printf("IO error while reading file\n");
}
```

(continued)

```
void do_save_as(void)
{
    FILE *outStr;
    result_t r;

    printf("Save as: ");
    scanf("%255s", fileName);

    outStr = fopen(fileName, "wb");
    if (outStr == NULL) {
        printf("Cannot open file\n");
        fileName[0] = '\0';
        return;
    }
    r = save(outStr);
    fclose(outStr);
    if (r == IO_ERROR) {
        fileName[0] = '\0';
        printf("IO error while writing file\n");
    }
}

void do_save(void)
{
    FILE *outStr;
    result_t r;
    char *tempName;
    char backName[256];
    char *dot_p;

    if (strlen(fileName) == 0) {
        do_save_as();
        return;
    }
    tempName = tmpnam(NULL);
    outStr = fopen(tempName, "wb");
    if (outStr == NULL) {
        printf("Cannot open new file\n");
        return;
    }
    r = save(outStr);
    fclose(outStr);
```

```
if (r == IO_ERROR) {
    printf("IO error while writing file\n");
    return;
}

strcpy(backName, fileName);
dot_p = strchr(backName, '.');
if (dot_p != NULL) *dot_p = '\0';
strcat(backName, ".bak");

remove(backName);
rename(fileName, backName);
rename(tempName, fileName);
}
```

width (macros inside string literals are not expanded). Therefore, we use the larger-than-necessary array size 256, and the format string `"%255s"` in `scanf()`.

The functions `do_load()` and `do_save_as()` are straightforward. Each obtains a file name from the user and tries to open the corresponding file (with mode `"rb"` for `do_load()` and `"wb"` for `do_save_as()`). If the file is successfully opened, the function calls `load()` or `save()` to perform the desired operation, then closes the file. An error message is printed if `load()` or `save()` returns an error code.

The function `do_save_as()` is not recommended for replacing an existing file with an updated copy. When a file is opened with w in the mode string, the current contents of the file are immediately discarded. If a system or program crash should occur while the new file is being written, then some data will be lost—perhaps all of it—because newly written data may not be made permanent until the file is closed. In the next section we will look at `do_save()`, which makes sure that a new file has been successfully written before changing the existing file into a backup file.

File Manipulation and a Save Operation for `info.c`

Most implementations supply a number of functions for manipulating disk files. Only four of these have been standardized. These standard functions provide some useful capabilities and an introduction to file manipulation. We can use them to create a temporary file, to create a temporary file name, to delete a disk file, and to change the external name of a disk file.

We can create a temporary file with `tmpfile()`, which is declared by

```
FILE *tmpfile(void);
```

The function opens a binary file for reading and writing (mode `w+b` or `wb+`) and returns the corresponding stream pointer, which is null if the file could not be opened. The name of the temporary file does not conflict with any existing file name, and the file is removed when it is closed or when the program terminates.

We can create a name suitable for a temporary file with `tmpnam()`, which is declared by

```
char *tmpnam(char *s);
```

The function returns a pointer to a file name that does not conflict with the name of any existing file name. If `s` is not null, it points to the array in which the file name is to be stored. The size of the array must be at least that given by the macro `L_tmpnam`. If `s` is null, `tmpnam()` stores the file name internally, where it will remain intact until `tmpnam()` is called again. The macro `TMP_MAX` gives the maximum number of temporary file names that can be generated. For many implementations, this number is in the tens of thousands and so is not a serious limitation.

Do not confuse a temporary *file* and a temporary *file name*. A temporary *file*, created and opened with `tmpfile()`, is automatically deleted when it is closed or when the program terminates. A temporary *file name*, created with `tmpnam()`, is just a computer-generated file name guaranteed not to be the same as the name of an existing file. Beyond that, the name is used just like any other file name. We create a corresponding file by opening it with `fopen()` and closing it with `fclose()`. If we want to delete the file, we must do so explicitly by calling `remove()`. We can retain the file indefinitely, if we wish, either under its temporary name or after changing the temporary name to one that is more meaningful to the user.

As mentioned, we delete a disk file by calling `remove()`, which is declared by

```
int remove(const char* filename);
```

The function returns zero if successful and a nonzero value otherwise. An open file should be closed before removing it.

The function `rename()` changes the name of a disk file from `old` to `new`:

```
int rename(const char *old, const char *new);
```

The function returns zero if successful and a nonzero value to signal an error. What happens when there is already a file with name `new` is implementation dependent.

We are now in a position to understand the `do_save()` function in Listing 7-3. We want to write a new version of a file without endangering the current version, which will be retained as a backup file. To be as cautious as possible, we do not want to change or delete any existing file until we know that a new version has been successfully written. We can proceed as follows:

1. Write the a new file using a temporary file name.

2. Delete any existing backup file.

3. Rename the current file as the backup file.

4. Rename the new file as the current file.

The temporary file name can be generated by `tmpnam()`, or it can be some valid but unlikely name such as $$$$$$$$.$$$.

For the name of the current file, `do_save_as()` uses the current contents of `fileName`, which is shared by `do_load()`, `do_save_as()`, and `do_save()`. This array is initialized to the null string and is set to the null string if an error occurs during a call to `do_load()` or `do_save_as()`. If `fileName` contains the null string, there is no valid current file name; in this case `do_save()` passes the call to `do_save_as()`, which will prompt the user for a new file name:

```
if (strlen(fileName) == 0) {
    do_save_as();
    return;
}
```

Next, the function creates a temporary file name with `tmpnam()` and opens a file with that name:

```
tempName = tmpnam(NULL);
outStr = fopen(tempName, "wb");
```

The data array is written to `outStr` as in `do_save_as()`.

We now need to construct a name for the backup file. This process is implementation dependent due to differing file-naming conventions. The example follows MS-DOS conventions, in which a file name ends with an optional extension consisting of a period and up to three characters (as in `items.dat` and `report.doc`). The name of the corresponding backup file is generated by replacing the extension with `.bak` (as in `items.bak` and `report.bak`) or by appending `.bak` to a file name that has no extension.

The program uses `strcpy()` to copy the current file name from `fileName` to `backName`. Then `strchr()` is used to find the period, if any. If a period is present, it is replaced by the null character, terminating the name at that point. Finally, `strcat()` is called to append the new extension `.bak`:

```
strcpy(backName, fileName);
dot_p = strchr(backName, '.');
if (dot_p != NULL) *dot_p = '\0';
strcat(backName, ".bak");
```

All that's left is the renaming. We first delete any existing backup file, an operation that can legitimately fail if no such file exists. Then the current file is renamed as the backup file and the newly written file is renamed as the current file:

```
remove(backName);
rename(fileName, backName);
rename(tempName, fileName);
```

Direct Access

Direct access files do not have to be designated in any special way. C allows direct access for any file whose storage device permits the current file position to be retrieved and changed. The only situation in which C forces sequential access is when a file is opened with a in the mode string. In that case, data can be written only at the end of the file, enforcing sequential access for writing.

C provides two pairs of functions for file positioning. The two differ mainly in how a file position is represented. For `fgetpos()` and `fsetpos()`, the position is stored as a value of type `fpos_t`, and the coding is implementation dependent. For `ftell()` and `fseek()`, the position is stored as a value of type `long`. For binary files, this `long` value can be interpreted as a byte number. A fifth positioning function, `rewind()`, is essentially a special case of `fseek()`.

The first two functions are declared as follows:

```
int fgetpos(FILE *stream, fpos_t *pos);
int fsetpos(FILE *stream, const fpos_t *pos);
```

The first argument of each function specifies the stream, and the second argument is the address of the variable that holds the file position. For example,

```
fpos_t cur_pos;
```

declares a variable for holding a file position. The call

```
fgetpos(ioStr, &cur_pos);
```

stores the current position of `ioStr` in `cur_pos`. If at some later time we wish to return to this position, we can do so with

```
fsetpos(ioStr, &cur_pos);
```

Because the coding of file positions is implementation dependent, we can neither interpret a position value obtained with `fgetpos()` nor create a position value for use with `fsetpos()`. All we can do is supply `fsetpos()` with position values that were previously obtained with `fgetpos()`.

Both functions return zero if successful and a nonzero value if an error occurred. A successful call to `fsetpos()` clears the end-of-file indicator for the stream, and discards any character "pushed back" into the stream by a previous call to `ungetc()`.

The other two positioning functions are declared as follows:

```
long ftell(FILE *stream);
int fseek(FILE *stream, long offset, int mode);
```

A call to `ftell()` returns the current file position as a `long` value; if the call is unsuccessful, −1 is returned. For a binary file, the return value is a byte offset from the beginning of the file: `ftell()` returns 0 for the first byte of the file, 1 for the second byte, and so on. For text files, the significance of the return value is still implementation dependent, because of uncertainties about how the ends of lines are coded.

For `fseek()`, the value of `mode` specifies how the value of `offset` will be interpreted. The three possible values of `mode` are given by `SEEK_SET`, `SEEK_CUR`, and `SEEK_END`. For binary files, the value of `offset` is the byte offset from a position determined by the value of `mode`:

MODE	MEANING OF OFFSET
SEEK_SET	Offset is from beginning of file.
SEEK_CUR	Offset is from current position.
SEEK_END	Offset is from end-of-file position.

For `SEEK_SET`, the first byte of the file has offset 0, the second has offset 1, and so on. For `SEEK_CUR`, the byte at the current position has offset 0, the byte following it has offset 1, the byte preceding it has offset −1, and so on. For `SEEK_END`, the end-of-file position has offset 0, the last byte in the file has offset −1, the byte before that has offset −2, and so on. Offsets returned by `ftell()` should be used with `SEEK_SET`.

For text files, the only numerical value we can safely specify as an offset is 0. Depending on the mode, offset 0 represents, respectively, the beginning of the file, the current position, or the end-of-file position. The only other offset values we can use are those returned by `ftell()`, and they must be used with mode `SEEK_SET`.

Note that the call

```
fseek(stream, 0L, SEEK_CUR);
```

does not change the current file position. We can use this call when we must call a positioning function to switch between reading and writing but we do not actually want to change the current position.

As with `fsetpos()`, a successful call to `fseek()` returns zero and clears the end-of-file indicator; an unsuccessful call returns a nonzero value.

We can set the file position indicator to the beginning of the file with `rewind()`, declared by

```
void rewind(FILE *stream);
```

This function calls `fseek(stream, 0L, SEEK_SET)`, then clears the error indicator for the stream.

Listings 7-4 and 7-5 show demonstration programs illustrating direct access. The program in Listing 7-4 writes four lines to a text file, then reads the lines back in an arbitrarily chosen order. The program in Listing 7-5 writes an array of structure objects to a binary file, then reads them back in an arbitrarily chosen order.

In Listing 7-4, a text file is opened with a temporary file name:

```
fileName = tmpnam(NULL);
ioStr = fopen(fileName, "w+");
```

Before writing each line, `fgetpos()` is called to store the current file position in one of the `fpos_t` variables, `line1`, `line2`, `line3`, or `line4`:

```
fgetpos(ioStr, &line1);
fputs("Now is the time\n", ioStr);
```

Listing 7-4

```
/* File demo1.c */
/* Demonstrate direct access to text file */

#include <stdio.h>
#include <stdlib.h>

int main(void)
{
   char *fileName;
   char lineBuf[80];
   FILE *ioStr;
   fpos_t line1, line2, line3, line4;

   fileName = tmpnam(NULL);
   ioStr = fopen(fileName, "w+");

   fgetpos(ioStr, &line1);
   fputs("Now is the time\n", ioStr);

   fgetpos(ioStr, &line2);
   fputs("for all good people\n", ioStr);

   fgetpos(ioStr, &line3);
   fputs("to come to the aid\n", ioStr);

   fgetpos(ioStr, &line4);
   fputs("of their country.\n", ioStr);

   fsetpos(ioStr, &line3);
   fgets(lineBuf, 80, ioStr);
   printf("%s", lineBuf);

   fsetpos(ioStr, &line1);
   fgets(lineBuf, 80, ioStr);
   printf("%s", lineBuf);

   fsetpos(ioStr, &line4);
   fgets(lineBuf, 80, ioStr);
   printf("%s", lineBuf);
```

(continued)

```
      fsetpos(ioStr, &line2);
      fgets(lineBuf, 80, ioStr);
      printf("%s", lineBuf);

      fclose(ioStr);
      remove(fileName);
      return EXIT_SUCCESS;
}
```

Before reading and printing each line, the program uses `fsetpos()` and an `fpos_t` variable to set the current file position to the beginning of one of the lines:

```
      fsetpos(ioStr, &line3);
      fgets(lineBuf, 80, ioStr);
      printf("%s", lineBuf);
```

The program prints the lines in the order in which they are read back from the file, producing the following output:

```
to come to the aid
Now is the time
of their country.
for all good people
```

The program in Listing 7-5 opens a temporary file with `tmpfile()`:

```
      ioStr = tmpfile();
```

Remember that `tmpfile()` opens a binary file with mode w+b.

The program defines a structure type `rec_t`, and it declares and initializes an array of six structure objects. This entire array is written to the binary file:

```
      fwrite(rec_array, rec_size, 6, ioStr);
```

Here, `rec_array` is the name of the array, and `rec_size` has been assigned the value `sizeof(rec_t)`.

We can now think of the file as containing six records, each corresponding to one array element. However, C knows nothing about these records, so it is up to us to specify the proper file position and the number of bytes for each record we want to read.

Assume that the records are numbered starting with 0, and the

Listing 7-5

```
/* File demo2.c */
/* Demonstrate direct access to binary file */

#include <stdio.h>
#include <stdlib.h>

typedef struct {
    int item;
    double price;
} rec_t;

rec_t rec_array[] = { {1000, 19.95}, {2000, 29.95},
                      {3000, 39.95}, {4000, 49.95},
                      {5000, 59.95}, {6000, 69.95}  };

int main(void)
{
    rec_t rec;
    size_t rec_num;
    size_t rec_size = sizeof(rec_t);
    FILE *ioStr;

    ioStr = tmpfile();        /* Opened with mode "w+b" */
    fwrite(rec_array, rec_size, 6, ioStr);

    rec_num = 4;
    fseek(ioStr, rec_num * rec_size, SEEK_SET);
    fread(&rec, rec_size, 1, ioStr);
    printf("Record %d: item = %d; price = %.2f\n",
            rec_num, rec.item, rec.price);

    rec_num = 0;
    fseek(ioStr, rec_num * rec_size, SEEK_SET);
    fread(&rec, rec_size, 1, ioStr);
    printf("Record %d: item = %d; price = %.2f\n",
            rec_num, rec.item, rec.price);

    rec_num = 2;
    fseek(ioStr, rec_num * rec_size, SEEK_SET);
    fread(&rec, rec_size, 1, ioStr);                 (continued)
```

```
    printf("Record %d: item = %d; price = %.2f\n",
            rec_num, rec.item, rec.price);

    rec_num = 5;
    fseek(ioStr, rec_num * rec_size, SEEK_SET);
    fread(&rec, rec_size, 1, ioStr);
    printf("Record %d: item = %d; price = %.2f\n",
            rec_num, rec.item, rec.price);

    rec_num = 3;
    fseek(ioStr, rec_num * rec_size, SEEK_SET);
    fread(&rec, rec_size, 1, ioStr);
    printf("Record %d: item = %d; price = %.2f\n",
            rec_num, rec.item, rec.price);

    rec_num = 1;
    fseek(ioStr, rec_num * rec_size, SEEK_SET);
    fread(&rec, rec_size, 1, ioStr);
    printf("Record %d: item = %d; price = %.2f\n",
            rec_num, rec.item, rec.price);

    return EXIT_SUCCESS;
}
```

---

number of the desired record has been assigned to rec_num. The offset of this record from the beginning of the file is

```
    rec_num * rec_size
```

and its size is, of course, rec_size. The following statements read the designated record into the rec_t variable rec:

```
    fseek(ioStr, rec_num * rec_size, SEEK_SET);
    fread(&rec, rec_size, 1, ioStr);
```

The program uses these statements repeatedly to read a record and to print the data contained in it:

```
rec_num = 4;
fseek(ioStr, rec_num * rec_size, SEEK_SET);
fread(&rec, rec_size, 1, ioStr);
printf("Record %d: item = %d; price = %.2f\n",
        rec_num, rec.item, rec.price);
```

The program reads and prints all six records in an arbitrary order, producing the following printout:

```
Record 4: item = 5000; price = 59.95
Record 0: item = 1000; price = 19.95
Record 2: item = 3000; price = 39.95
Record 5: item = 6000; price = 69.95
Record 3: item = 4000; price = 49.95
Record 1: item = 2000; price = 29.95
```

Controlling Buffering

You can use the following functions to control buffering for stream `stream`:

```
void setbuf(FILE *stream, char *buf);
void setvbuf(FILE *stream, char *buf, int mode, size_t size);
```

For `setvbuf()`, the argument `buf` points to a user-allocated buffer array, whose size is given by the argument `size`. If `buf` is null, `setvbuf()` will allocate the buffer array, which will be de-allocated when the file is closed.

The argument `mode` specifies the form of buffering to be used. Its value must be given by one of the following macros: `_IOFBF` for full buffering, `_IOLBF` for line buffering, or `_IONBF` for no buffering.

Function `setbuf()` specifies a default mode and the buffer size, the latter given by the macro `BUFSIZ`. Specifically, if `buf` is not null, `setbuf()` calls `setvbuf()` as follows:

```
setbuf(stream, buf, _IOFBF, BUFSIZ);
```

Argument `buf` must point to an array of at least `BUFSIZ` bytes. If `buf` is null, `setbuf()` calls `setvbuf()` as follows:

```
setbuf(stream, NULL, _IOFNBF, BUFSIZ);
```

We can only call `setbuf()` or `setvbuf()` immediately after a file is opened, before any other operations are performed on the stream. Note that the system normally makes reasonable provisions for buffering, so that we usually do not need to call `setbuf()` or `setvbuf()` to do buffering our way.

More About Error Handling

As we have gone along, we have discussed how the value returned by each function could be used to detect and diagnose errors. We now look at some additional functions that provide additional information about errors.

The end-of-file and error indicators can be accessed and cleared with the following functions:

```
int feof(FILE *stream);
int ferror(FILE *stream);
void clearerr(FILE *stream);
```

Functions `feof()` and `ferror()` return a nonzero value if the corresponding indicator is set and return zero otherwise. Function `clearerr()` clears both indicators.

If an error occurs or end-of-file is encountered while reading, the input function returns a value indicating that some of the requested input could not be read. After such an indication, we can use `ferror()` or `feof()` to determine whether an error occurred or end-of-file was encountered.

The header file `errno.h` defines a macro, `errno`, which behaves like a global variable. Some library functions, particularly math functions, assign a nonzero value to `errno` when an error occurs. Which functions make such assignments, and what the various error numbers mean, are largely implementation dependent.

The only I/O functions that are required to set `errno` are `fgetpos()`, `fsetpos()`, and `ftell()`. Other functions, such as `fopen()`, may well do so in a particular implementation, but they are not required to do so by the standard.

To use `errno`, a program must include `errno.h`. We set `errno` to zero just before calling a function and test it immediately afterwards:

```
errno = 0;
if ( fsetpos(stream, &pos) ) {
    /* Test value of errno */
}
```

The call to `fsetpos()` returns a nonzero value if an error occurred. In that case, the value of `errno` is checked in an attempt to obtain more information about the error.

Several facilities are provided for interpreting `errno` values. Header file `errno.h` defines a series of constants (represented as macros) that can be used to test the value of `errno` for various error conditions. All these macro names begin with E. The only ones that are specified in the standard are for math errors: EDOM for a domain error and ERANGE for a range error.

Header file `string.h` provides a function, `strerror()`, that returns an error message corresponding to a particular error number:

```
char *strerror(int errcode);
```

Thus `strerror(errno)` yields a pointer to the error message corresponding to the current value of `errno`.

Even more convenient is `perror()`, which prints (on `stderr`) the system error message along with one specified by the programmer. The function is declared in `stdio.h`:

```
void perror(const char *s)
```

If `s` is not null, the program first prints the string pointed to by `s` (the programmer's error message) followed by a colon, a space, the system error message, and a newline. The system error message is the same one that would be returned by `strerror(errno)`. Note that `perror()`, unlike `strerror()`, does not take an error number argument: `perror()` accesses the value of `errno` directly.

With the aid of `perror()`, our preceding example can be made somewhat more explicit:

```
errno = 0;
if ( fsetpos(stream, &pos) ) {
    perror("Cannot position file");
    /* Code to terminate program or
       recover from error */
}
```

Reading from and Writing to Strings

The functions `sscanf()` and `sprintf()` are similar to `fscanf()` and `fprintf()` except that the "s functions" read from and write to strings rather than streams. Specifically, the first argument of `sscanf()` points to the string containing the text to be read, and the first argument of `sprintf()` points to the character array in which the function will store its output. The output is stored as a string—a sequence of characters terminated by a null character.

For example, consider the following declarations:

```
char s[] = "100 1000000 1.75";
int m;
long n;
double x;
```

The statement

```
sscanf(s, "%d%ld%lf", &m, &n, &x);
```

reads from the string s using the given format string. Each of the three values in s is converted to binary form and assigned to a variable, exactly as if the input had been read from a stream.

For an example of output to a character array, consider the following declarations:

```
char ss[80];
int n_cats = 12;
int n_dogs = 9;
```

The statement

```
sprintf(ss, "She has %d cats and %d dogs", n_cats, n_dogs);
```

stores in ss the string

```
She has 12 cats and 9 dogs
```

This is the same string that `printf()` or `fprintf()` would have written to an output stream.

We see that `sscanf()` and `sprintf()` are not really I/O functions but rather powerful string-processing functions. With `sscanf()`, we can decompose a given string into individual data items, using the format string as a pattern or template to guide the decomposition. Likewise, `sprintf()` makes it easy to assemble a string from a series of constituent data items, the format string again serving as a template.

Like other `scanf()` functions, `sscanf()` returns `EOF` if no conversions can be done. Otherwise, it returns the number of items that were assigned to variables, which can be fewer than expected if an error occurred. The function `sprintf()` returns the number of characters written to the character array, not counting the terminating null character.

FUNCTIONS WITH VARYING NUMBERS OF ARGUMENTS

Many languages have input and output functions (or statements) that allow any number of values to be read or written in a single operation. Languages that do not provide this capability, such as Modula-2, demonstrate how tedious it is to have to make many separate function calls for reading or writing a single line. Some languages, such as Pascal, allow varying numbers of arguments only for input and output functions. In C, however, input and output functions are on the same footing as other library functions, so any capability needed for input and output must be made available to all functions.

In a function declaration, an ellipsis (. . .) stands for any number of additional arguments. For example, the functions in the `scanf()` and `printf()` families can be declared as follows:

```
int scanf(const char *format, ...);
int printf(const char *format, ...);

int fscanf(FILE *stream, const char *format, ...);
int fprintf(FILE *stream, const char *format, ...);

int sscanf(const char *s, const char *format, ...);
int sprintf(char *s, const char *format, ...);
```

The ellipsis must be the last item in the argument list, and it must be preceded by at least one declared argument.

The declared argument that immediately precedes the ellipsis serves as a starting point for accessing the remaining arguments, and is subject to some restrictions for that reason. The right-most declared argument must not have a type that is changed by the compiler—that is, it must not have an array or function type (although *pointers* to array elements and functions are OK), nor may it have any type that is subject to promotion. Also, it must not have storage class `register` because it can provide access to the remaining arguments only if it is actually stored in memory.

Basically, the function accesses the undeclared arguments by using the address of the right-most declared argument to calculate the address of the first undeclared argument. A pointer is initialized to this address and stepped through the undeclared arguments. The details of the process depend on the implementation, however. To hide these implementation-dependent details, the library provides a header file `stdarg.h` containing macros for accessing the undeclared arguments.

The macro `va_list` declares the pointer variable that will be used to access the arguments. The following declares `ap` as such an argument pointer:

```
va_list ap;
```

The function macro `va_start()` initializes `ap` to point to the first undeclared argument. The parameters for `va_start()` are the argument pointer and the right-most declared argument. Using the input and output functions as examples, assume that the right-most declared argument is `format`. Then the statement

```
va_start(ap, format);
```

initializes `ap` to point to the first undeclared argument.

The macro `va_arg()` returns the current argument (the one designated by the argument pointer) and steps the argument pointer to the next argument. The parameters of `va_arg()` are the argument pointer and the type of the argument to be fetched. For example, if the current argument has type `long`, we can fetch it and assign it to the `long` variable `arg` with the following:

```
arg = va_arg(ap, long);
```

The macro `va_end()` does any cleanup necessary for the function to return normally. It takes one parameter, the argument pointer:

```
va_end(ap);
```

Often, no final cleanup is needed, in which case `va_end()` has little or nothing to do. It must still be called, however, for the benefit of those implementations that need it.

After `va_start()` has been called, we can pass the argument pointer to another function, which can use `va_arg()` to get argument values. However, `va_end()` must be called by the same function that called `va_start()`.

As a simple example, Listing 7-6 shows a function `sum()` that can sum any number of integers. The first argument gives the number of values to be added; the remaining arguments are the values in question. For example,

```
n = sum(3, 7, 4, 9);
```

assigns n the value 20, the sum of 7, 4, and 9. Likewise,

```
n = sum(5, 1, 3, 5, 7, 9);
```

assigns n the value 25, the sum of 1, 3, 5, 7, and 9. We declare `sum()` as follows:

```
int sum(int count, ...);
```

Here, `count` is the required declared argument. The remaining arguments, which give the values to be added, are all undeclared.

In Listing 7-6, the following code fetches the undeclared `int` arguments and accumulates their sum in `total`:

Listing 7-6

```
/* File sum.c */
/* Function to sum a given number of integers */

#include <stdarg.h>

int sum(int count, ...)
{
    int i, total;
    va_list ap;

    total = 0;
    va_start(ap, count);
    for (i = 1; i <= count; i++)
        total += va_arg(ap, int);
    va_end(ap);

    return total;
}
```

```
    total = 0;
    va_start(ap, count);
    for (i = 1; i <= count; i++)
        total += va_arg(ap, int);
    va_end(ap);
```

Each call to va_arg() returns the value of another argument, which is added to the value of total.

To aid programmers in writing their own customized output functions, stdio.h provides three printf()-style functions that access the values to be printed via an argument pointer ap:

```
int vprintf(const char *format, va_list ap);
int vfprintf(FILE *stream, const char *format, va_list ap);
int vsprintf(char *s, const char *format, va_list ap);
```

These all work like the corresponding "non v" functions: values are printed to a stream or string under control of a format string. Instead of taking its own list of value arguments, however, each function uses ap to read arguments that have already been passed to another function, normally a customized output function. We must call `va_start()` before calling one of these functions and `va_end()` afterwards.

For example, if our program uses a window-style interface, we might want to write a function `wprintf()` whose first argument specifies the window that is to receive the output. Other arguments could specify other properties of the displayed text, such as position, size, color, and font. For this purpose, `vsprintf()` would likely be the most useful function. It would convert the desired output to a string, which could then be passed to the function for displaying a string in a given window.

The example in Listing 7-7 is considerably more modest. The function `nprintf()` numbers the lines it prints to `stdout`, preceding each line with a four-digit line number. The function assumes that each call prints only one line. If we use a format string that prints more than one line, the line numbering will not be correct. We declare `nprint()` just like the other functions in the `printf()` family:

```
int nprintf(const char *format, ...);
```

The current line number is stored in a static variable, `line_num`, which is initialized before program execution begins and retains its value from one function call to the next. The function begins by printing and incrementing the line number:

```
printf("%04d: ", line_num);
line_num += 1;
```

Next, `vprintf()` is called to print the undeclared arguments that were passed to `nprintf()`. We must call `va_start()` before calling `vprintf()` and `va_end()` afterwards:

```
va_start(ap, format);
retval = vprintf(format, ap);
va_end(ap);
```

Note that `vprintf()` is given the same format string that was passed to `nprintf()`. Also, because `format` is the only declared argument of `nprintf()`, it is the argument that `va_start()` uses to gain access to the undeclared arguments. Here is an example of the function in operation: the statements

```
nprintf("She has %d cats and %d dogs\n", 7, 6);
nprintf("He has %d cows and %d sheep\n", 17, 12);
nprintf("You have %d mice and %d ducks\n", 4, 2);
```

Listing 7-7

```
/* File nprintf.c */
/* Function to number lines of printed output */

#include <stdio.h>
#include <stdarg.h>

int nprintf(char *format, ...)
{
    static line_num = 1;
    int retval;
    va_list ap;

    printf("%04d: ", line_num);
    line_num += 1;

    va_start(ap, format);
    retval = vprintf(format, ap);
    va_end(ap);

    return retval;
}
```

produce the printout

```
0001: She has 7 cats and 6 dogs
0002: He has 17 cows and 12 sheep
0003: You have 4 mice and 2 ducks
```

CONDITIONAL DIRECTIVES

We conclude our study of C with an additional feature of the pre-processor. *Conditional directives* specify that certain program lines will be processed only under certain conditions, and skipped otherwise. Such directives are frequently found in header files, particularly if the implementation is intended for use with more than one computer, operating system, or memory model (memory models are discussed in Appendix 4).

The simplest conditional directive has the following form:

```
#if expression
    /* program text */
#endif
```

The expression, which must be built from integer constants (often represented by macros), yields zero for *false* and a nonzero value for *true*, as usual. If *expression* is *true*, the program lines between the #if and #endif directives are compiled (or preprocessed, if they are preprocessor directives). If *expression* is *false*, those lines are skipped.

A conditional directive can have an #else part:

```
#if expression
    /* program text */
#else
    /* program text */
#endif
```

If *expression* is *true*, the lines between the #if and #else directives are compiled. Otherwise, the lines between #else and #endif are compiled.

A conditional directive can have one or more #elif parts, which work like else-if parts in an ordinary if statement:

```
#if expression-1
    /* program text */
#elif expression-2
    /* program text */
#elif expression-3
    /* program  text */
#else
    /* program text */
#endif
```

Only one block of program text is compiled. If *expression-1* is *true*, the first block is compiled. Otherwise, if *expression-2* is *true*, the second block is compiled, and so on. If none of the expressions are *true*, the text between #else and #endif is compiled. For example,

```
#if _VERSION < 550
    typedef unsigned size_t;
#else
    typedef unsigned long size_t;
#endif
```

gives different definitions for `size_t` depending on the value of the macro `_VERSION`. Implementation-defined macro names often begin with an underscore. A version number such as 5.50 can be represented by an integer such as 550.

Compilers often define certain macros automatically, depending on choices that the programmer has made via command-line parameters or with menu and dialog-box selections. Also, some compilers allow the programmer to enter macro definitions that are to be assumed, even though they do not appear in the program text.

We (and the compiler) frequently use macro names as flags to represent various conditions that can affect a compilation. A macro name is defined if the corresponding flag is raised and not defined otherwise. We define and undefine such names as follows:

```
#define DEBUGGING_ON
    /* DEBUGGING_ON is defined */
    /* in this part of the program */
    /* ... */
#undef DEBUGGING_ON
```

We need not define any replacement text for a macro that is used as a flag.

The two expressions

```
defined macro-name
defined(macro-name)
```

both yield *true* only if the *macro-name* has been defined. Thus

```
#if defined(DEBUGGING_ON)
    printf("\nAt end of main loop:\n");
    printf("i = %d, j = %d, k = %d\n", i, j, k);
#endif
```

compiles the two debugging statements only if the macro `DEBUGGING_ON` is defined.

There are two directives that check directly whether a macro is defined:

```
#ifdef macro-name
#ifndef macro-name
```

These are equivalent, respectively, to

```
#if defined(macro-name)
#if !defined(macro-name)
```

For example,

```
#ifdef _SMALL_POINTERS
    #define NULL   0
#else
    #define NULL   0L
#endif
```

gives different definitions of NULL depending on whether _SMALL_POINTERS has been defined.

Some declarations and definitions occur in more than one header file and so may be included in a source file more than once. Multiple occurrences of function and macro definitions are allowed, provided all the occurrences are equivalent. Multiple occurrences of type definitions are forbidden, however. Even when multiple occurrences are allowed, we can save compile time if we can avoid compiling large numbers of redundant declarations or definitions.

We can use a macro name to prevent multiple declarations or definitions when they are forbidden or undesirable. For example, consider the following:

```
#ifndef ITEM_T_DEFINED
    #define ITEM_T_DEFINED
    typedef struct {
        unsigned long item_num;
        unsigned int quantity;
        double price;
    } item_t;
#endif
```

If ITEM_T_DEFINED has not been defined, the conditional lines remain in the program and define both ITEM_T_DEFINED and item_t. If another copy of this code is encountered later, ITEM_T_DEFINED will have been defined, and the conditional lines will be skipped.

EXERCISES

7-1. Sometimes rename() is more powerful than the renaming command provided by the operating system. In popular MS-DOS implementations, for example, rename() can rename a directory and move a file from one directory to another, neither of which are possible with the MS-DOS rename command. To make available or to explore the capabilities of rename() on your system, write a program change that changes a file name with rename(). The old and new names should be provided as command-line parameters; the program should print an error message if the number of parameters is incorrect or if rename() fails.

7-2. Write a program to merge two text files so that, if the lines in each input file are in lexicographical order, the lines in the merged output file will also be in order. The names of the input files and output file are passed to the program as command-line parameters. Use the following algorithm: Start by reading a line from each file. Repeatedly, compare the two lines, write the one that comes first to the output file, and replace it with the next line of the corresponding input file. When one input file is exhausted, copy the remainder of the other input file to the output file.

7-3. Write a function

```
void concat(char *s, int n, ...);
```

that concatenates n strings onto the end of string s. For example,

```
char ca[20] = "to";
concat(ca, 3, "get", "her", "ness");
```

set the contents of ca to "togetherness".

7-4. Write an enhanced version of printf(). The nature of the enhancement is left up to you, because what is realistic varies from system to system. Some possibilities are a function that writes to a given window or that writes text at a given screen position, in a particular color, or in a particular type font. Your function might also write to a printer, if it provides more possibilities for controlling the appearance of the printed text.

7-5. Write a simple disk-based text editor. As in our info.c example, the editor will have Load, Save, and Save As commands for loading, updating, and creating files. During editing, all text remains on disk, where it is read as needed. Lines in the current version of the disk file are read from that file; new lines typed by the user are stored in a work file.

The program maintains an array whose elements refer to lines. Specifically, each element contains the file position of a line and a flag stating whether the line is in the current file or in the work file. The order of the array elements reflects the order of the lines in the user's document. Each line is designated by a line number, which is one more than the subscript of the corresponding array element. The number of a line can change as the file is edited.

When a new file is loaded, the program reads through it, line by line, and builds the line array. The text read from the file is not retained, however, but will be read again as needed.

For simplicity, there are only three editing commands: List displays the lines having a given range of line numbers, Delete removes the lines having a given range of line numbers, and Insert allows one or more new lines to be inserted before the line with a given line number. The Insert command allows the user to enter as many lines as desired, then to terminate the command by typing a line containing a single period.

List does not change the line array or either file, though it may read from both the current file and the work file. Delete changes the line array, and Insert both changes the line array and writes new lines to the work file.

When the user issues a Save command, the program uses the line array to write a new text file, reading the lines from the current file and the work file as appropriate. At the same time, the line array is updated to reflect the positions of the lines in the new file. Then, as usual, any backup file is deleted, the current file is renamed as the backup file, and the new file is renamed as the current file. The work file is cleared, which can be done by closing it and then opening it again (with mode w+).

APPENDIX

1 *Keywords*

auto	extern	sizeof
break	float	static
case	for	struct
char	goto	switch
const	if	typedef
continue	int	union
default	long	unsigned
do	register	void
double	return	volatile
else	short	while
enum	signed	

2 Operators, Precedence, and Associativity

The following table lists all the C operators along with some of their properties. Horizontal lines group the operators according to precedence, so that all the operators in a given group have the same precedence. The groups are listed in order of decreasing precedence, so the operators in a given group have lower precedence than those in any preceding group and higher precedence than those in any succeeding group.

The *syntax* of an operator is *prefix* if the operator is placed before its operand, *infix* if it is placed between its operands, and *postfix* if it is applied after its operand. The *arity* of an operator is the number of operands it takes: *unary* for one operand, *binary* for two, and *trinary* for three operands. Note that C sometimes uses the same symbol for operators with different syntax and arity. The *associativity* indicates whether successive operators with the same precedence are grouped from *left to right* or from *right to left*.

The notations .*name* and ->*name* indicate that . or ->, *together with the following member name*, is classified as a postfix unary operator. The notation (*type*) designates a type-cast operator such as (int) or (double).

	SYMBOL	DESCRIPTION	SYNTAX	ARITY	ASSOCIATIVITY
Table A2-1	++	*postfix increment*	*postfix*	*unary*	*left to right*
C Operators and	--	*postfix decrement*	*postfix*	*unary*	*left to right*
Their Properties	[ ]	*subscript*	*postfix*	*unary*	*left to right*
	( )	*function call*	*postfix*	*unary*	*left to right*
	.*name*	*member selection*	*postfix*	*unary*	*left to right*
	->*name*	*indirect member selection*	*postfix*	*unary*	*left to right*
	sizeof	*byte size of object*	*prefix*	*unary*	*right to left*
	++	*prefix increment*	*prefix*	*unary*	*right to left*
	--	*prefix decrement*	*prefix*	*unary*	*right to left*
	&	*address of object*	*prefix*	*unary*	*right to left*
	*	*indirection*	*prefix*	*unary*	*right to left*
	+	*unary +*	*prefix*	*unary*	*right to left*
	-	*unary -*	*prefix*	*unary*	*right to left*
	~	*bitwise NOT*	*prefix*	*unary*	*right to left*
	!	*logical NOT*	*prefix*	*unary*	*right to left*
	(*type*)	*type cast*	*prefix*	*unary*	*right to left*
	*	*multiply*	*infix*	*binary*	*left to right*
	/	*divide*	*infix*	*binary*	*left to right*
	%	*remainder*	*infix*	*binary*	*left to right*
	+	*add*	*infix*	*binary*	*left to right*
	-	*subtract*	*infix*	*binary*	*left to right*
	<<	*left shift*	*infix*	*binary*	*left to right*
	>>	*right shift*	*infix*	*binary*	*left to right*
	<	*less than*	*infix*	*binary*	*left to right*
	<=	*less than or equal*	*infix*	*binary*	*left to right*
	>	*greater than*	*infix*	*binary*	*left to right*
	>=	*greater than or equal*	*infix*	*binary*	*left to right*
	==	*equal to*	*infix*	*binary*	*left to right*
	!=	*not equal to*	*infix*	*binary*	*left to right*
	&	*bitwise AND*	*infix*	*binary*	*left to right*
	^	*bitwise exclusive OR*	*infix*	*binary*	*left to right*
	|	*bitwise inclusive OR*	*infix*	*binary*	*left to right*
	&&	*logical AND*	*infix*	*binary*	*left to right*
	||	*logical OR*	*infix*	*binary*	*left to right*
	? :	*conditional*	*infix*	*trinary*	*right to left*

(continued)

	Symbol	Description	Syntax	Arity	Associativity
Table A2–1 *(continued)*	=	*assignment*	*infix*	*binary*	*right to left*
	*=	*multiply assign*	*infix*	*binary*	*right to left*
	/=	*divide assign*	*infix*	*binary*	*right to left*
	%=	*remainder assign*	*infix*	*binary*	*right to left*
	+=	*add assign*	*infix*	*binary*	*right to left*
	–=	*subtract assign*	*infix*	*binary*	*right to left*
	<<=	*left shift assign*	*infix*	*binary*	*right to left*
	>>=	*right shift assign*	*infix*	*binary*	*right to left*
	&=	*bitwise AND assign*	*infix*	*binary*	*right to left*
	^=	*bitwise exclusive OR assign*	*infix*	*binary*	*right to left*
	|=	*bitwise inclusive OR assign*	*infix*	*binary*	*right to left*
	,	*comma*	*infix*	*binary*	*left to right*

3 *Integrated Development Environments*

This appendix introduces the capabilities of integrated development environments in hopes of encouraging newcomers to explore these powerful and convenient programming tools. IDEs for MS-DOS include QuickC and C 6.0 from Microsoft, and Turbo C++ and C++ 2.0 from Borland. (The Borland C++ products also compile C programs.) For the sake of a concrete example, we will focus on Turbo C++, which, along with QuickC, was used to develop the programs in this book.

TOURING THE IDE

For newcomers to integrated programming environments and visual (mouse and menu) interfaces, Turbo C++ includes a guided tour in the form of the program TCTOUR.* The following commands run this tutorial program:

```
CD \TC\TOUR
TCTOUR
```

The Tour is far easier to learn from than any printed description of the integrated development environment. The program illustrates its instructions with IDE screens, and it mimics the responses of the IDE when the user carries out practice commands. In this appendix we will not go into such basic matters as pulling down menus, selecting commands, and using dialog boxes, because such skills are far

*In this appendix we follow the MS-DOS and Turbo C++ convention of displaying program, file, and directory names in all uppercase letters. When entering these names into the computer, however, you can type them in either uppercase or lowercase, the latter usually being more convenient.

better acquired from TCTOUR (or from experience with other visual interfaces).

Like many other interactive programs, the IDE has a menu bar listing the menus from which commands can be selected. In printed explanations, the Turbo C++ manuals use a notation of the form *menu | command* to indicate that a particular command is to be selected from a particular menu. For example, to choose File | Open means to pull down the File menu and select the Open command. To choose Edit | Paste means to pull down the Edit menu and select the Paste command.

The symbol ≡ represents the system menu, which can be pulled down by typing Alt-Spacebar. Thus to choose ≡ | Clear desktop means to pull down the system menu and to select the Clear Desktop command.

The menus also list shortcut *hot keys* that can be used to execute commands directly, without selecting from the menus. From the File menu, for example, we see that pressing F3 is equivalent to choosing File | Open, pressing F2 is equivalent to choosing File | Save, and pressing Alt-X is equivalent to choosing File | Quit.

RUNNING THE IDE

We run the IDE by executing the program TC, which is in the directory \TC\BIN. We *could* work with \TC\BIN as our current directory, in which case our C++ program files would be placed in \TC\BIN along with the implementation files. Usually, however, it is better to place our program files in a separate *working directory*. We can use different working directories for different programming projects, and if more than one person uses the computer, each person can use a different set of working directories.

Suppose that our working directory is \CPPWORK, which we can create with an MS-DOS MD (Make Directory) command:

```
MD \CPPWORK
```

To run the IDE with \CPPWORK as the current directory, we must (1) change the current directory to \CPPWORK with a CD (Change Directory) command, (2) specify \TC\BIN in a PATH command so that the system can find the TC program, and (3) run the TC program. Thus the following MS-DOS commands run TC from the working directory \CPPWORK:

```
CD \CPPWORK
PATH \TC\BIN
TC
```

THE DESKTOP

When the IDE is running, the screen usually shows a menu bar and one or more windows. A window is *opened* when it is created on the screen and *closed* when it is removed. Turbo C++ allows overlapping windows, so an open window may be hidden by other windows. The window in which you are currently working is the *active window*, which is designated by a bright double-line border.

Most of your work will be done in *edit windows*, each of which is labeled with the name of the file being edited. Turbo C++ has a multiple-file editor, so several files—and hence several edit windows—can be open at the same time. Some other important windows are the *Output window*, which is used to view program output, and the *Message window*, which is used to view compiler and linker error messages.

A particular configuration of open windows is called a *desktop*. When you exit from the IDE, it saves your current desktop, and restores it the next time the IDE is run. (If, as described shortly, you specify a project when you run the IDE, then the desktop last used *on that particular project* is restored.)

When you run the IDE for the first time, or when for some other reason there is no previously saved desktop, the IDE starts out with a default desktop containing a single, blank edit window labeled NONAME00.C. NONAME00.C is recognized as a dummy file name; the name of the first actual file that you open will replace NONAME00.C, and the file will be loaded into the renamed window.

When you run the IDE, it may present you with an old desktop in which you are no longer interested. In that case, you can clear the desktop—close all open windows—by choosing ≡ | Clear desktop.

COMPILING A PROGRAM WITH ONE SOURCE FILE

As an introduction to the IDE, we will see how to enter, compile, link, and execute the hello-world program in Listing 1-1.

Run the IDE from your working directory as just described. If the initial desktop contains anything other than the NONAME00.C window, clear it by choosing ≡ | Clear desktop.

We now need to choose a file name for the hello-world program. Turbo C++, which can compile both C and C++ programs, uses the file name extensions .H for header files, .C for C source files, and .CPP for C++ source files. The .C or .CPP extension determines whether the file will be compiled as a C or a C++ source file. Because the hello-world program is written in C, we give its source file the name `HELLO.C`. The default extension is `.C`, so C programmers can usually omit the extension, whereas C++ programmers must always write `.CPP`.

To open a file for the hello-world program, choose `File |  Open` or press F3. Enter `HELLO.CPP` in the dialog box that appears. If a blank `NONAME00.C` window is present, its name will change to `HELLO.C`; otherwise, a new window named `HELLO.C` will be opened. If the file `HELLO.C` already exists in your working directory, it will be loaded into the `HELLO.C` window. If no such file exists, the window will remain blank, and you can proceed to type in the desired text.

Assuming that you are creating a new file, type the text of Listing 1-1 into the `HELLO.C` window. When you are finished, choose `File | Save` or press F2 to save the file in your working directory.

To compile, link, and execute the hello-world program, choose `Run |  Run` or press Ctrl-F9. A Compiling window, and later a Linking window, will open and keep you informed as to which files are being compiled or linked. Note that most of the compile time is spent compiling the `STDIO.H` header file, which is much larger than the part of the program that you wrote.

When the hello-world program executes, the output it produces will flash on the screen too quickly to be seen. To study the output at leisure, open the Output window by choosing `Window |  Output`. The Output window shows a segment of recent output to the display; if you scroll to the bottom of this segment you should find the message `Hello,  world!` printed by the hello-world program. You can return to the edit window by pressing F6 until the edit window is active.

If your program contains errors, the IDE will aid you in locating and correcting them. To demonstrate this, let's introduce two errors into the hello-world program: delete the closing parenthesis in "`main()`" and delete the semicolon at the end of the output statement. Again, choose `Run |  Run` or press Ctrl-F9 to try to compile and run the program. After a while, a message at the bottom of the Compiling window will inform you that there are errors and instruct you to press any key.

When you press a key, the Compiling window will close and you will see that a Message window has opened. The Message window contains two error messages that correctly diagnose the two errors we introduced into the program. You can use the up- and down-arrow keys to move a highlight to each of the error messages; a corresponding highlight in the edit window indicates approximately where each error occurs. Note that, for both of the errors in our example, the highlight in the edit window indicates the line following the one on which the error actually occurs.

Pressing Enter will return you to the edit window so you can correct the errors. Once in the edit window, you can move the cursor to the approximate positions of the errors by typing Alt-F8 to go to the next error and Alt-F7 to go to the previous error. When you go to the location of an error with Alt-F7 or Alt-F8, the corresponding error message will appear highlighted at the bottom of the edit window.

The following three hot keys are useful for compiling, linking, and executing programs:

Alt-F9	Compile only; produces object file
F9	Compile and link; produces executable file
Ctrl-F9	Compile, link, and execute

Note that none of these keys does any more work than necessary. If a program has already been compiled, F9 will just link it and Ctrl-F9 will just link and execute it. If a program has already been compiled and linked, then Ctrl-F9 will just execute it.

COMPILING A PROGRAM WITH SEVERAL SOURCE FILES

Turbo C++ allows you to define a *project* consisting of all the source files that must be compiled and linked to produce a given executable file. Once you have defined a project, a program with several source files can be compiled and linked as easily as one with only a single source file. For example, typing Ctrl-F9 will compile all the source files in the project, link them, and execute the resulting program.

As mentioned, projects are also useful for managing desktops. If you specify a project when you run the IDE, the current desktop for that project will be restored. Because of this, it may be convenient to use projects even for programs with only one source file.

For example, let's create a project for our game-playing program in Chapter 4 (Listings 4-1 through 4-5). This program consists of two header files, `GAME.H` and `RANDOM.H`, and three source files: `CRAPS.C`, `GAME.C`, and `RANDOM.C`. Assume that these five files have been copied into your working directory. Run the IDE with the `TC` command; if the desktop contains anything other than the `NONAME00.C` window, clear it by choosing ≡ | `Clear desktop`.

To begin, choose `File` | `Open` (or press F3) five times, and each time enter into the dialog box the name of one of the five files. When you are through, your desktop should contain five overlapping windows, each labeled with the name of one of the five files.

Next, you must create a *project file*, which specifies the source files that belong to the project; project files have the extension `.PRJ`. Open a project window by choosing `Project | Open project`. A dialog box will appear for you to enter the name of the project file you are creating; let's call the file for the simulation project `CRAPS.PRJ`. When you have entered this name, an empty project window labeled `Project: CRAPS` will appear on the desktop.

You must now enter the name of each of the three source files in the project window. (Header files are *not* entered here.) Choose `Project | Add item`; a dialog box will appear for you to enter the name of the first source file (the names can be entered in any order). When you have done so, that name will appear in the project window and the dialog box will reappear. Continue until you have entered the names of all three source files, then press Esc to cancel the dialog box. When you are finished, the names of all three source files should be listed in the project window.

Setting up the project has been a bit tedious, but we are now ready to reap the benefits. Press Ctrl-F9 and watch as the IDE automatically compiles each of the three source files, links them, and executes the resulting program.

For projects, the three hot keys work as follows:

Alt-F9	Compile only source file in active window
F9	Compile and link all files in project
Ctrl-F9	Compile and link all project files, then execute

As before, F9 and Ctrl-F9 do no more work than necessary. To see an example of this, make a small change in one of the source files and press F9 or Ctrl-F9. Observe that only the source file you changed is recompiled; existing object files are used when the corresponding source files have not been changed.

Exit the IDE with Alt-X. Information about the project will be stored in the project file `CRAPS.PRJ`, and a description of the current desktop will be stored in a file `CRAPS.DSK`. To work further on the project, run the IDE and specify the project file as a command-line parameter:

```
TC CRAPS.PRJ
```

The IDE will restore the desktop to its previous state and load any other needed information about the project. In particular, it will recall which source files are part of the project, so that you can still compile and link the entire project with F9 or Ctrl-F9.

If your working directory contains only one project file, then you need not specify that file when you run the IDE. The project will be loaded automatically when you run the IDE with the command

TC

DEBUGGING

We have already seen how the IDE locates and informs us of syntax errors. The hardest errors to find, however, are the logic errors that manifest themselves only when the program is run. It wasn't too many years ago that finding such errors meant poring over pages or screens full of hexadecimal code. Fortunately, times have changed, and IDEs allow us to do our debugging in terms of such source-language constructs as variable names and program lines.

When we compile a program that we intend to debug, we must tell the compiler to insert special debugging code that helps the IDE monitor and control program execution. In Turbo C++, for example, we must indicate our desire to debug by selecting two options. We first choose `Options | Compiler | Code generation` (the third choice is from another menu that pops up) and check the option `Debug info in OBJs`. We then choose `Options | Debugger` and select the option `Source Debugging On`. Choosing `Options | Save` will cause the IDE to remember these choices, which should be in effect except when we are compiling the final delivery version of a program.

The first job of a debugger is to provide control over program execution, so that we can observe the effect of executing each line of the program. If, instead of typing Ctrl-F9 to execute a program, we press F7, then the first executable line of the program will be highlighted. If we press F7 again, that line will be executed, and the highlight will move to the next executable line. By repeatedly pressing F7, we can execute our program line by line.

If the highlighted line contains a function call, pressing F7 will move the highlight to the first line of the function, allowing us to trace the line-by-line execution of the function definition. If we do not want to trace into the function definition, we can press F8 instead of F7. F8 executes the entire function call before moving on to the next line of the program. We can trace the execution of a function only if it was compiled with debugging code. If it was not, as is true of library functions, then F7 has the same effect as F8.

To get quickly to a certain part of the program, we can position the cursor on a particular line and press F4. The program will execute normally until it reaches the given line, then stop with that line highlighted. Also, choosing `Debug | Breakpoints` allows us to set *breakpoints* on various lines. The program will execute normally until it encounters a line containing a breakpoint, then stop with the line highlighted. Typing Ctrl–F9 will cause the program to resume executing until the next breakpoint is encountered, at which time it will stop again.

When we stop the program at a certain point, we will normally want to look at the values of certain variables to see how the program's calculations are proceeding. Turbo C++ provides several ways of doing this. One way is to open an *inspector window* on a particular variable (by choosing `Debug | Inspect`). The inspector window shows the current value of the variable. If we step through the program or execute to another breakpoint, the inspector window will be updated to reflect the new value of the variable. The inspector window tries to provide whatever we might want to know about the value of a variable. For example, if the variable holds a structure object, the inspector window shows the values of the structure members. If the variable is a pointer, the inspector window shows both its value and the value to which it points.

Another way is to designate certain variables as *watch variables*. (`Debug | Watches` pops up a menu containing several commands that apply to watch variables.) Watch variables, together with their values, are listed in a separate window. As we step through the program or execute to breakpoints, the values of the watch variables are updated accordingly.

Something else we can examine is the *call stack*, which shows all functions that have been called but have not yet returned. The calls are displayed in reverse of the order in which they took place. For example, if `main()` has called `factorial()` with argument 5, `Debug | Call stack` displays the following:

```
factorial(5)
main()
```

Although these features do not make debugging fun (nothing could do that), they do make it a lot more tolerable. It is hard for the bug we are seeking to remain hidden for long when we can watch the values of the variables change as we step through the program.

4 MS-DOS Memory Models

One of the most popular operating systems for C programming is MS-DOS, which runs on processors in the Intel 80x86 family. Current versions of MS-DOS operate these processors in so-called real mode, which (at least as far as we are concerned here) mimics the behavior of the 8086, the original processor in the family. Because of the way the 8086 addresses memory, MS-DOS programmers must make certain decisions about how memory is to be organized and accessed. Popular MS-DOS compilers, such as the products mentioned in Appendix 3, systemize these decisions by offering the programmer a choice of six *memory models*.

The 8086 designates a memory location via a 16-bit *segment address*, which designates a particular 64K segment of memory, and a 16-bit *offset*, which designates a particular byte within the segment. Thus the address of an arbitrary byte is a 32-bit quantity consisting of a 16-bit segment address and a 16-bit offset.

The 8086 maintains a default code segment and a default data segment. If we place our code or data in the corresponding default segment, we can address it with 16-bit offsets, which take up less space and can be processed faster than 32-bit segment-offset addresses. But the drawback is that we are limited to 64K of code or data, which is insufficient for many programs.

The programmer must decide, then, whether to use short, fast 16-bit addresses (and accept the 64K memory limitation) or to go with the more cumbersome segment-offset addresses. This choice can be made separately for code and data, which leads to the following four basic memory models:

MODEL	CODE ADDRESS	DATA ADDRESS
Small	16 bits	16 bits
Medium	32 bits	16 bits
Compact	16 bits	32 bits
Large	32 bits	32 bits

If our code and data are each less than 64K, we can use the *small model*. If only our code exceeds 64K, we can use the *medium model*; if only our data exceeds 64K, we can use the *compact model*. If code and data both exceed 64K, we must use the *large model*.

Pointers can be 16 or 32 bits, depending on the model chosen and whether the pointer is to a function (code) or to an object (data). A 16-bit pointer is called a *near pointer*, because it can only point into the default code or data segment. A 32-bit pointer is called a *far pointer*, because it can point anywhere in the memory accessible to MS-DOS.

Variations on the small and large models yield two additional models, the tiny model and the huge model. The small model provides separate 64K code and data segments, allowing up to 128K for code and data combined. The *tiny model*, on the other hand, uses the same segment for both code and data, so that both, taken together, cannot exceed 64K. The compact and large models allow more than 64K of data overall, but no single data item can exceed 64K. The *huge model*, on the other hand, allows data items that exceed 64K.

The huge model modifies the behavior of pointers to support multisegment data objects. In general, a given byte can be designated by many different combinations of segment address and offset. Thus it is meaningless to compare the values of far pointers unless we know that they have the same segment address. In the huge model, however, pointers are stored in a normalized form so that each byte is designated by a unique pointer. Thus pointers can be compared even if they refer to bytes in different segments.

Also, when we carry out an arithmetic operation on a far pointer, such as p++ or p + 1, the operation is applied to the *offset only*. This means that if an arithmetic operation carries a pointer beyond the end of a segment, it will wrap around to the beginning of the segment—it will not go on to the next segment. In the huge model, however, this situation is detected and corrected, so that pointer arithmetic works correctly, independent of segments.

Far pointers that are stored in normalized form, and for which pointer arithmetic is corrected, are called *huge pointers*. Huge pointers are convenient—they let us forget about segments when comparing pointers and doing pointer arithmetic. But there is a penalty—the extra code needed to normalize pointers and correct pointer arithmetic means that operations on huge pointers can be considerably slower than the corresponding operations on near or far pointers. In general, the huge model must be chosen with caution—we must make sure that its advantages make up for the extra time required to manipulate huge pointers.

You can choose a model by making a menu selection in an IDE or passing a flag parameter to a command-line compiler. Note, however, that each model requires a separate library. If you want to be able to use any model, you must have all six libraries on your disk. This is why compiler installation programs often ask which models you want installed.

The area from which `calloc()` and `malloc()` allocate memory is called the *heap*. There are two possible heaps—the *near heap*, which is inside the default data segment, and the *far heap*, which is outside the default data segment. In the tiny, small, and medium models, `calloc()` and `malloc()` allocate from the near heap and return a near pointer; in the compact and large models they allocate from the far heap and return a far pointer. We cannot use `calloc()` and `malloc()` in the huge model; rather, we must use other allocation functions that are incompatible with `calloc()` and `malloc()`.

Glossary

actual argument An expression specifying a value to be passed to a function. When the function is called, the actual-argument expressions are evaluated, and the resulting values are passed to the function.

address A value used by the computer hardware to designate a memory location. C uses addresses in the form of *pointers*, which designate *objects*.

address–of operator (&) An operator that, when applied to the name of an object, yields the object's address. The name can be any *lvalue* except an lvalue that names a *bitfield* or a *register variable*.

alias Two *lvalues* that name the same object are said to be aliases.

alignment The requirement that the *address* of a location be a multiple of the number of bytes in the location. For example, the address of a two-byte location must be a multiple of 2, the address of a four-byte location must be a multiple of 4, and so on. Alignment can force unused bytes to be inserted in *structures* and *unions*.

arity The number of operands to which an operator is applied. A *unary operator* takes one operand, a *binary operator* takes two operands, and a *trinary operator* takes three.

array A sequence of objects having the same type and stored in consecutive memory locations. The objects are called the *elements* of the array. Individual array elements are designated via integer *subscripts*.

associativity The property of an operator that specifies how operators with the same precedence are grouped. For example, + associates from left to right, so 3+4+5 is grouped as (3+4)+5. On the other hand, := associates from right to left, so x:=y:=z is grouped as x:=(y:=z).

binary file A file containing a sequence of bytes all of which are considered as data bytes (rather than control codes) and none of which has any specific meaning to the system. Any desired structure, such as a division into records, must be imposed by the programmer.

binary operator An operator that takes two operands.

bitfield A sequence of bits that is part of a larger memory location. Because only whole memory locations can be designated by addresses, we cannot take the address of a bitfield with the *address-of operator*, nor can we designate a bitfield by a *pointer*.

block A sequence of program declarations and statements delimited by braces (the declarations must precede the statements). A block can be used anywhere that a single statement is allowed.

byte The smallest size of memory location that can be designated by an address. For modern computers, a byte almost invariably contains eight bits, although the C standard provides for larger (but not smaller) byte sizes.

byte-oriented memory A memory that is organized as a sequence of bytes. Larger locations are formed by combining consecutive bytes; the address of such a location is the address of its first byte.

command-line parameter A string that is passed to a program when the program is launched—that is, when its execution is initiated. For an operating system with a command-line interface, command-line parameters are typed on the same command line that launches the program. Most visual (mouse and menu) interfaces also have provisions for passing parameters to programs.

compound assignment operator An operator that carries out an operation and assigns the result to its left operand. Examples are += (add assign), *= (multiply assign), and <<= (left shift assign).

conditional directive A preprocessing directive that controls whether or not specified parts of a program will be compiled. The decision to compile or not compile depends on a given condition, which is often whether or not a specified macro name has been defined. Conditional directives simplify compiling different versions of a program, such as versions intended for different computers.

conversion specification A character sequence that, when used in a format string, describes how a data item is to be read with scanf() or written with printf(). A conversion specification always begins with a % sign. For example, we can use %d to read an int value and %8.3f to write a double value in an eight-character *field* with three digits to the right of the decimal point.

conversion specifier In a *conversion specification*, the letter or letters specifying the type of data to be read or written. For example, in the conversion specifications `%d`, `%ld`, and `%ud`, the conversion specifier `d` specifies that an `int` value is to be read or written, `ld` specifies a `long` value, and `ud` specifies an `unsigned int` value.

declaration A language construction that gives the type of object or function to which an identifier refers. For example,

```
double x, y, z;
```

declares `x`, `y`, and `z` as `double` variables, and

```
int fun(double, double);
```

declares `fun` as a function that takes two `double` arguments and returns an `int` value.

decrement operator (--) An operator that decrements an integer variable—decreases its value by 1—or changes the target of a pointer variable from an array element to the immediately preceding element. If used as a prefix operator, the decrement operator returns the decremented value; if used as a postfix operator, it returns the undecremented value—the value the variable had before the operator was applied.

direct access File access that allows data to be read or written at any specified position in the file. By changing this position appropriately, we can read data items in any desired order, independent of the order in which they are stored in the file. Also called *random access*.

element One of the objects making up an *array*. All the elements of an array have the same type. Individual elements are referred to by *subscripting* the array name. Thus if `a` is a one-dimensional array, `a[0]` refers to the first element of `a`, `a[1]` refers to the second element of `a`, and so on.

end-of-file indicator A logical value associated with a stream. The end-of-file indicator is normally *false*, but it is set to *true* if a program attempts to read beyond the end of the file to which the stream is attached.

enumeration type An integer type whose values are designated by user-specified identifiers. For example,

```
enum {RED, YELLOW, BLUE} color;
```

declares `color` as an integer variable whose possible values are represented by the constants `RED`, `YELLOW`, and `BLUE`.

escape sequence A sequence of characters that begins with a backslash, `\`, and that represents a single character. For example, `\n` represents the newline character, `\t` represents the tab character, `\15` represents the character with octal code 15, and `\x85` represents the character with hexadecimal code 85.

executable file	A file containing code that can be loaded by the operating system and executed by the computer. An executable file is produced by linking *object files* each of which was compiled from a *source file*.
expression statement	A program statement consisting of an expression followed by a semicolon. When the statement is executed, the expression is evaluated. Its value is discarded, however, so the expression is evaluated only for its *side effects*.
external linkage	Linkage of identifiers declared in different source files.
field	The area of the screen or printout in which a particular data item is printed. The number of characters in a field is its width. The printed item may have to be preceded or followed by spaces to achieve a specified field width.
file	Any source from which data can be read, or any destination to which data can be written. Disk files, keyboards, displays, printers, and communication devices all qualify as files.
file position indicator	A value that gives the position of the next byte to be read from or written to a *stream*.
file redirection	The process by which the operating system, at user request, connects the standard input and output streams to specified files.
file scope	The *scope* of an identifier whose declaration is not enclosed in any block. File scope extends from the declaration in question to the end of the source file.
formal argument	A variable designated to hold one of the argument values passed to a function. When the function is called, each formal argument is initialized to the value of the corresponding actual argument. Beyond this, a formal argument behaves just like a local variable.
format string	A string containing *conversion specifications* for data to be read with `scanf()` or printed with `printf()`. For printing, the format string may also contain text to be printed along with the data.
fully buffered	When a *stream* is fully buffered, characters are accumulated in a buffer and transmitted to or from the corresponding file only when the buffer is full.
function	In C, any subprogram other than a *macro*. Functions in C correspond to functions, procedures, and subroutines in other languages. Unlike many other languages, C does *not* restrict the term *function* to subprograms that return a value.
function declaration	A declaration that designates an identifier as a function name. In modern usage, a function declaration is always a *function prototype*, which gives the types of the function's arguments and return value.
function macro	A macro that takes arguments similar to those of a function. Often a

function macro is used in place of a function to eliminate the overhead of calling the function. Many library functions are also implemented as function macros for this reason.

function prototype A *function declaration* that gives the types of the function's arguments and return value. For example, the function prototype

```
long round(double x, int n);
```

states that `round()` takes a `double` argument and an `int` argument and returns a `long` result. The argument names `x` and `n` are not used and can be omitted.

handle An integer generated by the operating system and used to designate a file. The standard I/O functions do not use handles (they use *streams* instead). However, many implementation-dependent I/O functions require that files be designated by handles.

header file A file containing the definitions and declarations needed to use external identifiers—identifiers defined in other source files. Header files typically contain function declarations, macro definitions, and type definitions (that is, definitions of *typedef names*). The most common use for header files is to provide access to library functions.

identifier A name used to designate a program construction such as a variable, function, or macro.

include directive A preprocessing directive, beginning with `#include`, that causes the contents of a designated file to be inserted in the text of a source file before that text is passed on to the rest of the compiler. (The original source file is not altered.) The include directive is replaced by the contents of the designated file.

increment operator (++) An operator that increments an integer variable—increases its value by 1—or changes the target of a pointer variable from an array element to the immediately succeeding element. If used as a prefix operator, the increment operator returns the incremented value; if used as a postfix operator, it returns the unincremented value—the value the variable had before the operator was applied.

infix operator An operator that is placed between its two operands.

integrated development environment (IDE) A software tool that provides all the facilities needed to edit, compile, link, execute, and debug C programs. Common sequences of operations, such as compiling, linking, and executing a program, can be carried out with a single keystroke or menu selection. Also called an *integrated programming environment (IPE)*.

internal linkage Linkage of identifiers declared in the same source file.

iteration Repeated execution of a sequence of statements.

keyword A predefined word with a fixed meaning in C, such as `if`, `then`, `while`, `int`, or `double`. (The standard C keywords are listed in Appendix 1). A keyword cannot be used for any other purpose, such as an identifier.

library A large collection of predefined functions (and a small number of predefined variables). The header files provided with a library also define macros and types (*typedef names*). A standard library comes with every C implementation; other libraries can be written by the user or purchased from third parties.

line buffered When a stream is line buffered, a block of characters is transmitted to or from the attached file at the end of each line—that is, whenever a newline character is encountered.

local identifier An identifier that is declared inside a block. The scope of the identifier extends from the declaration to the end of the block, so a local identifier is inaccessible from outside the block in which it is declared.

lvalue A language construction that names an object. The simplest and most common lvalues are variable names, such as `x`, `count`, and `sum`. More complicated lvalues include subscripted array names (`a[n]`), references via pointers (`*p`), and member accesses (`s.m`, `p->m`). Note that, despite its name, an lvalue is a construction in a C program, not a data value.

macro An identifier that is defined to represent a segment of program text. Subsequent occurrences of the identifier (except inside string literals) are *macro calls*, which are *expanded* by replacing each call with the text specified in the definition. *Function macros* can be called with arguments (also called *parameters*), which are inserted into the specified text at designated positions before using the text to replace the macro call.

memory location A region of memory, that is, a sequence of consecutive bytes. The address of the first byte is the address of the memory location. In C, a memory location is also known as an *object*.

memory model A scheme for organizing memory on MS-DOS computers. The memory model determines (1) the amount of memory available for code and for data, and (2) the sizes of pointers to functions (code) and to data.

modifiable lvalue An *lvalue* designating an object whose value can be changed. Note that it is the value of the object, and not the lvalue, that is subject to change. Because an assignment operator changes the value of its left operand, the left operand of an assignment operator must be a modifiable lvalue.

multibyte character A character whose code requires more than one byte. Multibyte characters are needed in oriental languages, which have thousands of characters, as opposed to the hundreds that suffice for Western languages.

name space A collection of identifiers used for a specific purpose. For example, macro names belong to a separate name space from other identifiers, and tags belong to different name spaces than variable names. The name spaces to which identifiers belong determine (1) when two declarations of the same identifier conflict with one another, and (2) when one declaration of an identifier masks or hides another declaration of the same identifier.

nested constructions Language constructions such that one construction is contained within another construction of the same kind. For example, nested blocks occur when one block is contained within another block. Nested `if` statements occur when one `if` statement occurs as part of another `if` statement. Selection and iteration statements are frequently nested.

newline character The control character that terminates a line of text. In C, a line is always terminated by a single newline character, regardless of what scheme may be standard for the underlying operating system. The *escape sequence* for the newline character is \n.

null character The character with code 0. The null character can be represented by the escape sequence \0.

null pointer A pointer that has numerical value 0 and is guaranteed not to point to any valid object.

null string A string that contains no characters other than the *null character* that terminates a string.

object A region of memory containing data. The region of memory is also referred to as a *memory location*. Variables, arrays, and array elements are examples of objects. The use of this word in C differs from its use in object-oriented programming.

object file The file produced by the compiler when a source file is compiled. An object file cannot be executed by the computer, but must be linked with other object files (some or all of which are usually from the *library*) to form an *executable file*.

pointer The address of an object of a particular type. Thus we classify pointers as pointer-to-`int` (pointer to an object containing an `int` value), pointer-to-`long`, pointer-to-`double`, and so on. An address only locates the first byte of an object; the type is essential for determining the size of the object and the kinds of processing that can be carried out on its value.

pointer arithmetic   Arithmetical operations on pointers, which change the array element to which a pointer refers (pointer arithmetic is invalid for pointers that do not point to array elements). For example, `p + 5` points to the fifth array element after the one pointed to by `p`, and `p - 7` points to the seventh array element before the one pointed to by `p`.

postfix operator   A *unary operator* that follows its operand. The function call operator `( )` and the subscript operator `[ ]` are examples of postfix operators, as are the *increment* and *decrement operators*, `++` and `--`, which can be used (with different results) as either prefix or postfix operators.

precedence   A property of operators that determines the order in which operators are grouped with their operands. For example, the multiplication operator has higher precedence than the addition operator, so the expression

    3*4+5*6

is grouped as

    (3*4)+(5*6)

rather than as

    3*(4+5)*6

Because of its higher precedence, the multiplication operator "gets first chance at" the operands 4 and 5.

prefix operator   A *unary operator* that precedes its operand. The unary + and unary - operators, which are used in expressions such as `+x` and `-(y+z)`, are examples of prefix operators.

preprocessing   The first phase of compiling, in which the text of a source file is modified before passing it on to the rest of the compiler. Only the text that is passed on is modified; the original source file remains unchanged. Preprocessing is controlled by preprocessing directives embedded in the program. Each directive begins with a `#`, as in `#include` and `#define`. Important preprocessing operations are (1) processing *include directives*, which insert the contents of a specified file in the source text; (2) defining and expanding *macros*; and (3) processing *conditional directives*, which allow different versions of a program to be compiled from the same source file.

random access   See *direct access*.

register variable   A variable, declared with the storage specifier `register`, whose value is to be stored in a processor register (if possible) rather than in a main memory location. Processor registers can be accessed much faster than main memory locations. Because a processor register has no address, we cannot take the address of a register variable with the *address-of* operator, nor can we refer to a register variable via a pointer.

return code   An integer code returned to the operating system by a program to indicate whether the program executed successfully.

scope   The scope of an identifier is the region of the source file in which the declaration of the identifier is valid. An identifier is visible (that is, accessible) throughout its scope except where it may be masked by a declaration of another identifier with the same name.

selection   The process of determining which program statements will be executed, based on the outcome of tests carried out during program execution.

self-referential structure   A structure, one or more of whose members are declared as pointers to instances of the structure itself. It is physically impossible for a member variable to have the same type as the structure that contains it, but there is no problem with its *pointing to* an object with such a structure. *Tags* provide a convenient means for referring to a structure from within a member declaration, rendering declarations of self-referential structures simpler in C than in some other languages.

sequential access   File access that requires data items to be read in the order in which they are stored in the file or to be written in the order in which they are to be stored. C does not require sequential access, but some devices do. For example, characters can be read from the keyboard only in the order in which the user types them.

short-circuit evaluation   The process by which some parts of a logical expression are not evaluated if their values are not needed to determine the value of the expression. For example, in the expression

```
(x >= 0.0) && (sqrt(x) >= 5.0)
```

if the left operand of && yields *false*, the entire expression yields *false*, and so the right operand need not be, and is not, evaluated. This precludes the error that would otherwise result from attempting to evaluate `sqrt(x)` with a negative value for x.

side effect   Any effect of expression evaluation other than returning the value of the expression. For example, the expressions n := 5, m += 3, and ++p all have the side effect of changing the value of a variable.

source file   A file containing all or part of the text of a C program. Source files are compiled to *object files*, which are then linked to form the *executable files* that can be run on the computer.

storage duration (lifetime)   The time (during program execution) that an object remains in existence. For example, a local variable—a variable declared in a block—

is created when the computer encounters the variable's declaration and is destroyed when the computer leaves the block containing the declaration.

stream   Abstractly, a stream is a sequence of bytes from which bytes can be read, to which bytes can be written, and for which existing bytes can be altered. Concretely, a stream is a pointer to a `FILE` object describing the file or device that is the actual source or destination for bytes read from or written to the stream.

string   A sequence of characters terminated by a *null character*. A string is represented by a pointer to its first character.

string concatenation   In a C program, the process of combining string literals that are separated only by whitespace. For example,

```
printf("con" "cat"
       "e" "nation");
```

is equivalent to

```
printf("concatenation");
```

The preprocessor joins the four string literals in the first statement to produce the second statement, which is what is seen by the rest of the compiler.

string literal   A series of characters enclosed in quotation marks, such as `"computer"`. The literal corresponds to a string consisting of the enclosed characters followed by a terminating null character. The value of a string literal is a pointer to the first character of the corresponding string.

structure   A sequence of objects each of which can have a different type. The objects are called the *members* of the structure, and are referred to by identifiers called *member names*. What is called a structure in C is known as a *record* in many other languages.

subscript   An integer that designates an element of an array. A subscript expression enclosed in brackets, such as `[i+j]`, is a postfix operator that can be applied to an array name or a pointer. For example, if `a` is a one-dimensional array, `a[i+j]` designates the element corresponding to the value of `i+j`. If `p` points to an array element, `p[4]` points to the fourth element beyond the element pointed to by `p`, and `p[-5]` points to the fifth element before the element pointed to by `p`.

tag   A name that can be used to refer to a particular declaration of a structure, a union, or an enumeration. For most purposes, *typedef names* are more convenient than tags. However, tags are useful for defining *self-referential structures* and unions.

text file A file that is structured into lines and whose bytes are taken to represent characters. In C, the end of a line is represented by a *newline* character. When writing to or reading from a text file, the C implementation must translate newline characters to or from whatever coding the operating system uses to structure a file into lines.

trinary operator An operator with three operands. C has only one trinary operator, the conditional operator.

typedef name A name defined to represent a type. The type so named must be defined by some other C construction, such as a structure, a union, or an enumeration declaration.

unary operator An operator that takes only one operand.

unbuffered stream A stream for which bytes are transmitted to or from their destination or source as soon as possible, without their first being accumulated in a buffer. Specifying a C stream to be unbuffered affects only the C implementation. The operating system may still apply buffering over which the C implementation has no control.

union An object that can, at different times, store data items having different types. Each such item corresponds to a *member* of the union. Structures and unions are similar, because each declares members that can have different types. However, for a structure the members represent data items that can be stored in the structure object at the same time, whereas for a union the members represent alternative types for the single data item that can occupy the union object.

variable A memory location (that is, an *object*) named by an identifier.

whitespace A sequence of characters containing only spaces, tabs, newlines, and form feeds.

For Further Reading

C Standard

American National Standards Institute. *American National Standard for Information Systems: Programming Language C.* New York: American National Standards Institute, 1990.

Serious students of C will want a copy of this ANSI standard, which is now the ultimate authority on the language. As standards go, the C standard is relatively readable. Although not intended as a tutorial on the language, it makes a good reference on standard C.

Plauger, P. J. and Jim Brodie. *Standard C.* Redmond, Wash.: Microsoft Press, 1989.

This is another handy reference on standard C. Although it appeared before the standard was finalized, it coincides closely with the final standard. Some of the terminology is different, however. Pascal programmers will like this book because it uses their beloved "railroad diagrams" to describe syntax.

Kernighan, Brian W. and Dennis M. Ritchie. *The C Programming Language,* 2nd ed. Englewood Cliffs, N. J.: Prentice-Hall, 1988.

Before there was an ANSI standard, C was defined by Kernighan and Ritchie, or "K and R" for short. The second edition of this tutorial and reference manual has been revised to conform to the ANSI standard.

Library Functions

One thing you will need is a reference manual for the library functions provided by your implementation. In addition to whatever documentation the software vendor may supply, reference manuals for popular implementations are available from third-party publishers. Also available are reference manuals for the standard library—the library functions defined in the ANSI standard. The following are typical library reference manuals.

Barkakati, Nabajyoti. *The Waite Group's Microsoft C Bible,* 2nd ed. Indianapolis, Ind.: Howard W. Sams, 1990.

Barkakati, Nabajyoti. *The Waite Group's Turbo C++ Bible.* Indianapolis, Ind.: Howard W. Sams, 1990.

Plauger, P. J. *The Standard C Library.* Englewood Cliffs, N. J.: Prentice-Hall, 1992.

Schildt, Herbert. *C: The Complete Reference.* Berkeley, Calif.: Osborne McGraw-Hill, 1987.

C Tutorials

In times past, everybody learned C from Kernighan and Ritchie. Now the bookstore shelves are replete with C books. The following is a representative sample; the book by Hansen seems to be a particularly clear and straightforward introduction.

Hansen, Augie. *C Programming.* Reading, Mass.: Addison-Wesley, 1989.

Kochan, Stephen G. *Programming in C,* rev. ed. Indianapolis, Ind.: Hayden Books, 1988.

Schildt, Herbert. *Teach Yourself C.* Berkeley, Calif.: Osborne McGraw-Hill, 1990.

Siegel, Charles. *Teach Yourself C.* Portland, Ore.: MIS Press, 1989.

Townsend, Carl. *Understanding C.* Indianapolis, Ind.: Howard W. Sams, 1988.

Index